CRUCIAL MOMENTS
OF THE CIVIL WAR

Crucial Moments of the Civil War

Edited by

WILLARD WEBB
Brigadier General USAR

With an introduction by

BRUCE CATTON
Author of *A Stillness at Appomattox*
Senior Editor of American Heritage

Fountainhead Publishers, Inc.
475 Fifth Avenue, New York 17, N. Y.

Manufactured in the United States of America
by The Colonial Press Inc., Clinton, Mass.

To MARGARET and to MARTHA
from their affectionate grandfather

INTRODUCTION

Apparently there is some profound secret wrapped up in the story of the American Civil War. It is hard to say exactly what that secret is: it is all bound up with racial memories and re-told legends, with universal memories which are none the less real even though they deal with events which took place before any of us were born. Perhaps it is finally indefinable, in any precise terms. But to Americans of this generation an important part of the real truth about this country, its people and its inner meaning is somehow conveyed in the stories that come out of the war that is now a century old. Here is what we were, what we are now and what in the end we are all about, told in terms of a picture-book war which has the queer quality of being both entirely romantic and brutally realistic.

Perhaps it is the fact that its underlying meaning is literally beyond exact definition that keeps pulling so many of us back to the story of the Civil War. The story means so many different things. It emphasizes the point that any great historic truth has many facets; both sides were very often right and both sides were, in one or two ways, wrong; justice, heroism, dedication and endurance, not to mention meanness and folly and ordinary human wrong-headedness, were divided; it may be that another century must pass before we can finally weigh the whole business and make up our minds at last about its true significance. It is something for us now to brood over, and in our brooding we here and there touch the edges of some great force that was moving inexorably down through American life, expressing a fundamental fact about us but never quite holding still long enough to submit to scientific analysis.

It is a subject, in other words, for thoughtful students, for bookish men who examine the records and look for the significant moments. But it is also a subject for soldiers; for the record of this war is, after all, the record of things done by soldiers, by generals and by high privates, by the great American civilian who suddenly finds himself in uniform and who in that guise does remarkable things. This book has been compiled by a man who is both a bookish student and a combat soldier: by Brigadier General Willard Webb, a competent military man in one incarnation and, in another incarnation, a studious official of the Library of Congress; a man who knows both books and soldiers from first-hand experience and who is thus peculiarly fitted to bring together approximately a score of stories which give a new glimpse of the Civil War period.

Selecting these pieces, General Webb has drawn on varied sources. Some of the things he has chosen come from men who fought in the Civil War and who wrote while the heat of conflict was still on them—Frank Haskell, for instance, whose masterpiece on Gettysburg is perhaps the most moving of all accounts of that battle, was killed in action less than a year after he wrote this account. Others were written by newspaper correspondents, and some by modern historians who prowled back into the misty fields of conflict two or three generations after the guns were stilled. All of them put together recapture something of the heat and passion of the old days and convey to the modern reader an authentic picture of what the whole business was about and what it looked like and stood for.

These selections go from Bull Run to Appomattox. They are not all-embracing. They could not be, because the subject is too vast. (The only all-embracing work on the Civil War is that ponderous compilation, "The Official Records of the War of the Rebellion," which runs to something like 163 fat volumes and still leaves something to be said.) But they make up a moving set of pictures of certain crucial moments in the war; the moments in which that long-gone war speaks to modern Americans in terms that will always be moving.

PREFACE

Once, many years ago, when I was a young reference assistant at the Library of Congress, a somewhat eccentric reader handed me a slip which read: "My subject for today is history from the dawn to the inauguration of Calvin Coolidge. Please let me have any material on this subject." The analogy with the problem of selecting a single volume of stories on the American Civil War is not too far-fetched. For each one which is selected a dozen must, regretfully, be rejected. Obviously, from the table of contents, a formula of something old, something new has been used here.

Diversity of geography and type of activity were also considered. There are those who contend that realists like Sherman make the best workmen at the craft of war (though some may suggest in rebuttal the names of Stuart and Custer). But whatever the points of that argument, it is the romanticist like Thomason (with no mean combat record himself) who writes best about it.

Surely there has never been such a literary interest in any war in all history as there has been in the American Civil War. There are multi-volume biographies, economic studies of such commodities as salt, studies of soldier life, of desertion, of foreigners, books on tactics, on strategy, books in profusion dealing with this war in great detail. Most of the chroniclers of war have been romantics and this war has furnished themes for stories since it began. So some extracts here have been selected from fiction with the hope that some of the flash of saber and the fascinating, frightening roar of troops in the assault may for a while be recalled.

In these days of supersonic push buttons we need again recall that every gadget, that all fantastic devices, must be used by men. And no science fiction weapon can completely replace the imponderables of the human spirit. The courage, the character, the self-sacrifice of the men of a nation are in the ultimate what enables a nation to become great, indeed to survive. In our own Civil War these factors were present to a flamboyant degree. And the war has been chronicled for nearly 100 years by men of skill.

It was in World War II on Okinawa, in a blackout command tent, located with the tanks, between the artillery position and the infantry lines, that I read Colonel Henry's *First with the Most.* The artillery preparation for the advance across the Chinen Peninsula was in progress. The noise was great. I read by candlelight under the worst conditions for concentrating but such was the magic of Colonel Henry's prose that I became oblivious to the din of cannonading around me, and for a while I rode across northern Mississippi in the hurrying column of Bedford Forrest. The incessant clatter of hoofs, the squeak of stirrup straps and a sense of urgency to cut off Streight blotted out the jolting wham of a battery of long toms close by.

May these selections bring to you some of the pleasant hypnosis they have brought to me.

Clifton, Virginia

TABLE OF CONTENTS

CONTRIBUTING AUTHORS AND SOURCES

LIST OF ILLUSTRATIONS

17

SECTION TWO

1

THE BATTLE OF BULL RUN

By Edmund Clarence Stedman
(ARMY CORRESPONDENT, THE NEW YORK WORLD.)

After the bombardment of Fort Sumter and the call to arms, the Union military forces took the initiative. The fundamental purpose of war is to impose our will on the enemy. The Confederate's strategy was passive. They withdrew from the Union. It was not necessary for them to do more than repel possible invasion. On the other hand, the Federal Government was determined to hold the Union together, by force if necessary. It, therefore, behooved them to disperse any obstacle resisting the normal exercise of sovereignty. They must, in a word, advance to accomplish this.

The Confederate Army under Beauregard took up a position generally along the line of the meandering and beded little stream called Bull Run, with outposts thrown out to the neighborhood of Fairfax Court House and Vienna. A second force under Johnston was located in the general neighborhood of Harpers Ferry to protect the access corridor of the Shenandoah Valley. When the major Federal effort was developed it was expected that either of these two forces might be moved to support the other, as needed.

In July, the Federals started the first of the overland "On to Richmond" thrusts under the command of General McDowell and Johnston's force moved swiftly to reinforce the troops on the line of Bull Run.

The Union Army moved down the turnpike leading to Warrenton, which crossed Bull Run on the Stone Bridge. When they

*reached the tactically important plateau at Centreville they paused
to feel out the enemy. A reconnaissance in force against the Confederate right was repulsed and convinced McDowell that the Bull
Run line was too strongly held to be breached by direct assault.
He, therefore, resolved to effect a fairly close envelopment of the
Gray left. In the meantime, he would send a vigorous feint straight
down the highway to make the enemy believe that his main effort
was directly across the bridge. By happenstance, the enveloping
movement was discovered by a signal station at Manassas, several
miles away. Confederate forces on the left flank were quickly
shifted to refuse that flank. As more Union forces completed the
envelopment march, they were brought up on the right of the
developing fire fight and to oppose them more and more Southern
units were moved from right flank to left flank. The Gray forces
were driven back to form an obtuse angle with the Stone Bridge—
which was never captured—as the apex. In rallying the troops of
his brigade, which was falling back, Brig. Gen. Bernard E. Bee
pointed to a line of troops on the high ground of the Henry Hill
and shouted, "See there stands Jackson, like a stonewall."*

*The troops on both sides were courageous and completely in-
experienced. After the battle wavered for several hours, the
Union forces gave way into what became for many units a somewhat
disorderly retreat.*

*The die was cast. Each side had found the enemy more compe-
tent than he had anticipated. Each side girded himself for what
now, obviously, would be a stern and demanding war.*

WASHINGTON, MONDAY, *July* 21, 1861.
At two o'clock this morning I arrived in Washington, having witnessed the great conflict near Manassas Junction from beginning
to end, and the gigantic rout and panic which broke up the Federal
army at its close. I stayed near the action an hour or two later than
my associates, in order to gather the final incidents of the day,
and fully satisfy myself as to the nature and extent of the misfortune.

And now in what order shall the event of yesterday be described? Even now how shall one pretend to give a synthetic nar-

ration of the whole battle, based on the heterogeneous statements of a thousand men; a battle whose arena was a tract miles
in breadth and length, interspersed with hills and forests; whose
contending forces were divided into a dozen minor armies, continually interchanging their positions, and never all embraced
within the cognizance of any spectator or participator. Even the
general commanding the Federal columns was ignorant, at the
close, of the positions of the several corps; was ignorant, at the
beginning, of the topography of the dangerous territory on which
he attacked an overpowering foe. Was either general of division
better informed of the movements even of his own forces? I doubt
it. I only know that at sunset last evening, generals, colonels, and
majors, were all retiring, devoid of their commands, no more
respected or obeyed than the poorest private in the broken ranks.
I know that a grand army, retreating before superior numbers, was
never more disgracefully or needlessly disrupted, and blotted, as
it were, out of existence in a single day. This is the truth, and why
should it not be recorded? And why should I not tell the causes
which produced this sad result? Weeks will be required for the
proper summing up of details. At present, for one, I acknowledge
my inadequacy to describe more than the panorama which passed
before my own eyes, and the result decided by the combination of
this with much that was seen and done elsewhere.

The affair of Thursday last was like a spectacle in an amphi-
theatre, visible in its oneness to all who were on the sides of that
mountain valley. But those who were on yesterday's field now
understand how little of a great battle in a hilly region is known
or seen by curious lookers-on; how much less by those actually
engaged in its turmoil. But let me give the plan and commencement of the engagement on our side, the progress of that portion
which was within my ken, and the truth in relation to the result.

On Friday, the day succeeding our repulse at Bull Run, Major
Barnard, topographical engineer of the general staff, escorted by
Company B of the Second Cavalry regiment (under Lieutenant
Tompkins), made a wide reconnaissance of the country to the
north, in order to examine the feasibility of turning the enemy's
rear by a strategic movement in that direction.

A route was discovered by which it appeared that such a measure might be successfully executed. In a letter on the defences of
Manassas Junction, I pointed out the different roads leading thith-
erward from Centreville. One—the most direct—is that passing
through Thursday's battlefield; another, further north, leading,
when produced, to Warrenton, beyond the Manassas Gap Railroad. From the latter, a minor road, branching off still more to the
north, was found to open at a fork half-way between Centreville
and the Bull Run ravine. This road could be used for the rapid
advance of men and artillery, preceded by a corps of sappers
and miners.

A plan was at once projected by General McDowell for a decisive attack upon the enemy's line of defence, to be made simul-
tanously by three advancing columns, from the several points of
approach. The various division encampments were already advantageously located for the inception of such a movement, and
orders were swiftly issued for the entire army to start at six o'clock
on Saturday afternoon. It was afterwards discovered that our stock
of heavy ammunition embraced no more than nineteen rounds to
each gun, and that we must send to Fairfax for a better supply.
It was also thought advisable to have the army arrive in sight of
the enemy at sunrise, and the first orders were accordingly coun-
termanded, and fresh ones issued, appointing two o'clock of the
ensuing morning for the hour of leaving camp. Three days' rations
were to be served out by the commissary, and the tents of each
regiment to remain standing and under guard.

In the moonlight of the stillest hour of the night our force of
36,000 men began to move, in pursuance of the following arrangement for the advance. On the left, or southernmost road, the gallant Colonel Richardson, be it remembered, had continued to
hold the approach to the field where he fought so bravely on
Thursday, his command consisting of the Fourth Brigade of Tyler's Division, viz. the Second and Third Michigan, the First
Massachusetts, and the Twelfth New York regiments. It was
rightly determined that these troops, if they fought at all, should
be apportioned to the ground of which they already had partial
knowledge. Behind Richardson, and near Centreville, Colonel
Miles was to take up his position in reserve, with his entire First

and Second Brigades. These included the Eighth (German Rifles) and Twenty-ninth New York regiments, the Garibaldi Guard and the Twenty-fourth Pennsylvania, the Sixteenth, Eighteenth, Thirty-first, and Thirty-second New York regiments, and the Company G (Second Artillery) battery—the one lately brought from Fort Pickens. Thus Richardson could call to his support, if necessary, a reserve of 7,000 men, in addition to the 4000 with which he was instructed to hold his position, to prevent the enemy from moving on Centreville past our left, but not to make any attack. The centre, on the Warrenton road, commanded by General Tyler, consisted of the First and Second Brigades of the Tyler Division, embracing the First and Second Ohio, and Second New York regiments, under General Schenck, and the Sixty-ninth, Seventy-ninth and Thirteenth New York, and Second Wisconsin, under Colonel Sherman. Carlisle's, Rickett's, and Ayre's battery, accompanied this important column, which numbered 6000 men, and which was supported in the rear by the Third Tyler Brigade, under Colonel Keyes, consisting of the First, Second, and Third Connecticut regiments, and the Fourth Maine,—a force of 3000, available at a moment's call. On the extreme right, Colonel Hunter took the lead, with the two brigades of his division, viz. the Eighth and Fourteenth New York regiments under Colonel Porter, with a battalion of the Second, Third, and Eighth Regular Infantry, a portion of the Second Cavalry, and the Fifth Artillery Battery, under Colonel Burnside; the First and Second Ohio, the Seventy-first New York, and two New Hampshire regiments, with the renowned Rhode Island Battery. After Hunter's followed Colonel Heintzelman's Division, including the Fourth and Fifth Massachusetts and the First Minnesota regiments, with a cavalry company and a battery, all under Colonel Franklin, and the Second, Fourth, and Fifth Maine and Second Vermont regiment under Colonel Howard. To about 14,000 men was thus intrusted the difficult and most essential labor of turning the enemy by a circuitous movement on the right, and these troops, as it eventuated, were to experience the larger part of the sanguinary fighting of the day.

On the night preceding the battle General Cameron visited the camp, reviewed the Third Tyler brigade, passed a few hours with

General McDowell, and then left for Washington, in spirits depressed by no premonition of the disaster which was to befall our arms, and the private grief which would add a deeper sorrow to the feelings he now experiences. After midnight a carriage was placed at General McDowell's tent, which was to bear him to the scene of action. In order to be ready to move with the army I went down to the familiar quarters of Lieutenant Tompkins, whose company was attached to the General's escort, and there slept an hour while our horses ate the only forage they were to have for a day and a half. At two o'clock we were awakened; the army had commenced to move.

There was moonlight, as I have said; and no moonlight scene ever offered more varying themes to the genius of a great artist. Through the hazy valleys, and on hill-slopes, miles apart, were burning the fires at which forty regiments had prepared their midnight meal. In the vistas opening along a dozen lines of view, thousands of men were moving among the fitful beacons; horses were harnessing to artillery, white army wagons were in motion with the ambulances—whose black covering, when one thought about it, seemed as appropriate as that of the coffin which accompanies a condemned man to the death before him. All was silent confusion and intermingling of moving horses and men. But forty thousand soldiers stir as quickly as a dozen, and in fifteen minutes from the commencement of the bustle every regiment had taken its place, ready to fall in to the division to which it was assigned. General McDowell and staff went in the centre of Tyler's, the central column. At 2:30 A.M. the last soldier had left the extended encampments, except those remaining behind on guard.

The central line appeared to offer the best chances for a survey of the impending action, and in default of any certain pre-knowledge, was accompanied by all non-participators whom interest or duty had drawn to the movement of the day. In order to obtain a full review of its moonlight march to the most momentous effort of the campaign, I started at the extreme rear, and rapidly passed along to overtake the van of the column. For some way the central and right divisions were united, the latter forming off, as I have explained, about a mile beyond Centreville. So, leaving

camp a mile below the village, I enjoyed the first spectacle of the
day—a scene never to pass from the memory of those who saw
it. Here were thousands of comrades-in-arms going forward to lay
down their lives in a common cause. Here was all, and more than
one had read of the solemn paraphernalia of war. These were not
the armies of the aliens to us, but, with the dress, the colors, the
officers, of every regiment, we were so familiar that those of each
had for us their own interest, and a different charm. We knew the
men, their discipline, their respective heroes; what corps were
most relied on; whose voice was to be that of Hector or Agamem-
non in the coming fray. How another day would change all this!
How some long-vaunted battalions would perhaps lose their, as
yet, unearned prestige, while accident or heroism should gild the
standards of many before undistinguished! Then, as I followed
along that procession of rumbling cannon-carriages and caissons,
standards and banners, the gleaming infantry, with their thousands of shining bayonets, and the mounted officers of every
staff, what fine excitement was added to the occasion by the salu-
tations and last assurances of the many comrades dearer than the
rest! The spirit of the soldiery was magnificent. They were all
smarting under the reproach of Thursday, and longing for the
opportunity to wipe it out. There was glowing rivalry between
the men of different States. "Old Massachusetts will not be
ashamed of us to-night." "Wait till the Ohio boys get at them."
"We'll fight for New York to-day," and a hundred similar utter-
ances, were shouted from the different ranks. The officers were as
glad of the task assigned them as their men. I rode a few moments with Lieutenant Colonel Haggerty, of the Sixty-ninth. He
mentioned the newspaper statement that he was killed at the
former battle, and laughingly said that he felt very warlike for
a dead man, and good for at least one battle more. This brave
officer was almost the first victim of the day. The cheery voice of
Meagher, late the Irish, now the American, patriot, rang out
more heartily than ever. Then there were Corcoran, and Burnside, and Keyes, and Speidel, and many another skilled and gallant officer, all pushing forward to the first fruition of their three
months' patient preparation. In the ranks of the Connecticut and

other regiments, were old classmates and fellow-townsmen, with whom it was a privilege to exchange a word on this so different occasion from any anticipated in those days when all the States were loyal, and the word "disunion" was a portion of an unknown tongue.

General McDowell's carriage halted at the junction of the two roads, a place most favorable for the quick reception of dispatches from all portions of the field. The column assigned to Colonel Hunter here divided from the main body and went on its unknown, perilous journey around the enemy's flank.

A mile along—and by this time the white morning twilight gave us a clearer prospect than the fading radiance which had thus far illumed the march—we could look across an open country on the left to the farm-house, where we knew Colonel Richardson was stationed, and to the blood-stained valley beyond, whose upper reaches were now to be the arena of a larger conflict. But it was after sunrise when the van of General Tyler's column came to the edge of the wooded hill overlooking those reaches. The sun had risen as splendid as the sun of Austerlitz. Was it an auspicious omen for us, or for the foe? Who could foretell? The scenery was too beautiful and full of nature's own peace, for one to believe in the possibility of the tumult and carnage just at hand, or that among those green oak forests lurked every engine of destruction which human contrivance has produced, with hosts of an enemy more dangerous and subtle than the wild beasts which had once here made their hiding-places. Then, too, it was Sunday morning. Even in the wilderness, the sacred day seems purer and more hushed than any other. It was ours to first jar upon the stillness of the morning, and becloud the clearness of that serene atmosphere with the rude clangor of the avant messenger that heralded our challenge to a disloyal foe.

From the point I mention, where the road slopes down to a protected ravine, we caught the first glimpse of the enemy. A line of infantry were drawn up across a meadow in the extreme distance, resting close upon woods behind them. We could see the reflection of their bayonets, and their regular disposition showed them expectant of an attack. After a moment's inspection, General

Tyler ordered Carlisle to advance with his battery to the front, and here one could think of nothing but Milton's line:

"Vanguard! to right and left the front unfold."

The ancient order for the disposition of advance ranks is still in military usage. For the Second and Third Tyler brigades under Schenck, were at once formed in line of battle, in the woods on either side—the First Ohio, Second Wisconsin, Seventy-ninth, Thirteenth, and Sixty-ninth New York Regiments, succeeding each other on the right, and the Second Ohio, and Second New York being similarly placed on the left, while the artillery came down the road between.

A great 32-pound rifled Parrot gun—the only one of its caliber in our field service—was brought forward, made to bear on the point where we had just seen the enemy (for the bayonets suddenly disappeared in the woods behind), and a shell was fired at fifteen minutes past six A.M., which burst in the air; but the report of the piece awoke the country, for leagues around, to a sense of what was to be the order of the day. The reverberation was tremendous, shaking through the hills like the volley of a dozen plebeian cannon, and the roar of the revolving shell indescribable. Throughout the battle that gun, whenever it was fired, seemed to hush and overpower everything else. We waited a moment for an answering salute, but receiving none, sent the second shell at a hill-top, two miles off, where we suspected that a battery had been planted by the rebels. The bomb burst like an echo close at the intended point, but still no answer came, and General Tyler ordered Carlisle to cease firing, and bring the rest of his battery to the front of the woods and our column, ready for instant action. It was now about seven o'clock. For half an hour but little more was done; then skirmishers were deployed into the forest on each side, in order to discover the whereabouts of our nearest foes. Before us lay a rolling and comparatively open country, but with several hills and groves cutting off any extended view. In the western distance on the left we could see the outskirts of Manassas Junction. The woods at whose edge our line of battle formed, extended half around the open fields in a kind of semicircle, and it was into the arms of this crescent that our skirmishers advanced. Soon we began to hear random shots exchanged in the thicket on the left, which proved the existence of an enemy in that direction. (What can be done against men who, to all the science and discipline of European warfare, add more than the meanness and cowardly treachery of the Indian? We had, all through the day, to hunt for the foe, though he numbered his myriads of men.) At the same time, a scout on the right captured a negro native, who was led to the general, shaking with fear, and anxious to impart such information as he had. Through him we learned that the rebels were quartered among the woods on the right and left, and in the groves in the open country; that they had erected a battery on the distant hill, and had kept him at work for three days, assisting to fell trees, so that a clear range of the road we occupied could be obtained.

By this time our scouts reported the enemy in some force on the left. Two or three Ohio skirmishers had been killed. Carlisle's battery was sent to the front of the woods on the right, where it could be brought to play where needed. A few shell were thrown into the opposite thicket, and then the Second Ohio and Second New York marched down to rout out the enemy. In ten minutes their musketry was heard, and then a heavy cannonade answer. They had, without doubt, fallen upon a battery in the bushes. For a quarter of an hour their firing continued, when they came out in good order, confirming our surmises. After advancing a furlong they saw the enemy, who exchanged their fire and retired through the forest. Suddenly from a different direction a voice was heard, exclaiming, "Now, you Yankee devils, we've got you where we want you!" and several heavy guns were opened upon them with such effect that Schenck finally ordered them to retire, which they did in perfect order. The boys came out indignant at the practices of the rebels, and swearing they would rather fight three times their force in the open field than encounter the deadly mystery of those thickets. No soldiers are willing to have their fighting entirely confined to storming infernal earthworks at the point of the bayonet. Every regiment, yesterday, was at times a forlorn hope.

A few dead and wounded began to be brought in, and the battle of Manassas had commenced. Carlisle's howitzers and the great rifled gun were opened in the direction of the battery, which answered promptly, and a brief, but terrific, cannonading ensued. In less than half an hour the enemy's guns were silenced, two of Carlisle's howitzers advancing through the woods to gain a closer position. But a fatal error was here made, as I thought, by General Tyler, in not ordering in a division to drive out the four rebel regiments stationed behind the battery, and to seize its eight guns. Through some inexplicable fatuity he seemed to assume that when a battery was silenced it was convinced, and there it remained, with its defenders, unheard from and unthought of until the latter portion of the day, when it formed one cause of our final defeat. It is actually a fact, that while our whole forces were pushed along the right to a co-operation with Hunter's flanking column, and a distance of miles in advance, this position on the left, close to the scene of the commencement of the fight, and just in front of all our trains and ammunition wagons—a position chosen by all spectators as the most secure—was, through the day, within five minutes' reach of a concealed force of infantry, and a battery which had only been silenced. No force was stationed to guard the rear of our left flank. It was near this very point, and with the assistance of this very infantry, that the enemy's final charge was made, which created such irretrievable confusion and dismay. And after the first few hours no officer could be found in this vicinity to pay any attention to its security. All had gone forward to follow the line of the contest.

Meantime, Richardson, on the extreme left, could not content himself with maintaining his position, for we heard occasional discharges from two of his guns. However, he took no other part in the action than by shelling the forces of the enemy which were sent rapidly from his vicinity to the immediate point of contest. From the hill behind we could see long columns advancing, and at first thought they were Richardson's men moving on Bull Run; but soon discovered their true character. Indeed, from every southward point the enemy's reinforcements began to pour in by thousands. Great clouds of dust arose from the distant roads. A person who ascended a lofty tree could see the continual arrival of cars at the nearest point on the Manassas Railroad, with hosts of soldiers, who formed in solid squares and moved swiftly forward to join in the contest. The whistle of the locomotive was plainly audible to those in our advance. It is believed that at least fifty thousand were added during the day to the thirty thousand rebels opposed to us at the onset. It was hard for our noble fellows to withstand these incessant reinforcements, but some of our regiments whipped several corps opposed to them in quick succession, and whenever our forces, fresh or tired, met the enemy in open field, they made short work of his opposition.

At 10:30 A.M. Hunter was heard from on the extreme right. He had previously sent a courier to General McDowell, reporting that he had safely crossed the run. The general was lying on the ground, having been ill during the night, but at once mounted his horse and rode on to join the column on which so much depended. From the neighborhood of Sudley Church he saw the enemy's left in battle array, and at once advanced upon them with the Fourteenth New York and a battalion of regular infantry— Colonel Hunter ordering up the stalwart Rhode Island regiments (one led by the model of the American volunteer, Burnside), the Second New Hampshire, and our own finely-disciplined Seventy-first. Governor Sprague himself directed the movements of the Rhode Island Brigade, and was conspicuous through the day for gallantry. The enemy were found in heavy numbers opposite this unexcelled division of our army, and greeted it with shell and long volleys of battalion firing as it advanced. But on it went, and a fierce conflict ensued in the northern battle ground. As soon as Hunter was thus discovered to be making his way on the flank General Tyler sent forward the right wing of his column to co-operate, and a grand force was thus brought to bear most effectually on the enemy's left and centre.

The famous Irish regiment, 1,600 strong, who have had so much of the hard digging to perform, claimed the honor of a share in the hard fighting, and led the van of Tyler's attack, followed by the Seventy-ninth (Highlanders) and Thirteenth New York, and Second Wisconsin.

It was a brave sight—that rush of the Sixty-ninth into the death-struggle! With such cheers as those which won the battles in the Peninsula, with a quick step at first, and then a double quick, and at last a run, they dashed forward and along the edge of the extended forest. Coats and knapsacks were thrown to either side, that nothing might impede their work, but we knew that no guns would slip from the hands of those determined fellows, even if dying agonies were needed to close them with a firmer grasp. As the line swept along, Meagher galloped toward the head, crying "Come on, boys! you've got your chance at last!" I have not since seen him, but hear that he fought magnificently, and is wounded.

Tyler's forces thus moved forward for half a mile, describing quite one-fourth of a circle on the right, until they met a division of the enemy, and of course a battery of the enemy's most approved pattern.

It was noon, and now the battle commenced in the fierceness of its most extended fury. The batteries on the distant hill began to play upon our own, and upon our advancing troops, with hot and thunderous effect. Carlisle answered for us, and Sherman for Hunter's Division, while the great 32-pounder addressed itself resistlessly to the alternate defences of the foe. The noise of the cannonading was deafening and continuous. Conversely to the circumstance of the former engagement, it completely drowned, at this period, the volleys of the musketry and riflemen. It blanched the cheeks of the villagers at Centreville, to the main street of which place some of the enemy's rifled shell were thrown. It was heard at Fairfax, at Alexandria, at Washington itself. Five or six heavy batteries were in operation at once, and to their clamor was added the lesser roll of twenty thousand small-arms. What could we civilians see of the fight at this time? Little: yet perhaps more than any who were engaged in it. How anxiously we strained our eyes to catch the various movements, thoughtless of everything but the spectacle, and the successes or reverses of the Federal army. Our infantry were engaged in woods and meadows beyond our view. We knew not the nature or position of the force they were fighting. But now and then there would be a fierce rush into the open prospect, a gallant charge on one side and a retreat on the other, and we saw plainly that our columns were gaining ground, and steadily pursuing their advantage by their gradual movement which continued toward the distance and the enemy's centre.

We indeed heard continuous tidings of heroism and victory; and

those in the trees above us told us of more than we could discover
with our field glasses from below. We heard that Hunter had fairly
rounded the enemy's flank, and then we listened for ourselves to
the sound of his charges in the northern woods, and saw for ourselves the air gathering up smoke from their branches, and the wavering column of the Mississippians as they fled from their first battery and were forced into the open field. Then we saw our own
Sixty-ninth and Seventy-ninth, corps animated by a chivalrous national rivalry, press on to the support of the more distant column.
We could catch glimpses of the continual advances and retreats;
could hear occasionally the guns of a battery before undiscovered;
could guess how terribly all this accumulation of death upon
death must tell upon those undaunted men, but could also see—
and our cheers continually followed the knowledge—that our
forces were gradually driving the right of the enemy around the
second quarter of a circle, until by one o'clock the main battle was
raging at a point almost directly opposite our standing-place—
the road at the edge of the woods—where it had commenced six
hours before.

There was a hill at the distance of a mile and a half to which I
have heretofore alluded. From its height overlooking the whole
plain, a few shell had reached us early in the day, and as it was
nearer the Manassas road than almost any other portion of the
field, more of the enemy's reinforcements gathered about its ridge
than to the aid of the beaten rebels in the woods and valleys. Here
there was an open battery, and long lines of infantry in support,
ready, for a wonder, to let our wearied fellows see the fresh forces
they had to conquer.

As the Sixty-ninth and Seventy-ninth wound round the meadows
to the north of this hill, and began to cross the road apparently
with the intention of scaling it, we saw a column coming down from
the farthest perspective, and for a moment believed it to be a portion of Hunter's Division, and that it had succeeded in completely
turning the enemy's rear. A wild shout rose from us all. But soon
the lookouts saw that the ensigns bore secession banners, and we
knew that Johnston, or some other rebel general, was leading a
horde of fresh troops against our united right and centre. It was
time for more regiments to be sent forward, and Keyes was ordered

to advance with the First Tyler Brigade. The three Connecticut regiments and the Fourth Maine came on with a will; the First Connecticut was posted in reserve, and the other three corps swept up the field, by the ford on the right, to aid the struggling advance.

All eyes were now directed to the distant hilltop, now the centre of the fight. All could see the enemy's infantry ranging darkly against the sky beyond, and the first lines of our men moving with fine determination up the steep slope. The cannonading upon our advance, the struggle upon the hilltop, the interchange of position between the contestants, were watched by us, and as new forces rushed in upon the enemy's side the scene was repeated over and over again. It must have been here, I think, that the Sixty-ninth took and lost a battery eight times in succession, and finally were compelled, totally exhausted, to resign the completion of their work to the Connecticut regiments which had just come up. The Third Connecticut finally carried that summit, unfurled the stars and stripes above it and paused from the fight to cheer for the Union cause.

Then the battle began to work down the hill, the returning half of the circle which the enemy, driven before the desperate charges of our troops, described during the day, until the very point where Tyler's advance commenced the action. Down the hill, and into the valley thickets on the left, the Zouaves, the Connecticut and New York regiments, with the unconquerable Rhode Islanders, drove the continually enlarging but always vanquished columns of the enemy. It was only to meet more batteries, earthwork succeeding earthwork, ambuscade after ambuscade. Our fellows were hot and weary; most had drunk no water during hours of dust, and smoke, and insufferable heat. No one knows what choking the battle atmosphere produces in a few moments, until he has personally experienced it. And so the conflict lulled for a little while. It was the middle of a blazing afternoon. Our regiments held the positions they had won, but the enemy kept receiving additions, and continued a flank movement toward our left—a dangerous movement for us, a movement which those in the rear perceived, and vainly endeavored to induce some general officer to guard against.

Here was the grand blunder, or misfortune, of the battle. A misfortune, that we had no troops in reserve after the Ohio regiments were again sent forward, this time to assist in building a bridge across the run on the Warrenton road, by the side of the stone bridge known to be mined. A blunder, in that the last reserve was sent forward at all. It should have been retained to guard the rear of the left, and every other regiment on the field should have been promptly recalled over the route by which it had advanced, and ordered only to maintain such positions as rested on a supported, continuous line. General Scott says, today, that our troops had accomplished three-days' work, and should have rested long before. But McDowell tried to vanquish the South in a single struggle, and the sad result is before us.

As it was, Captain Alexander, with his Sappers and Miners, was ordered to cut through the abattis by the side of the mined bridge, in the valley directly before us, and lay pontoons across the stream. Carlisle's Artillery was detailed to protect the work, and the Ohio and Wisconsin reserve to support the artillery. Meanwhile, in the lull which I have mentioned, the thousand heroic details of federal valor and the shamelessness of rebel treachery began to reach our ears. We learned the loss of the brave Cameron, the wounding of Heintzelman and Hunter, the fall of Haggerty, and Slocum, and Wilcox. We heard of the dash of the Irishmen and their decimation, and of the havoc made and sustained by the Rhode Islanders, the Highlanders, the Zouaves, and the Connecticut Third; then of the intrepidity of Burnside and Sprague—how the devoted and daring young governor led the regiments he had so munificently equipped again and again to victorious charges, and at last spiked, with his own hands, the guns he could not carry away. The victory seemed ours. It was an hour sublime in unselfishness, and apparently glorious in its results!

At this time, near four o'clock, I rode forward through the open plain to the creek where the abattis was being assailed by our engineers. The Ohio, Connecticut, and Minnesota regiments were variously posted thereabout; others were in distant portions of the field; all were completely exhausted and partly dissevered; no general of division, except Tyler, could be found. Where were our officers? Where was the foe? Who knew whether we had won or lost?

The question was quickly to be decided for us. A sudden swoop, and a body of cavalry rushed down upon our columns near the bridge. They came from the woods on the left, and infantry poured out behind them. Tyler and his staff, with the reserve, were apparently cut off by the quick maneuver. I succeeded in gaining the position I had just left, there witnessed the capture of Carlisle's battery in the plain, and saw another force of cavalry and infantry pouring into the road at the very spot where the battle commenced, and near which the South Carolinians, who manned the battery silenced in the morning, had doubtless all day been lying concealed. The ambulances and wagons had gradually advanced to this spot, and of course an instantaneous confusion and dismay resulted. Our own infantry broke ranks in the field, plunged into the woods to avoid the road, got up the hill as best they could, without leaders, every man saving himself in his own way.

By the time I reached the top of the hill, the retreat, the panic, the hideous headlong confusion, were now beyond a hope. I was near the rear of the movement, with the brave Captain Alexander, who endeavored by the most gallant but unavailable exertions to check the onward tumult. It was difficult to believe in the reality of our sudden reverse. "What does it all mean?" I asked Alexander. "It means defeat," was his reply. "We are beaten; it is a shameful, a cowardly retreat! Hold up, men!" he shouted, "don't be such infernal cowards!" and he rode backwards and forwards, placing his horse across the road and vainly trying to rally the running troops. The teams and wagons confused and dismembered every corps. We were now cut off from the advance body by the enemy's infantry, who had rushed on the slope just left by us, surrounded the guns and sutlers' wagons, and were apparently pressing up against us. "It's no use, Alexander," I said, "you must leave with the rest." "I'll be damned if I will," was his sullen reply, and the splendid fellow rode back to make his way as best he could. Meantime I saw officers with leaves and eagles on their shoulder-straps, majors and colonels, who had deserted their commands, pass me galloping as if for dear life. No enemy pursued just then; but I suppose all were afraid that his guns would be trained down the long, narrow avenue, and mow the retreating thousands, and batter to pieces army wagons and everything else which crowded it. Only one field officer, so far as my observation extended, seemed to have remembered his duty. Lieutenant Colonel Speidel, a foreigner attached to a Connecticut regiment, strove against the current for a league. I positively declare that, with the two exceptions mentioned, all efforts made to check the panic before Centreville was reached, were confined to civilians. I saw a man in citizen's dress, who had thrown off his coat, seized a musket, and was trying to rally the soldiers who came by at the point of the bayonet. In reply to a request for his name, he said it was Washburne, and I learned he was the member by that name from Illinois. The Honorable Mr. Kellogg made a similar effort. Both these Congressmen bravely stood their ground till the last moment, and were serviceable at Centreville in assisting the halt there ultimately made. And other civilians did what they could.

But what a scene! and how terrific the onset of that tumultuous retreat. For three miles, hosts of Federal troops—all detached from their regiments, all mingled in one disorderly rout—were fleeing along the road, but mostly through the lots on either side. Army wagons, sulters' teams, and private carriages, choked the passage, tumbling against each other, amid clouds of dust, and sickening sights and sounds. Hacks, containing unlucky spectators of the late affray, were smashed like glass, and the occupants were lost sight of in the debris. Horses, flying wildly from the battlefield, many of them in death agony, galloped at random forward, joining in the stampede. Those on foot who could catch them rode them bareback, as much to save themselves from being run over, as to make quicker time. Wounded men, lying along the banks—the few neither left on the field nor taken to the captured hospitals— appealed with raised hands to those who rode horses, begging to be lifted behind, but few regarded such petitions. Then the artillery, such as was saved, came thundering along, smashing and overpowering everything. The regular cavalry, I record it to their shame, joined in the melée, adding to its terrors, for they rode down footmen without mercy. One of the great guns was overturned and lay amid the ruins of a caisson, as I passed it. I saw an artilleryman running between the ponderous fore and after-wheels of his gun-carriage, hanging on with both hands, and vainly striving to jump upon the ordnance. The drivers were spurring the horses; he could not cling much longer, and a more agonized expression never fixed the features of a drowning man. The carriage bounded from the roughness of a steep hill leading to a creek, he lost his hold, fell, and in an instant the great wheels had crushed the life out of him. Who ever saw such a flight? Could the retreat at Borodino have exceeded it in confusion and tumult? I think not. It did not slack in the least until Centreville was reached. There the sight of the reserve—Miles's Brigade—formed in order on the hill, seemed somewhat to reassure the van. But still the teams and foot soldiers pushed on, passing their own camps and heading swiftly for the distant Potomac, until for ten miles the road over which the grand army had so lately passed southward, gay with unstained banners, and flushed with surety of strength, was covered with the fragments of its retreating forces, shattered and panic-stricken in a single day. From the branch route the trains attached to Hunter's Division had caught the contagion of the flight, and poured into its already swollen current another turbid freshet of confusion and dismay. Who ever saw a more shameful abandonment of munitions gathered at such vast expense? The teamsters, many of them, cut the traces of their horses and galloped from the wagons. Others threw out their loads to accelerate their flight, and grain, picks, and shovels, and provisions of every kind lay trampled in the dust for leagues. Thousands of muskets strewed the route, and when some of us succeeded in rallying a body of fugitives, and forming them in a line across the road, hardly one but had thrown away his arms. If the enemy had brought up his artillery and served it upon the retreating train, or had intercepted our progress with five hundred of his cavalry, he might have captured enough supplies for a week's feast of thanksgiving. As it was, enough was left behind to tell the story of the panic. The rout of the Federal army seemed complete.

The sight of Miles's reserve drawn up on the hills at Centreville, supporting a full battery of field pieces, and the efforts of the few officers still faithful to their trust, encouraged many of the fugitive infantry to seek their old camps and go no farther. But the majority pushed on to a point near the late site of Germantown, where Lieutenant Brisbane had formed a line of Hunt's artillerists across the road and repulsed all who attempted to break through. I particularly request attention to the service thus rendered by this loyal young officer.

While he was thus engaged, a courier arrived with the news that Colonel Montgomery was advancing with a New Jersey Brigade from Falls Church, and that the retreat must be stopped, only the wagons being allowed to pass through. Some thousands of the soldiery had already got far on their way to Washington. Poor fellows! Who could blame them? Their own colonels had deserted them, only leaving orders for them to reach Arlington Heights as soon as they could. A few miles farther I met Montgomery swiftly pressing to the rescue, and reported the success of Lieutenant Brisbane's efforts. And so I rode along, as well as my wearied horse could carry me, past groups of straggling fugitives, to Fairfax, where Colonel Woodbury was expecting, and guarding against, a flank movement of the enemy, and on again to Long Bridge and the Potomac. But the van of the runaway soldiers had made such time that I found a host of them at the Jersey intrenchments begging the sentinels to allow them to cross the bridge. Today we learn of the safe retreat of the main body of the army; that they were feebly followed by the rebels as far as Fairfax, but are now within the Arlington lines, and that McDowell, a stunned and vanquished general, is overlooking the wreck of his columns from his old quarters at the Custis mansion.

The list of the killed and wounded in this wide-spread action will not be found proportionate to the numbers engaged on either side, and to the duration of the conflict. The nature of the ground, and the fact that the struggle was confined to attacks upon batteries and ambuscades, made the whole affair a series of fiery skirmishes, rather than a grand field encounter. Men fought with a kind of American individuality—each for himself—and the musketry firing was of the most irregular character. There were few such heavy volleys as those which made the hills echo last Thursday.

It would not be surprising if our entire loss in killed and wounded should prove to have been not over a thousand men. The rebels must have suffered twice as much from the terrific cannonading of our artillery in the forenoon, and from the desperate charges of the Zouaves, the Sixty-ninth, and the other corps which were especially distinguished in the engagement. The Zouaves captured two batteries, fought hand to hand with the Carolinians in a furious bowie-knife conflict, routed the famous Black Horse Cavalry, and only broke ranks when victory became hopeless.

Nine-tenths of our killed and wounded were perforce left on the field, and in the hospitals at either end; and as the enemy retains possession of the ground, we can get no accurate details of our losses. From prisoners taken by us we learned that the rebel leaders, determined to have no incumbrances on their hands, issued orders to give no quarter. It is positively known that many of our comrades were bayoneted where they fell. All the wounded Zouaves suffered this inhuman fate.

Rickett's, Carlisle's, and the West Point batteries remain in the enemy's possession. Twenty-three of our guns, including the thirty-two pound siege pieces, were taken. But Sherman, who went into action with six cannon, came out with eight—two of them dragged from the rebel embrasures. Large numbers of sutlers' and train wagons are probably cut off, and abandoned arms and munitions have fallen into the enemy's hands. At the date of this letter, it is uncertain whether any of our regiments which were intercepted at the time of the panic have surrendered themselves to the rebels; but this must be the case with many of the infantry who, ignorant of the country, starving and exhausted, dashed into the forests in their retreat. Every hour, however, is reducing our list of missing, as the stragglers reach their old camps along the Potomac.

The disastrous result of the action was perhaps inevitable— even though no panic had occurred at the close—from the three causes against which the noblest soldiery can never successfully oppose their daring. First, the enemy's forces had been largely underrated, and nearly doubled our own in number; second, the onus of the attack rested entirely upon us, and the natural and scientific defences of the rebels made their position almost impregnable; third, many of our leaders displayed a lamentable want of military knowledge. There was little real generalship in the field. There was no one mind of the Napoleonic order, at once centralizing and comprehending the entire movement of the day. There was no one to organize our regiments in strong, swift-moving columns, and hurl them powerfully against the foe. Nor were the generals of division more competent to their work. They exhibited personal bravery, but advantages gained were not secured; important points were abandoned as soon as carried; and a reckless, fatiguing pursuit preferred, until Beauregard and Davis, who commanded in person, led us on to positions thoroughly available for the attack of their final reinforcements. As for us, no one had thought of providing that reserve absolutely necessary to the sealing and completion of a battle's successes. It is the last conflict of the day that decides the victory and defeat. We had no cavalry to rout our retreating foe. Our artillery was not rendered efficient in the afternoon. General Tyler neglected to guard his rear, and to check the pushing forward of his trains. As for the colonels, many of those who were not wounded or killed in the engagement exhibited not merely inefficiency, but the pusillanimity which I have before recorded. To conclude: before we can force our way through a country as well adapted for strategic defence as the fastnesses of the Piedmontese, the defiles of Switzerland, or the almost unconquerable wilds in which Schamyl so long held the Russians at bay—before we can possess and advance beyond the scientific intrenchments with which the skill of disloyal officers has made those Virginia forests so fearfully and mysteriously deathful to our patriotic soldiery, we must discover the executive leader whose genius shall oppose new modes of subduing a novel, and thus far successful method of warfare, and whose alert action shall carry his devices into resistless effect.

2

WHITE OAK SWAMP AND MALVERN HILL

By Samuel M. Schmucker

The James River, and the York with its complex of tributaries, flow eastward to the sea only a few miles apart. The frequently marshy area between them is known as the Peninsula. At the start of the Civil War the Federal forces had held on to Fortress Monroe at the seaward end of this strip.

After McDowell's defeat at the first battle of Bull Run another General, George B. McClellan, a West Pointer with a great gift for organization, was called from the west to take command of the Union forces. He spent the winter in organizing and training the troops. As spring came on he assumed executive command of the Army of the Potomac. These troops he moved to the Peninsula, disembarking them at Fortress Monroe. This was sound strategy, for not only did the rivers secure his flanks but both the rivers were navigable, and his supply bases could be moved forward as his lines moved forward.

The Confederates moved troops from the Bull Run-Centreville area to counter this. While artillery, which defended dams on transverse streams, slowed the Federal advance, McClellan did move slowly but inexorably up the Peninsula until his lines were within seven miles of Richmond and his troops could hear church bells ring there.

At this point the Confederate General Joseph E. Johnston was wounded and he was replaced by General Robert E. Lee. Lee planned and executed almost immediately a bold and vigorous offensive resulting in the series of battles usually known as the Seven Days. Generally speaking, he drove in the Federal right, forcing the army back down the Peninsula, and against the bank of the James River. McClellan finally rested against the river in an extremely strong position on high ground known as Malvern Hill. When the Confederates attacked him there, however, they were quickly and bloodily repulsed.

Lee's great ascendancy over his troops and his people was established and the second On to Richmond move was rendered impotent.

A very brief period for repose was allowed to the Federal troops. They had indeed won the race to White Oak swamp; but the vast army of the Rebels was in eager pursuit of them, and in a short time was upon their rear. Then followed another desperate engagement, named after the locality in which it took place. Soon after crossing the White Oak creek the Federal generals formed their new line of battle with great energy and promptness. The chief of these officers were Heintzelman, Sumner, Kearney, Porter and Hancock. The new position of the Federal forces extended about four miles in length. On the extreme right wing General Hancock was posted with his brigade. Next to him were placed the troops of Brooks and Davidson. The batteries belonging to this division were commanded by Captain Ayres. Then came the divisions of Sumner, Heintzelman and Porter.

The battle commenced with an attack by the enemy on the column of General Hancock. They opened with about twenty batteries, which were served with such vigor and skill that they soon blew up several of Captain Mott's caissons, shattered his guns and spread confusion among the teamsters, cannoniers and troops who came within their range. It was at this period that so complete a terror pervaded some of the regiments, that one of them, the Twentieth New York, fled in the utmost disorder and scattered in fragments in every direction. For this disgraceful proceeding General McClellan, on the following day, ordered the provost marshal to arrest all the stragglers as they came into camp.

After a short time, however, the Federals who had been attacked recovered their self-possession, and their guns responded to those of the enemy. The latter had not yet crossed the White Oak creek, and the engagement was still confined to the operations of the artillery. At length a portion of the Rebels made an attempt to cross the stream, but were met and repulsed with success by General Smith, whose brisk fire of infantry extended continuously along whole columns. Finding it impossible to cross in front, the enemy detached a powerful force to proceed four miles due south to Charles City Cross Roads, for the purpose of interposing between the Federal forces and James River, thereby intercepting their retreat. The position which they purposed to reach was within a mile and a half of Turkey Bend on that river; and had they succeeded in their intention, they would have inevitably accomplished the ruin of the army, and prevented its successful establishment at Harrison's Landing. Fortunately, information of this movement of the Rebels was obtained in time; and Generals Porter and Keyes so marshaled their wearied troops as to prevent its achievement.

They reached the advancing columns of the enemy at four o'clock in the afternoon, and attacked them. The Rebels fought desperately and their artillery produced a dreadful havoc in the Federal ranks. The latter were nearly dead already from the effects of heat, exhaustion and thirst; and so little discipline remained that a portion of those regiments which were nearest the James River, at one time broke ranks, rushed to its shores, plunged in, and after slaking their thirst returned to their colors, and resumed the fight. But the resistance of the Federal troops gradually became weaker. Human nature could endure no more.

The fresh masses of the exultant Rebel army continued to press forward with still greater resolution. An overwhelming and decisive victory seemed about to crown the persevering efforts of the Rebel hosts, when, at the critical moment, a deliverer suddenly appeared. As at Pittsburg Landing, so in the present instance, the gallant navy of the Union rescued the land forces from destruction. At that crisis the gunboats on the James River opened their fire upon the enemy. At five o'clock the enormous rifled guns of the Jacob Bell, Golena, and Aroostook, which were anchored in Turkey Bend, belched forth their colossal shells, with a detonation which completely drowned the feebler chorus of all the artillery on land, and terrified the foe by the unexpected presence of a more formidable antagonist. As the shells descended upon the serried masses of the Rebels and burst among them, whole ranks were battered to the earth by the flying fragments. Horrible havoc ensued. Confusion and terror were quickly diffused through their columns; and they who, a few moments before, were confident of driving the Federal army into the James River or of compelling it to surrender, themselves began to give way.

Encouraged by the evident effect of the shot of the gunboats, the Federal commanders, of whom the most distinguished on this memorable field was General Heintzelman, determined to recover the fortunes of the day by making a combined and desperate charge. The gunboats were therefore signalled to suspend their fire. Preparations were quickly made to effect the intended movement. The great-hearted veteran whom we had just named galloped from column to column. He announced the purpose to charge in brief and thrilling words. He then returned to his position, and passed down, to right and to left, the stern order to advance. The bugles sounded; and like the surging of a mighty deluge which had long been compressed within narrow limits, that mass of heroes, having caught new energy and strength from reviving hope, moved forward sublimely to the assault. The steady Massachusetts men of Grover, the fierce and fiery brigades of Meagher and Sickles, the well drilled soldiers of Hooker, Kearney with his brave Jersey Blues, the resolute troops of Heintzelman, and others equally gallant, marched defiantly against the foe, with the determination to conquer or to perish. The enemy met their rushing tides at first with firmness; but nothing could long resist such a delirium of fortitude as seemed to pervade and to inflame their assailants. They gradually gave way; their lines broke; and they eventually fled from the field in complete confusion.

During this famous battle-shock, many were slain on both sides, and many prisoners were taken. The Rebels had previously captured a large number of guns, being portions of the batteries of Randall, Mott and Ayres. In the entire engagement at White Oak swamp the Federal loss in killed and wounded was not less than three thousand five hundred. That of the enemy was undoubtedly as great, if not much greater. But the contest saved the Federal army from ruin or from capitulation, and covered both the generals who commanded and the soldiers who fought in it, with enduring renown. In vain had the best Rebel officers repeatedly put in practice their favorite tactics, of hurling fresh masses of troops on the Federal lines, first on one wing, then on the other, and suddenly in the centre. All was in vain. The goal had been safely reached. The glancing placid waters of the James River had at last greeted the longing eyes of the soldiers of the Union; and the possibility of their destruction or of a still more disastrous capture was forever averted.

At the close of the battle of White Oak swamp the Federal army took possession of Malvern Hill in the vicinity of the river. General McClellan had selected Harrison's Landing, six miles below, as his future permanent camp, and thither the convoy of wagons, ammunition stores, and supplies of all sorts continued to be directed. The James River was crowded with transports and vessels of all kinds, to assist in the work of transportation. During Monday night the heroes of a seven-days battle rested from their herculean labors. But their task was not yet completed. On Tuesday, July the 1st, the last of this memorable series of engagements, the battle of Malvern Hill, was fought.

As an attack from the enemy was anticipated, the Federal army was drawn out in battle array at an early hour. Their line formed a magnificent semicircle, which presented a formidable front. General Keyes with his command was posted on the extreme right. General Franklin's corps came next, then the troops of Sumner comprising the divisions of Sedgwick and Richardson. The extreme left was occupied by Fitz John Porter. Heintzelman's corps, embracing the divisions of Hooker, Kearney and Couch, occupied the centre. Fifty heavy guns bristled along the lines from their freshly made earthworks.

The battle commenced about noon with a vigorous cannonading on both sides. The enemy were commanded by Generals Lee, Magruder and Jackson, and opened the engagement with great spirit. Several hours passed away before the infantry came into action. At four o'clock the Rebels advanced, fiercely attacked the troops commanded by General Couch and attempted to break the

Federal line. The effort failed, and the assailants were driven back with great slaughter at the point of the bayonet. But they were not easily disheartened. After a short interval they made a still more desperate effort to accomplish their purpose. The Rebel commanders threw forward heavy masses of troops, assisted and protected by artillery, against the ranks of Porter and Couch, and continued for more than an hour to hurl forward fresh columns upon the Federal line.

At one crisis their determined efforts seemed about to be successful in driving back the Federals. At that critical moment General Porter dispatched a messenger to General Sumner, requesting immediate reinforcements. The Irish brigade of Meagher, who's valorous troops seemed, in almost every emergency, to be the protecting aegis of the Federal army in the peninsula, were immediately sent to the rescue. They advanced to meet the enemy with their usual enthusiasm. The wavering Federal lines were quickly steadied; the Rebel host in turn recoiled; and the periled fortune of the day was recovered. Thus the fight was continued until after nightfall. At ten o'clock the last gun was fired.

During the progress of the engagement the most signal service had been rendered by the gunboats on James River. The immense shells from their rifled cannon tore shrieking and howling through the forests, and often exploded within the lines of the enemy with a concussion which shook the solid earth, and scattered piles of dead and wounded on every hand. In all their efforts to drive the Federal forces from their position, the enemy had signally failed. After each advance they had been repulsed with heavy losses. The battle was to them an unqualified defeat. To prove that this statement should not be regarded as exaggerated or inaccurate, we might adduce many admissions made by the Rebels themselves. One of the most impartial of these will suffice. A leading Richmond journal said: "Officers and men went down by the hundreds; but yet, undaunted and unwavering, our line dashed on, until two-thirds of the distance across the interval was accomplished. Here the carnage from the withering fire of the enemy's combined artillery and musketry was dreadful. Our line wavered a moment, and fell back into the cover of the woods. Twice again the effort to carry the position was renewed, but each time with the same results. Night at length rendered a further attempt injudicious; and the fight until ten o'clock was kept up by the artillery on both sides.

"The battle-field, surveyed through the cold rain of Wednesday morning, presented scenes too shocking to be dwelt on without anguish. The woods and the field before mentioned were, on the western side, covered with our dead, in all the degrees of violent mutilation, while in the woods on the west of the field lay, *in about equal numbers,* the blue uniformed bodies of the enemy."

Thus ended the battle of Malvern Hill. Thus terminated the last assault made by the troops of the Rebel Confederacy at this period, upon the army of the Union in the Peninsula. Thus concluded one of the most extraordinary series of engagements which has ever occurred in the blood-stained annals of ancient or modern warfare. The losses endured on both sides were appalling; and impartial history will hereafter affirm from her high seat, that the Rebels had little of which to boast, in the incidents and results of the battles which were fought near their capital. It is unquestionably true, that the Federal forces would have been withdrawn to the James River without these assaults having been made upon them.

While, therefore, the Confederates inflicted superfluous wounds and death upon them, they were themselves in turn punished and mulcted to a much more destructive and ruinous extent. The Federal losses in these various engagements were as follows: in the battle of Mechanicsville, the number in killed and wounded was about one thousand; in that of Gaines' Mill, three thousand; in that of Peach Orchard, five hundred; at Savage's Station, one thousand; in White Oak Swamp, three thousand five hundred; at Golding's Farm, four hundred; at Malvern Hill, two thousand; making a grand total of eleven thousand four hundred. This estimate does not include the missing, whose exact numbers are unknown. It is probable that the losses of the Rebels were fully twice as great as those which had been inflicted on the Federal troops.

During Tuesday night, and on Wednesday the 2d of July, the concentration and establishment of the Union forces at Harrison's Landing were completed. The enemy were too much broken and exhausted to continue the pursuit or to renew the assault. Their self-imposed task had been finished, with greater infliction of suffering and calamity on themselves than on their opponents.

The new position which General McClellan had selected, consisted of a strip of land along the northern bank of the James River, five miles in length, where a number of suitable wharves existed, at which the transports could discharge their cargoes of supplies; and whose external form toward the enemy was admirably adapted to the purpose of defense. It was soon made impregnable against all attacks by the skillful use of the spade; for such formidable breastworks were quickly thrown up, as to convince the Rebels of the impolicy of any attempt to carry them by assault.

On the 4th of July General McClellan issued an address to his troops, in which he bestowed upon them that praise for heroism and endurance which they had richly merited; and which will continue to be, until the end of time, the just reward of the brave and patriotic men, whose undying glory and misfortune it was to have belonged to the Federal army in the Peninsula.

The repose of that army at Harrison's Landing remained undisturbed by the enemy during the period of nearly a month. It was not until the night of the 31st of July that their hostile presence and spirit were again exhibited. The Rebels had crossed the James in considerable numbers, above the Federal camp; had posted several batteries opposite to the Landing, and in the vicinity of the Union fleet of transports; and then began a vigorous cannonading, both upon the camp and the fleet. The assault continued during an hour and a half. Their guns threw shell of six and twelve pounds weight, both round and conical. They effected but little damage, inasmuch as they generally fell short of their mark. A few of them exploded within the Federal camp, and some of them reached the shipping. In consequence of the fact that no attack was expected from the foe in that direction, all the Federal guns had been posted in the front; so that a considerable interval elapsed before a sufficient number could be transferred to the proper position to respond to the enemy. In half an hour the latter commenced to reply, and in a short time the Rebels were silenced.

They had made a futile assault; for although they discharged several hundred shells, so inaccurate was their aim that the loss on the Union side was only six killed and nine wounded. During the attack the Rebels frequently changed the position of their batteries, and as the night was extremely dark, it was only by the flashes of the guns that their location could be discovered. The vessels on the James River did not return any shots, as by so doing they would have revealed their own location more distinctly to the enemy.

This brief and unimportant episode was the mere prelude to the last military operation which was destined to take place between the Federal and Rebel armies in the Peninsula. The hideous carnival of blood and death which had rendered that spot so sadly famous in all coming time, was now about to terminate with the second battle at Malvern Hill.

On Monday, the 4th of August, a portion of the Federal army was ordered to make a reconnaissance in the direction of the Rebel lines. It consisted of the divisions commanded by Generals Hooker and Sedgwick, a brigade of cavalry under General Pleasanton, and four batteries. General Hooker was chief in command. Leaving the camp at four o'clock in the afternoon, they marched along the road to Charles City for some distance. They then diverged through several by-roads as far as Nelson's Farm. At that point they bivouacked for the night. Early on the following morning they resumed their march, and in an hour they reached the rear of Malvern Hill, upon which the enemy were posted. They thus occupied a position between the latter and the remainder of their army, as well as their depot of supplies at Richmond. An admirable opportunity was thus afforded to surround and capture a large portion of the Rebel force.

Immediately after coming within view of the latter, the Federal troops were formed in line of battle. The artillery were posted in the front, the cavalry and infantry were ranged on the flanks. The Rebels commenced the battle promptly at six o'clock with their guns. The Federal cannon responded with spirit. The enemy were much inferior in number to the Union troops; comprising only three regiments of infantry, a small portion of cavalry, with four pieces of artillery. They maintained the contest during two hours with great determination; but the vast superiority of the Union troops in numbers rendered a further resistance on their part useless. They then retired in good order toward the James River. The

Federal victors did not pursue. Their loss was only six killed and twenty-four wounded. The enemy took with them all their guns, their killed and their wounded. This fight enabled General Hooker to take possession of Malvern Hill, which gave him a position six miles nearer to Richmond than that at Harrison's Landing.

On Tuesday afternoon General McClellan, accompanied by a number of officers, visited the spot, and greatly commended General Hooker for his achievement. It was perfectly evident however, that though the small body of Rebel troops stationed there had been overpowered, large reinforcements would be quickly sent from Richmond to recover the lost position. A general engagement would therefore soon occur, to decide the permanent possession of the place.

Accordingly, General McClellan immediately sent messengers to his camp, ordering a large number of his troops to march toward Malvern Hill, to support the column already posted there. If these troops had arrived in time, the issue of the subsequent operations might have been different. But the messengers who conveyed the order pursued the wrong road, were unaccountably delayed on their journey and thus the reinforcements did not approach until the position had been hopelessly lost. Only a portion of those Federal troops which were sent arrived, and these made their appearance only in time to join in the general retreat.

On Wednesday the Rebels marched to Malvern Hill in large masses, and as the Federal forces, by this maneuver, would have been greatly inferior in numbers, a retrograde movement was precipitately made to Harrison's Landing. Thus ended the capture, the occupation and the evacuation of the position at Malvern Hill. The Federal loss during the operation was four killed and fifteen wounded.

It had now become evident to the Federal Government that the expedition against Richmond, through the Peninsula, had proved a total and irremediable failure. It was quite as evident that the longer delay of the army of the Union in that unpropitious clime would be productive of no good, while it would entail a continued and lavish waste of the national treasure and of valuable lives. General McClellan therefore received orders to evacuate Harrison's Landing. This order was obeyed on the 16th and 17th of August,

1862. Through the energy and skill of Colonel Ingalls, all the stores of subsistence and ammunition were safely removed on board the fleet of Federal transports which then lay at Harrison's Landing. Nothing of the least value was left behind.

The Rebel commanders, intensely gratified to witness the departure of their formidable visitors, did not offer any resistance to the movement. The army crossed the Chickahominy by a pontoon bridge two thousand feet in length, consisting of a hundred boats. The troops then marched forward toward Williamsburg, while the transports and gunboats sailed down the James to Fortress Monroe.

The future destination of the Army of the Peninsula was then as yet unknown. It was, however, intended to be consolidated with the forces which had been placed under the orders of General Pope. This arrangement was afterward completed; and the fortunes of war were again tried under new auspices, against the desperate, yet by no means contemptible conspirators, who had risen in rebellion against their legitimate government, and had thus far struck, with such marvelous energy, ferocity and skill, against its sacred bosom.

Nor can the patriot and philanthropist fail to experience the most poignant emotions of regret, when reflecting upon the varied incidents and results of the campaign in the Peninsula:—when he remembers the brilliant hopes which threw so bright and fair a radiance around the advance of the Union army toward the Rebel capital; when he recalls the many glorious prodigies of heroism and valor which were vainly performed by the soldiers and officers of that army, in the sanguinary battles which they fought; when he computes how many thousands of valiant and devoted men, from different and distant portions of the continent, were left behind by their departing comrades to moulder in their unknown and unhonored graves, the victims of a climate and of labors more deadly than the bullets and cannon of the foe; in a word, when he meditates upon the complete and melancholy discomfiture of one of the greatest and noblest enterprises which the checkered page of history presents.

3

THE BATTLE OF SHILOH

By Samuel M. Schmucker

When the Germans invaded Russia in 1940, they employed as a basic tactic what they called kiel und kessel, *wedge and kettle. These were comparatively small scale double envelopments. By encirclement of areas the Russian forces left in that area could be chewed up in detail.*

If the Federal Government had a Grand Strategy in the Civil War it was to fragment the Confederacy and then again split the fragments. The obvious and essential first cleavage was the Mississippi River.

A major achievement in this direction was made when the Cumberland and Tennessee Rivers were opened by Grant's capture of Forts Henry and Donelson. In continuing the operation, the Federals concentrated at Pittsburg Landing and the Confederates at Corinth. On April 6, 1862 while Grant was not present, the Confederates, under Albert Sidney Johnston, attacked with considerable success. Grant returned and, on the 7th, reversed the battle, no doubt partly due to the death of General Johnston.

Here, from Schmucker, is a brief tactical account of the engagement and a consideration of some of the possibilities of the battle.

The first great battle of the war, employing troops in large masses, was fought in connection with this. Possession of the little chapel of Shiloh was not of itself important. Like other operations, this was a part of the fight to determine possession of the Mississippi River.

Within the account of Major Truman is a quotation from General Grant pointing out that he considered up until the time of Shiloh that one decisive victory by the Union forces would cause the rebellion to collapse. This made the battle crucial to him. He got his victory but the war went on for three years, lacking two days. From this point on Grant became increasingly a factor in Federal decisions and Federal victory. His realization that a long, costly and determined war lay ahead, was more "crucial" than the tactical decision.

The Federal forces which had crossed the Mississippi River were posted westward from Pittsburg Landing (Shiloh) in a curved line along the banks, and extended a distance of three and a half miles; the centre facing the road to Corinth. They were commanded by Generals Prentiss, Sherman, Hurlbut and McClernand. As Corinth was a position admirably adapted for defense, it was not suspected that the enemy would abandon the advantages which it afforded and venture on an advance. Hence it must be admitted that their attack was in a great measure unexpected.

They marched out of Corinth on Saturday, April 5th, seventy thousand in number, in three grand divisions. Sidney Johnston was in command of the centre; Braxton Bragg and Beauregard commanded the two wings; Hardee, Polk, Breckinridge, and Cheatham held inferior positions. Their plan of attack was, to assault the centre of the Federal lines, consisting of the divisions of Prentiss and McClernand, penetrate them, and then assail each of the wings on the front and flank. Having thus divided and overpowered the Federal army, their purpose was to compel them to surrender, or drive them into the Tennessee River, and thus complete either the capture or the ruin of the whole.

During the night of Saturday their numerous forces lay at no very great distance from the Federal camp. Their proximity evidently began to be suspected; for at two o'clock in the morning of Sunday, the 6th, Colonel Peabody, of General Prentiss's division, sent forward four hundred men beyond his lines, to ascertain whether any Rebel troops lay in that vicinity. These had scarcely proceeded half a mile when they encountered a large body of Rebels approaching them. The latter opened their fire immediately, and drove the Federals with great slaughter, back toward their camp. They followed promptly, and actually reached the position of Colonel Peabody as his regiment, aroused by the distant firing, were falling into line. The gray mists of morning were then about ascending, and throwing a partial, hazy light over the scene, so soon to become the arena of one of the bloodiest struggles of modern times. Many of the officers had not yet risen, many of the men were not yet armed, when the whole Federal camp became aware that a vigorous attack had commenced upon some portion of their line.

The Twenty-fifth Missouri regiment, belonging to General Prentiss's division, was the first to feel the assault of the approaching enemy, who were firing volleys of musketry as they advanced. Their cannon, already in position and unlimbered, were tossing shells into the heart of the Federal encampment. During this process the Federal army was gradually dressing, arming, and falling into line; but this was not accomplished until a decisive advantage had been gained by the enemy.

The whole of General Sherman's division was the first to confront the Rebels in line of battle. It was now six o'clock. Sherman's troops withstood the shock for some time with heroism; but being overpowered by superior numbers, were compelled to give way. As they retreated the balls of the enemy ploughed through their living masses with fearful slaughter. The divisions of Generals Sherman and Buckland abandoned their camp equipage, and some of them retreated in disgraceful disorder. Several of the Ohio regiments, especially the Fifty-third, commanded by Colonel Appler, fled without firing a single gun, and covered themselves with ignominy.

In vain did General McClernand order forward a portion of his left, to support the scattering and fugitive troops of Buckland. In vain did General Sherman exert himself to stop the flight of his own men, dashing bravely along the lines amid a hailstorm of bullets. The advancing billows of the Rebel host overwhelmed every thing before them; and while portions of the Federal regiments occasionally paused a few moments to stop the tide of fugitives and pursuers, the great mass rolled onward in a tumultuous chaos toward the river.

Then it was that General Prentiss, having succeeded in making a stand for a time, and having been left unsupported on the field, was encompassed by the enemy. A wall of bayonets closed around his men, and after a short but desperate combat they were made prisoners. Three regiments having laid down their arms, were marched toward the rear of the enemy.

It was now ten o'clock. One whole division of the Federal army had retreated, leaving a frightful gap in the centre of their lines. Just then the division of General W. H. L. Wallace was deployed into the vacant territory; and they held their position with great resolution till toward the end of the day.

By this time General Grant arrived on the field from Savannah, and immediately placed guards in the rear to stop the retreating soldiers. The temporary flight was thus terminated, the officers became reassured, and succeeded in bringing their troops, many of whom had begun to waver, into order of battle. Then ensued a more regular, universal and desperate combat.

The battle raged along the whole line; for the enemy had now all reached the scene of conflict, and every portion of both armies was brought into action. The roar of the cannon and musketry was deafening; the earth trembled under their shock. The fiercest struggle was in the centre, between the enemy and the troops who had taken General Sherman's position. A furious charge was made upon the Fourteenth Ohio battery, and after a long contest it was captured by the Rebels. A similar onslaught was made upon the Fifth Ohio battery, which resulted in the capture of three of its guns. The left wing of the Federal forces also encountered and resisted a ferocious assault. The Rebels, by a sudden dash, captured a part of the battery of Waterhouse, together with that of Beer.

For nearly two hours a lurid sheet of fire blazed between the two columns, hurling destruction into each other's ranks. Three different times the Federals, weakened by the deadly fire of the Mississippi riflemen, were compelled slowly to retire toward the river; and three times they regained the lost advantage. Dresser's battery of rifled guns on two occasions made the enemy recoil with fearful losses.

Thus till after three o'clock the combat raged with appalling fury. The air seemed filled with sulphurous hail; the wide-spread scene of conflict was covered with a far ascending curtain of smoke, within which the rushing, advancing, receding masses of men might be dimly seen, plunged into the mortal struggles of the conflict. At one time the fire of the enemy appeared to be concentrated toward the centre. At another it would expand and extend itself up and down the line, to right and to left.

By this time the ground was covered with the wounded and the slain of both armies. Successive bayonet charges had been made at intervals during the day by both sides. Thus, repeatedly was the terrific spectacle exhibited during that long and desperate combat, of a thousand men, sometimes five thousand, summoned by the sound of the bugle, forming into line, rushing forward with fixed bayonets as if impelled by a single animating spirit, rending the air with their yells, sheets of flame darting forth from their advancing lines, then the shock of the collision, the reverberation of the blows, the clashing of steel, and at last the necessary recoil, as the one party or the other, possessing greater momentum and strength than their adversaries, remained masters of the position. Then were heard the piercing shrieks of the wounded, the melancholy groans of the dying, the vociferous shouts of the victors.

All this had frequently been enacted during the long progress of that day. For the most part, the superiority of numbers which the rebels possessed generally gave them the advantage. As the sun was descending the western heavens, the Federal army was gradually retiring toward the river, unable to resist with success the ponderous and infuriated masses opposed to them. By this time the enemy had full possession of the camps of Sherman, Prentiss, and McClernand. The whole front line, except Stuart's brigade, had given way. To the last the divisions of W. H. L. Wallace and Hurlbut made a heroic stand, and maintained their positions. Hurlbut had been encamped at the end of the line nearest the river. His troops consisted chiefly of Kentucky, Indiana and Iowa regiments. Having open fields before them, they raked the approaching enemy with terrible effect. They held their position from ten in the forenoon until half past three. No officer on the field deserved greater praise for his heroism and gallantry than

General Hurlbut. His example and his exertions served greatly to avert the horrors of an universal defeat, which impended over the army of the Union on that memorable day.

Next in line to his brigade was that of General W. H. L. Wallace, who commanded the troops which had formerly been under the orders of General Charles Ferguson Smith, whom sickness prevented from being present in this engagement. General Wallace entered into the conflict about ten o'clock. He and his men fought with the utmost resolution till half past three. Four separate times the Rebel generals attempted to turn them by the most furious charges. Just as often their advancing masses were compelled to recoil and retreat with fearful losses.

The powerful batteries from Missouri, commanded by Stone, Weber, and Richardson, were admirably served, and greatly contributed to the partial success of the day, in this portion of the field. But when the general retreat began, and the whole line commenced to retire, they were compelled to yield, for it would have been madness to remain. As the division began to fall back, General Wallace was severely wounded. His soldiers were the last to give way, at that desperate moment when the Federal line was driven back within half a mile of Pittsburg Landing, with the victorious masses of the Rebels crowding within a thousand yards of their confused and retreating ranks.

And now the last horrible tragedy of this day seemed about to be consummated. The Rebels at length occupied all the camps of the Federal army. The latter were crowded in wild confusion around Pittsburg Landing, within the circumference of half a mile. In vain had the soldiers of the Union expended prodigies of valor, in the most desperate attempts to resist their fate. They had now fallen back as far as the nature of the ground would permit. There seemed to be no alternative but to surrender, or to perish beneath the tranquil and brightly glancing waves of the Tennessee River; for sufficient transports had not been provided to convey over even a small proportion of the multitude of the fugitives.

Never had the fate of any army seemed more desperate, its ruin more inevitable. During the day General Buell had been repeatedly telegraphed to hasten his tardy legions; but he had been unable as yet to reach the scene of conflict.

Certain destruction thus appeared to impend over the Union army, when a sudden deliverance unexpectedly arose. The gunboats Lexington and A. O. Tyler having opportunely arrived from Savannah, were at that moment able to bring their guns to bear upon the masses of the victorious Rebels; and having steamed up the mouth of Licking Creek, they opened a deadly fire upon their right wing. Broadside after broadside of sixty-four pounders were discharged as rapidly as the most skillful gunnery could send their shells into the serried ranks of the foe.

At the same time the long-wished-for advance guard of Buell's army appeared on the high bluffs which lined the opposite banks of the river. Their presence at once inspirited the Federal troops, and shout after shout ascended to greet them. But no time was to be lost, and quickly several transports which had been tied along the opposite bank were loosed, and filled with artillery and troops. But before they could arrive, Colonel Webster, the chief of General Grant's staff, had collected all the guns which remained untaken, had formed them into a semicircle bearing upon the Rebel army, and had opened a formidable assault upon their line.

These combined salutes, while they raised the courage of the Federal forces, which had been fighting for so many hours, disheartened the enemy. The death of General Sidney Johnston now became known, which misfortune added to their panic. Their commanders at length discovered that their successes for that day were ended; and that no further advantage could possibly be gained. They therefore withdrew as far as the Federal camps which they had taken, and prepared to renew the contest with more decisive results, as they hoped, on the ensuing day.

The night of Sunday was industriously employed in transporting the troops of General Buell across the river. As soon as the successive regiments arrived, they proceeded to take their positions in the Federal lines. The gunboats continued their bombardment during the whole night. They soon made the position occupied by the centre and the right of the Rebels, at the close of Sunday, untenable, and compelled them to fall back from point to point, so that they evacuated more than half the ground they had gained by the retreat of the Federal army toward the river. This circumstance will account for the mysterious fact that the Rebels made no assault during the night, as had been confidently expected; and it also prevented them from commencing the battle at daybreak on Monday.

During the hours of that memorable night, while a furious tempest raged, and a deluge of rain descended, the Federal commanders were busy in making preparations for resuming the contest. New dispositions had been formed. Ammon's brigade was placed on the extreme left, that of Bruce in the centre, that of Hazen on the right of Nelson's division.

At seven o'clock on Monday the action began, by a simultaneous advance on both sides; for both sides seemed equally eager for the combat. General Lewis Wallace opened the engagement by shelling the enemy opposed to him. He was answered by a powerful Rebel battery, and a duel between artillery ensued. The result here was, that a body of Federal infantry having been sent across a ravine to attack the flank of this portion of the enemy's line, the guns of the latter were soon limbered up and hastily withdrawn.

General Nelson at the same time attacked the enemy opposed to him. His large mass of troops renewed the contest in all its fury; the action soon became general along the whole line; and the rattle of small arms, and the louder, heavier tones of the artillery reverberated without intermission over the far-extending scene of conflict. The Rebels attacked the Federal centre and right with the utmost desperation.

At half past ten the Federals had regained nearly all the ground from which they had been driven on the preceding day. At that moment the enemy concentrated their efforts to make a grand assault. Suddenly, and with much concert, their generals hurled their furious squadrons on the lines of the advancing Federals. Stunned by the shock, the latter reeled, and for a time gave way on the entire right. The ground there was fiercely contested, and the issue would have been doubtful, perhaps disastrous; but just at the critical moment General Buell arrived on that part of the field and assumed the command. He soon comprehended the relative positions of the combatants, and ordered a forward double-quick movement by brigades. The Rebel lines were then driven back for a quarter of a mile. Soon the deserted camps of the Federals were reached, and repossessed by their former owners.

By half past two the entire right of the enemy was routed; they had lost all in that portion of the field which they had gained; the captured guns of the Federals were retaken; and some additional trophies were wrested from the retreating enemy.

In that part of the Federal lines where the brigades of Crittenden, McCook, Smith, and Boyle were posted, a contest of equal intensity took place. At one time the Federal troops were overpowered and retreated. The day was recovered by a spirited cannonade poured into the Rebel masses by the batteries Mendenhall and Bartlett. After a long contest the enemy here also began to retire, and to leave the field in the possession of their antagonists.

On the extreme right, where the gallant Hurlbut and McClernand commanded, the vicissitudes of the day were equally varied, to be terminated at last by a result equally honorable to the Federal arms. Four times McClernand lost and regained the position which he occupied at the commencement of the engagement. The troops in the centre of the Federal army, commanded by General Sherman, overpowered by a terrific assault of artillery, in which Watson's Louisiana battery was remarkable for its prodigious effects, were compelled at one time to give way. But after a long struggle they recovered their advantage, aided by the efficient batteries of Thurber and Thompson.

By four o'clock, an hour and a half later than the victory on the left, the enemy commenced to retire here also before Sherman's advancing lines. Then the retreat became general, and the whole Rebel army, disheartened and essentially weakened by the immense though futile struggles of the day, withdrew in comparative order toward Corinth. The Federal forces then reoccupied their original camp, and took possession of almost every trophy which, on the preceding day, had fallen into the possession of the temporary victors.

During the progress of this memorable engagement, Generals Grant, Buell, Sherman, Nelson, the Wallaces, Hurlbut, McClernand and McCook, greatly distinguished themselves. They were present in every portion of the field, and exhibited the utmost skill and coolness in every emergency. Very many of the inferior commanders were equally valiant and equally worthy of commendation. But it must also be admitted, that some of the subaltern officers disgraced themselves during the combat by their cowardice. General Grant was compelled to order a number of these under arrest on the battlefield. The results of this great conflict were important. Their defeat greatly dispirited the Rebel leaders; while it covered the Federal arms with immortal renown.

The chief glory of this victory will be ascribed by posterity to the two generals who were highest in command, Generals Grant and Buell.

CHAPTER 3, PART 2

A SPECTACULAR BATTLE AND ITS "IFS"
(COMMENTARY)

By Major Ben C. Truman

After these many years—thirty-seven—the most troublesome battle of the Civil War to the historian and for the digestion of the general reader is Shiloh, fought on April 6 and 7, 1862. It is the only stupendous conflagration of our great internecine struggle that remains in a state of impossible settlement,—and what has brought about the complete perpetuation of this unsettlement is not so conspicuously sectional as heterogeneous, for there has been no concert of agreement between the leading spirits in that spectacular baptism of fire and flood on either side; and as all the noted participants of that majestic episode have passed away, Shiloh must ever remain the one sanguinary sanctuary that will ever be quarreled over so long as two of its survivors are alive.

There are just two things upon which all agree, and they are, the heroism of both armies, and that Shiloh (or Pittsburg Landing) was one of the three most desperate and important battles of the war. All previous actions, including even Bull Run and Mill Spring, had been skirmishes in comparison. There were thousands of raw troops on either side, many unskillful officers of all grades, inefficient camp police operations, far too much sutlerism, and only that discipline engendered by sustained familiarity of the Western and Southern kind. The fighting, therefore, on the whole, was not scientific, but it was dramatic, resolute, intrepid, and effective.

There were no intrenchments, so to speak, on either side, and few opportunities for splendid maneuvering; but two long lines of impetuous new soldiery stood up against each other for two days in an indescribably tempestuous duel amid a sublime thunder-roll that was lost in reverberating diminuendos twenty-odd miles up and down the serpentine shores of the Tennessee River. There was a crash of small arms from daylight to dark on Sunday, and a roar of artillery, and a hissing and screeching of shot and shell, and falling of tops of great monarchs of the woods, and explosions of caissons, and oaths of horsemen, and cries of wounded, that made a diapason whose rumblings were heard for many miles away in all directions.

That night it rained furiously on more than two thousand dead and ten thousand wounded wearers of the blue and the gray. The entire Union army had been beaten back to a dreadful danger line, and the Confederates were occupying our field of the morning before. But while the victorious men in gray were vociferating their joy over their accomplishment and drinking deep from the spirituous tierces abandoned by the Federal sutlers, Buell, like Blücher, had come up, and amidst the pyrotechnics of sky and cannon had crossed the river with three of his divisions,—Crittenden's, McCook's, and Nelson's,—and Lew Wallace, who had been so anxiously looked for all the fiery day, came just at dark with five thousand fresh fighters.

The battle was resumed early Monday morning by the Union army, and so terrific was the assault on the Confederates, who were unaware of the tremendous re-enforcements hurled against them, that what seemed almost a victory twenty-four hours before had been turned into a repulse, and a Union success was recorded at sundown. Never after did either side distrust the thorough and tenacious courage of its adversary, and never before in America had life been rated so cheaply nor death met with such scornful effrontery and lofty unconcern.

The loss (official) on the Union side was 1,754 killed, 8,408 wounded, and 2,885 prisoners,—13,047; and on the Confederate side, 1,728 killed, 8,012 wounded, and 957 prisoners—10,697; 23,744, in all, or 19,902 in killed and wounded.

Now, if all that can be said of Shiloh could be elaborated from the above fact, it would be well and good, and it could be gloriously gazetted with other illustrious encounters. But this can never be. There is a division of opinion as to whether Grant was or was not surprised, and this division of opinion has prevailed about equally on both sides. The Army of the Tennessee, naturally, denies the allegation almost to a man. Halleck, Buell, Thomas, Stanton, Rosecrans, McClellan, and many expert military critics, have thought otherwise. All the correspondents of Northern newspapers—and they were all friendly to Grant—and a number of high officers of the Army of the Tennessee at the time declared that our army was surprised,—to some extent, it undoubtedly was,—and several regiments that had never been under fire before and were unwisely put in front, broke and ran away. They could hardly have done so had the battle been opened by the gradual pressing in of a proper skirmish line, and it was assumed by conservative and unprejudiced observers and thinkers that the Confederate forces fell upon a portion of our line in order of battle, just as Hardee fell upon McCook at Stone River, with a shock which was clearly a surprise.

The fact that General Grant was breakfasting with Mr. and Mrs. W. H. Cherry, at Savanna, ten miles below Pittsburg Landing, after the battle had commenced, does not more fully emphasize the fact of the surprise, however, as he had a habit of going to Savanna each evening for nearly two weeks; but neither General Grant nor any other commander ever had his headquarters at such a distance from his army, with a river between them, after that.

On the other hand, the surprise was not so absolutely an astonishment as the word might simply betray, as there had been more or less skirmishing for three or four days, and our pickets had been driven in by an advance of Hardee's corps on Thursday, the 3d, on the Bark road, and again at Mickey's. On Friday, the 4th, there was feeble skirmishing here and there all along the line. That evening, during a drenching shower, our abandoned picket post was briskly attacked, and Lieutenant Heaton and seven men of the Seventieth Ohio were captured. The next day there were more exchanges of shot on the picket line and three Georgia cavalrymen were brought in. Therefore, if Grant was actually surprised at Shiloh, he ought not to have been, because he knew there was a big army in front of him, commanded by Albert Sidney Johnston, with Beauregard second in rank, and that there had been skirmishing for four or five days.

Another paradox has grown out of the statement of Grant in the first volume of his memoirs,—although he carefully presents it on the authority of Adam Badeau, whom the Grant family have pronounced a fraud since,—that Prentiss and most of his division were captured along about four o'clock in the afternoon of Sunday, while for twenty years before, the descriptions of Prentiss's capture early in the morning by all the correspondents and general officers on both sides, had never been contradicted. Some twelve years ago I met Prentiss in Cincinnati and asked him if he remembered the exact time of his capture. He answered me, "Exactly half-past five." Had I known him familiarly, I would have come back with "Morning or evening?"

For twenty years, then, Prentiss's capture was made early Sunday morning. But for some fallacious reason, or to serve some partisan historian on our side, the record has been changed. "I held my ground," he continued, "until half-past five in the evening, several hours after Sherman had given way on my left and the line on my right had been broken and driven back. The early reports state, and it has gone down to history, that I was captured in the morning; but this is an untruth, or, at least, a straight-out general uncontradicted mistake." The General also informed me that he had seen Grant and had received orders from him as early as eight. Surely this is a mistake, as Grant was not on Prentiss's part of the field at any time before ten. It is such a reversing of records that tangles up the historian when he tackles Shiloh.

Opinion is divided as to the results had not Buell thrown three divisions into Monday's fight. Grant has gone so far as to say that he did not need them—that with Lew Wallace's five thousand men, who came from Crump's Landing at nightfall on the 6th, he could have won over Beauregard easily. Not a great many Northern soldiers and only few Southern ones have ever believed this. For some unaccountable reason—no superior military one, for Grant had ordered him twice during Sunday to the field of action,—Wallace merely listened to the cannonade only a few miles away, and nearly essayed the role of a Grouchy at Waterloo when he might have illumined a career as did Desaix at Marengo. Grant criticises Wallace's action in his memoirs, and between his lines he uses more than a switch.

Unfortunately for history, the Southerners have also disagreed regarding their share in Shiloh, and the partisans of Johnston and Beauregard are still quarreling, a large majority favoring the distinguished abilities of the former over those of the latter, with the North almost a unit in their claims of Johnston having been much the greater soldier of the two. There are many Federal officers and European critics who have always maintained that had Johnston not been killed at the very zenith of his day's effort it would have been all up with Grant before nightfall. But of this there can never be anything but fallacious and unsatisfactory speculation. There is no poorer place in the world for "Ifs" than on the battlefield. The results are victories or defeats for one side or the other, and no "Ifs" can tarnish the one or repair the other.

It was unfortunate for the South that there was such a pronounced difference of opinion between Johnston and Beauregard. The former, first in command, purposed an immediate and effective attack, and the latter, the popular hero of Bull Run, opposed it. Beauregard wished to pursue the policy in the West which Lee was pursuing in the East so effectively,—to prolong the war, wear out the North, and keep his own army intact by a defensive campaign. Johnston overruled all opposition. He ended the council of war on Saturday afternoon with the decisive declaration: "We shall attack at daylight to-morrow. I would fight them if they were a million!" A stray bullet cut an artery in his leg, early in the afternoon, while victory seemed about to perch upon his banner. It was his Austerlitz! Beauregard assumed command. It was his Waterloo!

As I have heretofore stated, the difficulty which must be overcome by the historian in aggregating the stubborn facts of Shiloh was curiously emphasized in the two articles that appeared in the same number of the *Century Magazine* some sixteen or seventeen years ago,—the one by General Grant, the other by Colonel William Preston Johnston, a son of General Johnston, and on the staff of Jefferson Davis. One gives, of course, the Federal, and the other the Confederate side. Not only in their interpretation of the aims and purposes of the combatants, and in their estimate of the significance and result of the first day's battle, do they differ, but also in their accounts of events, even in minor details.

Thus Colonel Johnston credits Grant with an army of 58,000 nearly 50,000 of whom were effectives, while he allows the Confederate commander 50,000 of whom but 40,000 were available for combat. General Grant, on the contrary, gives the entire strength of the Federal army of 38,000, of whom not more than 25,000 were in line on the first day. Of course, General Grant's statement of his own forces is official and conclusive; but the fact illustrates the discrepancies of history.

The man of Northern prejudices at that day read General Grant's paper carefully and only glanced at Colonel Johnston's. The man of Southern prejudices consoled himself with Colonel Johnston's conviction that the battle of Shiloh was won on the first day, and was lost on the second only because the Confederate commander was killed. The impartial historian accepting the veracity, but not necessarily the judgments, of both authors will compare the two papers to reach a true understanding of this momentous battle, and will find in General Grant's frank confession of his misapprehension of the strength of the Confederacy, and in Colonel Johnston's disclosure of the divided counsels in the Confederate army, two leading clews to the true interpretation of the events of the day.

"Up to the battle of Shiloh," says General Grant, "I, as well as thousands of other citizens, believed that the rebellion against the Government would collapse suddenly and soon if a decisive victory could be gained over any of its armies." This was substantially the universal opinion in the North. It was even shared by many in the South. The fall of Forts Donelson and Henry apparently opened the whole Southwest to the Federal army. The North believed that further resistance would be in vain. Thousands in the South shared that belief. General Grant, as soon as the dilatory Halleck gave him opportunity to move, acted in accordance with his subsequent instructions to General Sheridan before Rich-

mond, and pushed things. He hurried his army forward after the
retreating Confederate forces, meaning to give them no time to
recover from their demoralization. He expected no other than a
Fabian policy of slow retreat and sullen but not aggressive resistance. Assuming that the Confederates would retreat if pushed,
he threw up no earthworks. He put raw levies at the front. He telegraphed to Halleck on Saturday night (April 5th), "I have scarcely
the faintest idea of an attack (general one) being made upon us."
The army, catching the contagion of his confidence, perhaps
neglected to keep out scouts in the front. This was charged at the
time by newspaper correspondents, and is not specifically denied by General Grant, who does specifically deny some analogous
charges. While General Grant was thus taking for granted that
the Confederate forces would not venture on an aggressive campaign, the Confederate Generals themselves were in fiery debate
upon that very point. General Johnston, as I have once before
stated, purposed an attack. General Beauregard opposed it.

Thus both sides entered the first day's battle under tremendous disadvantages. The Federal forces were not expecting an
attack, and were not, therefore, adequately prepared for it. Even
when it came, they regarded it at first as only a reconnaissance in
force. General Sherman, who was at the front, so interpreted it.
"Beauregard," he said, "is not such a fool as to leave his base of
operations and attack us in ours." On the other hand, the Confederates entered on an aggressive campaign with divided counsels.
The second in command was half sick, had no faith in an assault,
and no expectation of success.

General Grant in his *Century Magazine* article, and also in his
book, insists that the Federal forces were not defeated on the first
day. But, really, the facts do not bear out this claim. His front had
been forced back nearly, or quite, two miles. General Prentiss's
division had been captured en masse,—2,200 officers and men.
The Federal camps were in the possession of the enemy. What
the Confederates could or would have done on the morrow if
their leadership had remained unchanged must always remain a
matter of opinion, a chapter of "Ifs." That the wearied assailants
could have driven the Federal forces into the river or cut off their

retreat, and enforced their surrender, is at least problematical, but not strictly incredible, even if the Federal army had not been re-enforced on the morrow by part of General Buell's forces and by the gunboats. But the attempt was not even made, which incorporates another chapter of "If's."

The death of General Johnston threw the command on General Beauregard, and the change of commanders brought a change of policy. At the council of war on Saturday afternoon General Beauregard had urged that the army withdraw to Corinth. On Monday morning he ordered that withdrawal to take place. The first day battle of Shiloh was a Confederate attack under one commander. The second day's battle was a Confederate retreat under another commander. Both were measurably successful. It is, indeed, rarely the case that a change of command and a change of policy takes place on the field of battle with so little disaster to the army as resulted to the Confederates from their change of commanders and policy at the battle of Shiloh.

This battle singularly illustrates how far the fortunes of war depend upon what we call accident. If General Johnston had lived he would have pursued on Monday the aggressive policy of Sunday, and his army would have either won a magnificent victory or suffered a tremendous defeat. And that he did not live was due to accident. A stray shot cut an artery in his leg. An extemporized tourniquet would have stopped the bleeding. But half an hour earlier he had dismissed his surgeon-in-chief—who up to that time had accompanied him—to attend wounded Federal prisoners. There was no one present at the moment who knew enough to tie up the artery, and General Johnston bled to death. It may be gloriously said of the distinguished Confederate commander that his lofty humanity to Federal prisoners cost him his life. On the other hand, General Grant, Colonel McPherson, and Major Hawkins, reconnoitering the field together, suddenly found themselves subjected to a sharp musket-fire from a concealed battery. Major Hawkins lost his hat, Colonel McPherson's horse was shot through the body and lived just long enough to take him out of danger, and the scabbard of General Grant's sword was taken off by a ball. If the one ball had missed General Johnston, and the other had struck General Grant, the commander of the Federal forces, not of the Confederate forces, would have been changed, and the issue of the battle of Shiloh might have been altogether different. What a great contribution Shiloh has been to the achievements of war! What a glowing chapter on the eloquent impotence of "Ifs"!

4

THE MONITOR AND MERRIMAC

By Frank B. Butts

A most important factor in the defeat of the Confederacy was the economic strangulation imposed by the Northern Navy's blockade. Before the arrival of the airplane the counter weapon to a ship of war was another ship of war. The Confederacy, primarily an agrarian society, was born and all its life spent under war conditions. It had not the remotest possibility of ever equaling the North in the technological requirements of building and maintaining a fleet. In countering this situation, Southern ship designers built an ironclad, revolutionary in design and deadly in combat effectiveness. Greatly daring, her commander tried her against the strong wooden ships of the Federal fleet—and in a few hours the timbered warships of the world were outmoded. Technically the ironclad had many deficiencies—too deep a draft and an inadequate power plant. But for these—and the arrival of a new type Federal ship—the whole strategic planning of the North would have been changed. During the hours when the Virginia (neé Merrimac) and the Monitor slugged it out, the future of naval warfare hung in the balance.

The Monitor left New York on the afternoon of March 6, 1862, with a fair indication of good weather, in tow of the tug Seth Low, and accompanied by the gunboats Currituck and Sachem. They proceeded without incident until the next day at noon, when they

71

had reached the Capes of Delaware, and the water began to sweep over the deck of the Monitor and broke into the vessel under the turret and through the hawser pipe. The wind and sea increased during the afternoon, and the water broke over the blower pipes into the ventilating machinery, which soon became useless and stopped the draft of the furnaces. The engine room was immediately filled with gas, which prostrated the engineers and firemen, who had to be carried to the top of the turret in order to revive. At this time the voyage had a most discouraging outlook. The motive power was checked, and the water was breaking into the ship in considerable quantities. Commander Worden ordered the hand pumps started and the men to bailing. The vessel was headed in shore and the sea having smoothed down after an hour or two, the blowers were put in order, and the vessels were put on their course again. About midnight, when they were crossing a shoal, the water again broke over the blower pipes, causing a renewal of the accident and wetting the wheel ropes, which jammed and, until the shoal was crossed or for half an hour, the Monitor was at the mercy of the sea. Damages were again repaired and the vessel proceeded smoothly until they were passing Cape Henry light, when heavy firing was heard in the direction of Fortress Monroe. They were not mistaken in thinking that the Merrimac had come out and that an engagement was going on with our fleet at Hampton Roads. The decks were cleared and the Monitor made ready for action, as it was thought the Merrimac would attempt to escape to the North. Here for the first time quarters was beat on board the Monitor, and a drill was had in handling the guns and ammunition. When about a dozen miles from Fortress Monroe a pilot was taken on board, from whom was learned the true state of affairs at Hampton Roads. He recounted the disasters to the Cumberland and Congress, the formidable character of the Merrimac and the gloom that overshadowed all who had witnessed the fight.

Such was the state of affairs when the Monitor arrived at Hampton Roads, that the sturdy commanders trembled in face of the coming day, and all was silence and gloom. The sloop-of-war Cumberland, having a crew of three hundred men, and mounting twenty-four guns, now lay on the bottom with only her topgallant masts and pennant above the water, marking the spot where one hundred and seventeen mangled bodies lay buried beneath the waves. The Congress, a fifty-gun frigate, had also met her destruction, and now lay on shore with the flames kindled by hot shot of the Merrimac sweeping out her hull. The Roanoke and Minnesota, steam frigates of forty guns each, the pride of the navy and the most perfect of any men-of-war of the period, lay hard and fast on shore, with broken machinery and as powerless as if they had been unarmed. The capture or entire destruction of the Federal fleet at Hampton Roads and the escape of the Merrimac and the rebel cruisers seemed inevitable.

At 9 o'clock, P.M., of this memorable day, March 8, 1862, the Monitor anchored near the Roanoke, and Lieutenant Worden immediately reported on board to Captain Marston, where he spent much of the evening, and the crew was given a short drill of half an hour. The working of the guns and the movements of the turret were new to all on board, but were readily learned by these practical gunners. When Captain Worden had finished his interview with the senior officer and returned, the Monitor was got underway, and at 2 o'clock on the morning of the 9th anchored near the frigate Minnesota at Newport News. An incident occurred at this time reflecting great credit upon a man of whom very little, if anything, has ever been said.

Pilot Samuel Howard, attached to the United States bark Amanda, went on board the Monitor as soon as she was seen coming into the Roads, and remained with her until brought alongside the Roanoke. When it was decided that the Monitor should proceed up the Roads and protect the Minnesota, Captain Worden inquired of the flag-officer for a pilot. Mr. Howard volunteered, to which the Captain of the Amanda objected, as he was already short of officers. A pilot who had been left on the bark was sent for, but he declined to go. Two other pilots were then sent for from the pilot boat, but they declined to go, assigning as a reason that they knew nothing about the Roads. Mr. Howard then volunteering again was permitted to go. The night was hazy, the smoke of the battle having settled upon the water. He proceeded by the north star and the light of the burning Congress, and laid the Monitor alongside the Minnesota ready for battle the next day.

There were at that time in Hampton Roads sixteen of all classes of war vessels, mounting 298 guns, which that day had proven their utter worthlessness to engage a mailed vessel. Tired and exhausted with the constant employment of the past three days, in view of the work that would be needed of them on the morrow, the crew of the Monitor was allowed sleep and rest. "It was a most glorious sleep," said one of them to me. "I closed my eyes with my thoughts filled with the horror of that day's work of destruction, and depressed by the burden of what was depending upon us on the morrow. Overcome with fatigue, dreams of the victory that awaited us added pleasure to my sleep. I was hardly more delighted when the Merrimac withdrew from the fight than when I awoke from my vision. I was invigorated with strength and courage,—a victory seemed sure."

At half-past five in the morning all hands were called, and the ship was immediately cleared of her sea-rig and got ready for battle, shot were hoisted into the turret, and a thorough inspection made, so that everything about the ship should be in working order. Breakfast was soon over, and it seemed as quiet and solemn as if preparing for the funerals of those who had been slain the day before. At half-past seven o'clock a long line of black smoke was seen, preceded by the steamers Jamestown, Patrick Henry and Teazer. It was the signal for battle. The crews of the different vessels stood by their guns, fuses in hands. The Monitor steamed slowly from beneath the bows of the Minnesota, where she had been partly concealed, to meet the challenger in an open field. It was alike an astonishment to the rebels and our own people; neither had seen her when she arrived, and many were the conjectures of what she could be. Some said a huge water tank; others an infernal machine; none that she had guns, and not till they saw steam rise from her deck did they think she had power to move herself. Onward, with the brave Worden at her wheel, she was steered straight for the Merrimac, whose consorts, loaded with spectators and soldiers, had dropped astern and out of the channel. Onward in a straight line the Monitor kept her course. Her diminutive size, for only the turret could be seen by those who were a mile or more away, made her seem like a rat attacking an alligator. The Merrimac stopped her engines, as if to survey and wonder at the audacity of the nondescript. The Monitor was approaching on her starboard bow. Then, as if seized with impulsive rage, and as if a huge breath would waft her enemy away, the Merrimac poured a broadside of solid shot at her. For an instant she was enveloped in smoke, and people who were looking on held their breath in doubt of seeing the Monitor again. It was a moment of great suspense. Then as a gentle breeze swept over the scene the Monitor appeared. At this instant the flash of her own guns was seen, and then their report, louder than any cannon that had ever been heard, thundered across the sea. It seemed to jar the very earth, and the iron scales of the invincible crumbled and cracked from their fastenings. One on board the Merrimac at this time has told me that, though at first entirely confident of victory, consternation took hold of them all. "Damn it!" said one, "the thing is full of guns!"

The enthusiasm at this moment among the thousand of civilians and soldiers, who lined the shore to witness the fight, was beyond description and their own control. Such a spontaneous burst of cheers was never before heard. Men were frantic with joy.

The Monitor continued her approach, reserving fire that every shot might take effect, until she came parallel with the Merrimac, but heading in the opposite direction. In this way they passed slowly within a few yards of each other, both delivering and receiving the other's fire. Some anxiety had been felt about the turret machinery, many persons having thought that a heavy shot striking the turret with great velocity would damage it so as to stop its working, but finding that it was revolving freely, and that the Monitor was apparently uninjured, Captain Worden headed again towards the Merrimac with renewed confidence and engaged her at close quarters.

Again they joined in close combat, the Monitor lying bow on, at times touching, both delivering their fire as rapidly as possible. At the same time the marines on the Merrimac poured an incessant fire of musketry at the peek-holes about the pilot house and turret. The speed of the two vessels was about equal, but the light draught of the Monitor gave her an advantage. The rebels finding that they could make nothing of the invulnerable "cheesebox," as they called her, and foiled and maddened at the loss of their coveted prize, turned towards the Minnesota, determined, if possible, to destroy her. The Merrimac went head on and received a full broadside of the Minnesota. Fifty solid nine-inch shot struck square. Any wooden vessel that ever floated would have gone to pieces under such a fire. The Merrimac was unharmed. She returned the fire with her forward rifle guns. One shell passed through four rooms, tearing away partitions and setting the ship on fire. Another passed through the boiler of the steamer Dragon which lay alongside, blowing her up and killing and wounding seventeen men. Before a third was fired the Monitor interposed, compelling the Merrimac to change her position. The two combatants then made a complete circle in their endeavors to get a favorable position, each seeking to discharge a broadside into some vital part. The Merrimac then turned sharp and made a plunge towards the Minnesota, but Worden was vigilant, and crossed the stern of the Merrimac, sending two solid shot into her. To get back again between her and the Minnesota, the Monitor had almost to cross her bow. The Merrimac steamed up quickly, and finding that the Monitor would be struck with her prow Worden sheered towards the enemy's stern, avoiding a direct blow, and as they came into collision, each vessel delivered a broadside into the other. At this point a shell from the Merrimac struck the pilot-house exactly over the peek-hole through which Captain Worden was looking. The shell exploding, filled his face and eyes with powder and fragments of iron, utterly blinding and for a time rendering him unconscious. Lieutenant Greene, who had been in charge of the turret division, immediately left the guns and spent full thirty minutes nursing the wounded commander, during which time the gunners shotted the guns, and, as the Merrimac was turning away, discharged them at close range into her stern, a blow that made her whole frame shudder and seemed at once to be fatal. There was no officer to direct the movements of the vessel except the pilot Howard. As the two combatants parted from the struggle they were headed in opposite directions, both away from their goal. Presuming that the fight would be continued, Pilot Howard ran the vessel a short distance down the channel and turning brought her again close to the protection of the Minnesota, when Lieutenant Greene stepped into the pilot-house and assumed command. It was then observed that the Merrimac had taken the channel and was heading towards Norfolk. She was soon joined by her consorts, and taken up to their refuge under the batteries of Craney Island, the Merrimac apparently sagging down astern.

Thus ended the greatest naval battle of the world. The Cumberland went into action with 376 men. When the survivors were mustered there were only 255. The crew of the Congress were 434; of these 298 got to shore. Three were killed and sixteen wounded on the Minnesota. One sloop-of-war 24 guns, and one frigate 50 guns, totally destroyed. One first-class steam frigate, carrying 40 nine-inch Dahlgren guns, disabled. Two others were driven off, glad of the low water which kept the Merrimac away.

When the sun went down the 8th of March it appeared to those who were acquainted with the appalling facts that the cause of the Union was well nigh, if not utterly lost. No victory with such decided results for the present, or with such bright hopes for the future, was gained by the rebels either before or after. That night was one of exultation among the conspirators wherever the telegraph could carry the news. The easy and entire destruction of the Union navy, the capture of Washington, the laying of the northern cities under contribution, the raising of the blockade, recognition in Europe; in short the complete triumph of the rebel cause seemed the natural consequence of that day's work. The rebels knew of nothing between them and entire success, and our government had no means of arresting this impending ruin, except an experimental and most diminutive war-ship, in which experienced naval officers and scientific naval constructors had little or no confidence, and which had not even reached the scene of action.

The importance of this battle to the cause of the Union can only be estimated from revelations of the secret archives department, which appear to prove that England and France were watching the result of this very affair, resolved to take the side of Southern secession had the Northern fleet been vanquished. The result of this day's conflict proved to them the entire worthlessness of their wooden navies, and that their ships were safer in their own waters. When the tidings of this fight crossed the Atlantic, the London *Times* affirmed that England had on the day before 149 first class war-ships, now there were only two; beyond these there was not one that could safely be pitted against the Monitor, and even these were not invulnerable, for, being iron-plated only amidships, they would be set in a blaze at either extremity in a few minutes by shell from this new war-ship.

After the battle Captain Worden was taken at once to Washington and an incident, connected with him there, illustrates the character of Abraham Lincoln. A cabinet meeting was in session, when it was told the President that the wounded commander of the Monitor was in the city. He instantly rose, took his hat saying, "Excuse me, gentlemen, I must see this fellow," and went immediately to his room. Worden was on a sofa, his eyes bandaged, his face swollen and bloody. The President was announced, and he took his hand in silence. "Mr. President," said the wounded officer, "You do me great honor by this visit." "Sir," replied Mr. Lincoln, while the tears ran down his cheeks, "I am the one who is honored by this interview."

The only perceptible danger to those on board the Monitor, after the first round from the Merrimac, was to those in the turret, who were in great danger from the flying of bolt-heads driven with great force across the turret, and, from the concussion, which would for a time paralyze a man if he should in any way be in contact with the turret when struck by a shot. There were several sight-holes, through the turret, about an inch and a quarter in diameter, through which now and then a musket bullet, fired by the Merrimac marines, would enter the turret.

The Monitor was struck during the engagement twenty-one times. Eight times on the side armor, seven times on the turret, four times on the deck and twice on the pilot-house. None of the marks was very large, hardly indented into the armor plating sufficient to hold as much as a common tea-saucer, and only two that crooked or bulged the iron on the inner side of the turret. The pilot-house was a clumsy affair, built of eight-inch iron beams placed log-house fashion and bolted together. The one hit when Captain Worden was wounded was cracked and slightly turned out of place. The Monitor also received seven other hits from the Minnesota as she lay at times between the two vessels enveloped in smoke, but these were mere scratches compared with the scars of the Merrimac.

.   .   .

It is hardly possible for a person unaccustomed to the relative size of vessels to make a correct comparison between the Monitor and her opponent as they appeared together during the engagement. The Merrimac being five times her tonnage, it may be imagined she was a very large vessel, the other a very small one. Thus it was that during the engagement our people viewing the fight could not always see the Monitor, and only the sound of her guns gave evidence of her existence, whose echoes sounded over sea and land, mingled with the cheers of thousands, whose throbbing hearts gave impulse to their joy.

In order clearly to understand the honor and fame that has been awarded to the Monitor for her victory, something should be known of the build and formidable character of the vessel with which she was engaged, as well as the amount of property saved from destruction, and the damage the Merrimac and the two rebel cruisers would have done if they had escaped to sea.

What I am to state was told me by mechanics who worked in raising her, and getting her ready for sea, also from those who were on board during the fight, or went in her consorts as spectators.

In 1855, the United States built, at different navy yards, four steam frigates: the Merrimac, the Wabash, the Minnesota, the Roanoke, and, by contract, at a private yard, the frigate Niagara. They were all nearly alike, of about 3,500 tons burden, carrying a heavy battery of nine and ten-inch Dahlgren guns. In April, 1861, the Merrimac was at Norfolk navy yard undergoing repairs. When the navy yard was abandoned she was scuttled and set on fire, but, it being low tide, she only sunk to the gun-deck, and the fire was extinguished. She was soon raised by the Confederates, and the dry-dock, which had by accident or misfortune escaped destruction, was opened for her reception. After an examination, it was found that the bottom of the hull and the engines and boilers were entirely uninjured, and John M. Brooke, formerly a lieutenant in the United States navy, and John L. Porter, Confederate naval constructor, reported plans for her reconstruction into a shot-proof steam battery.

There is not room here for comment upon the battle fought by the Merrimac and Monitor. If their commanders had known exactly how much their own vessels could be depended upon, and the strength and impregnability of their opponent, the battle would have ended sooner, with a far different result. It would have been unwise for the Merrimac to have risked a battle with the Monitor without trying to escape to sea, where she could have done more damage than to have sunk a dozen iron-clads, and accomplished the mission that was intended, without any permanent injury. The Monitor had an advantage on the waters where they fought by being of less draft, and the long high sides which the Merrimac exposed enabled the gunners to train the guns without missing a shot. No guns of such caliber as the Monitor's had ever been experimented with, and a charge of fifteen pounds of powder, such as Captain Worden had been instructed with caution to use, was thought to be enormous, and all that the guns would bear. Subsequent tests have proved that thirty pounds would not have been an overcharge, while even forty pounds might have been used with impunity. With such a charge of powder as either of these a shot would have bored the Merrimac through and through, and the battle could not have lasted after a second round.

Of the condition of the Merrimac after the battle, the most reliable account I have ever had was given to me by a ship carpenter who was employed at the Norfolk navy yard during the time it was in possession of the Confederate government. From his experience I should think he was fully capable of making a correct estimate in such a matter. He told me that the Merrimac was in a disabled condition and could not have been engaged any longer; that a shot had entered one of the forward ports, disabling two guns and killing and wounding nineteen men; that the water had entered through her battered sides in such a quantity that she was obliged to retire. He further said that he worked on her after she had been taken into the dry-dock, and that the armor was torn off and bent into every conceivable shape; that her whole frame was battered and shaken beyond repair, and it was with the gravest fears that she was held in defence of the city of Norfolk.

The Merrimac and Monitor never met again. For a month they lay watching each other, neither side caring to take the chances of losing a battle.

On the 3d day of May, General Magruder retired from York-town. Norfolk was abandoned, the strong positions at Sewell's Point and Craney Island evacuated, and the rebel troops were concentrated for the defence of Richmond. The Merrimac was shut out from her retreat, and all day and night they worked to lighten her, in order to cross the shoals so as to take her up the James River. In this they did not succeed. The poor old commander, Joseph Tatnall, who had spent his whole life in the naval service of the United States, saw nothing to be done but to destroy his vessel. So he ran her ashore, landed the crew and set her on fire, fore and aft. She burned fiercely for an hour, and on the morning of May 11, 1862, she blew up. Thus ended the Merrimac.

5

THE RED PLAINS OF MANASSAS—
THE SECOND BULL RUN

By D. Augustus Dickert

*After Lee defeated McClellan on the Peninsula, the Federals or-
ganized a new army under John Pope. After it began to gather
strength, this army moved into Virginia and down to the line of
the Rapidan River. General Lee, keeping a wary eye on the forces
left at Harrison's Landing under McClellan, moved Jackson out
to confront Pope on the Rapidan. When he was convinced that
McClellan intended no further aggressive action, he moved with
Longstreet to join Jackson. In a series of attempts to bring Pope to
battle under conditions favorable to the Confederates, Lee only
succeeded in maneuvering Pope back to the lines of the Rappahannock.*

*After one more effort Lee tried the big solution. Longstreet's
corps, spread thin and with vigorous bluffing, absorbed the positions which had been held by Jackson's corps. Jackson's foot
cavalry, once out of the lines, formed column and marched off to
their left flank. For two days they advanced, passed through the
Thoroughfare Gap, turned hard right and came down like a wolf
on Pope's supply lines at Bristowe station, then moved up the
railroad tracks to the great Federal supply depot at Manassas
Junction. After gluttoning his troops and destroying any supplies
that were left, he disappeared so far as Pope's intelligence was
concerned. With characteristic taciturnity he concealed his real
destination. North of the highway that runs from Washington and*

Alexandria, there was an unfinished railroad; the grading had been done but no tracks laid. Behind this ready-made breastwork, Jackson literally hid his corps. This was a strong defensive position. Its left flank rested on the historic little stream called Bull Run. Its right flank was refused in defensible terrain. Back of the line were passes in the Bull Run mountains through which the gray-coats could withdraw. In front of the railroad grade the ground sloped gently down to the highway, affording perfect fields of fire.

As the pinch of his severed supply lines began to be felt, Pope ordered a regrouping around Manassas. As the Federal Division of Rickett's marched down the Warrenton Pike headed for Centreville, Jackson issued one of the most tactically impertinent and strategically sound orders in the history of warfare. He moved out from his position and attacked the marching blue column in flank. Thus he brought the enemy to battle at the exact time and place of his choosing. Darkness terminated this brief fight but Pope proceeded to order a concentraton at the point of impact to "bag Jackson." For three days Pope attacked the troops behind the railroad grade in a series of frontal assaults, each of which was repulsed.

In the meantime Lee with Longstreet's corps moved up over the route Jackson had followed and prorogued Jackson's right flank at a 90° angle. As the Federal attacks began to weaken, Longstreet's artillery opened a devastating enfilade fire and, with the joining point as a hinge, Lee swung Longstreet's corps like a gate and smashed Pope's army. Virginia was thus freed of Federal forces and the stage was set for the invasion of Maryland.

The enemy lay quietly in his camps at Harrison's Landing for a few days, but to cover his meditated removal down the James, he advanced a large part of his army as far as Malvern Hill on the day of the 5th of August as if to press Lee back. Kershaw, with the rest of McLaws' Division, together with Jones and Longstreet, were sent to meet them. The troops were all placed in position by nightfall, bivouacked for the night on the field, and slept on their arms to guard against any night attack. The soldiers thought of tomorrow—that it perhaps might be yet more sanguinary than any of the others. Our ranks, already badly worn by the desperate conflicts at Savage Station, Frazier's Farm, Cold Harbor, etc., still showed a bold front for the coming day. Early in the morning the troops were put in motion, skirmishers thrown out, and all preparations for battle made, but to the surprise and relief of all, the "bird had flown," and instead of battle lines and bristling steel fronts we found nothing but deserted camps and evidences of a hasty flight. In a few days we were removed further back towards Richmond and sought camp on higher ground, better to guard against the ravages of disease and to be further removed from the enemy. The troops now had the pleasure of a month's rest, our only duties being guard and advance picket every ten or twelve days.

While McClellan had been pushing his army up on the Peninsula the Federals were actively engaged in organizing a second army in the vicinity of Manassas and Fredericksburg under General John Pope, to operate against Richmond by the flank. General Pope from his infamous orders greatly incensed the people of the South, and from his vain boasting gained for himself the sobriquet of "Pope the Braggart." He ordered every citizen within his lines or living near them either to take the oath of allegiance to the United States or to be driven out of the country as an enemy of the Union. No one was to have any communication with his friends within the Confederate lines, either by letter or otherwise, on the penalty of being shot as a spy and his property confiscated. Hundreds of homes were broken up by the order. Men and women were driven south, or placed in Federal prisons, there to linger for years, perhaps, with their homes abandoned to the malicious desecration of a merciless enemy, all for no other charges than their refusal to be a traitor to their principles and an enemy to their country.

Pope boasted of "seeing nothing of the enemy but his back," and that "he had no headquarters but in the saddle." He was continually sending dispatches to his chief General Halleck, who had been appointed Commander in Chief of all the Federal forces in the field, of the "victories gained over Lee," his "bloody repulses of Jackson," and "successful advances," and "the Confederates on the run," etc., while the very opposites were the facts. On one occasion he telegraphed to Washington that he had defeated Lee, that the Confederate leader was in full retreat to Richmond, when, as a fact, before the dispatch had reached its destination his own army was overwhelmed, and with Pope at its head, flying the field in every direction, seeking safety under the guns at Washington. It is little wonder he bore the name he had so deservedly won by his manifestoes, "Pope the Braggart."

About the middle of July, Jackson with Ewell and A. P. Hill, was sent up to the Rapidan to look after Pope and his wonderful army, which had begun to be re-enforced by troops from the James. On the 9th of August Jackson came up with a part of Pope's army at Cedar Mountain, and a fierce battle was fought, very favorable to the Confederate side. A month after Jackson had left Richmond, Longstreet, with three divisions, headed by Lee in person, was ordered to re-enforce Jackson, and began the offensive. While the Federal commander was lying securely in his camp, between the Rappahannock and the Rapidan, unconscious of the near approach of the Confederate Army, his scouts intercepted an order written by General Lee to his cavalry leader, giving details of his intended advance and attack. Pope, being thus apprised, hurriedly recrossed the Rappahannock and concentrated his forces behind that stream. Lee followed his movements closely, and while watching in front, with a portion of his army, he started Jackson on his famous march around the enemy's rear. Pulling up at night, Jackson marched to the left, crossed the Rappahannock on the 25th, and by the night of the 26th he had reached the railroad immediately in Pope's rear, capturing trains of cars, prisoners, etc.

On learning that large quantities of provisions and munitions of war were stored at Manassas Junction, feebly guarded, General Trimble, with a small number of brave Alabamians, Georgians, and North Carolinians, not five hundred all told, volunteered to march still further to that point, a distance of some miles, notwithstanding they had marched with Jackson thirty miles during the day, and capture the place. This was done in good time, defeating a brigade doing guard duty, and capturing large number of prisoners, one entire battery of artillery, and untold quantities of provisions.

Jackson now appeared to retreat, but only withdrew in order to give Longstreet time to come up, which he was doing hard upon Jackson's track, but more than twenty-four hours behind. This was one of the most hazardous feats accomplished by Lee during the war, with the possible exception of Chancellorsville, "dividing his army in the face of superior numbers," a movement denounced by all successful Generals and scientists of war. But Lee attempted this on more occasions than one, and always successfully.

Jackson concealed his forces among the hills of Bull Run, giving time for Longstreet, who was fighting his way through Thoroughfare Gap at the very point of the bayonet, to come up, while Pope was racing around the plains of Manassas, trying to intercept Jackson's imaginary retreat. It seems as if the one single idea impressed itself upon the Federal commander, and that was that Jackson was trying to get away from him. But before many days Pope found the wily "Stonewall," and when in his embrace endeavoring to hold him, Pope found himself in the predicament of the man who had essayed to wrestle with a bear. When the man had downed his antagonist he had to call lustily for friends. So Pope had to call for help to turn Jackson loose—to pull him loose.

On the 29th the forces of Pope, the Braggart, came upon those of Jackson hidden behind a railroad enbankment on the plains of Manassas, and a stubborn battle ensued, which lasted until late at night. Longstreet came upon the field, but took no further part in the battle than a heavy demonstration on the right to relieve the pressure from Jackson. Longstreet's left, however, turned the tide of battle. Lee turned some prisoners loose at night who had been captured during the day, leaving the impression on their minds that he was beating a hasty retreat. Reporting to their chief that night, the prisoners confirmed the opinion that Pope was fooled in believing all day, that "Lee was in full retreat," trying to avoid a battle. Pope sent flaming messages to that effect to the authorities at Washington, and so anxious was he lest his prey should escape, he gave orders for his troops to be in motion early in the morning.

On the 30th was fought the decisive battle of Second Manassas, and the plains above Bull Run were again the scene of a glorious

Confederate victory, by Lee almost annihilating the army of John Pope, the Braggart. Had it not been for the steady discipline, extraordinary coolness, and soldierly behavior of Sykes and his regulars at Stone Bridge, the rout of the Federal Army at Second Manassas would have been but little less complete than on the fatal day just a little more than one year before.

At Ox Hill, 1st September, Pope had to adopt the tactics of McClellan at Malvern Hill, face about and fight for the safety of his great ordnance and supply trains, and to allow his army a safe passage over the Potomac. At Ox Hill, the enemy under Stephens and Kearny, displayed extraordinary tenacity and courage, these two division commanders throwing their columns headlong upon those of Jackson without a thought of the danger and risks such rash acts incurred. Both were killed in the battle. Philip Kearny had gained a national reputation for his enterprising warfare in California and Mexico during the troublesome times of the Mexican War, and it was with unfeigned sorrow and regret the two armies heard of the sad death of this veteran hero.

During the time that all these stirring events were taking place and just before Magruder, with McLaws' and Walker's divisions, was either quietly lying in front of Richmond watching the army of McClellan dwindle away, leaving by transports down the James and up the Potomac, or was marching at a killing gait to overtake their comrades under Lee to share with them their trials, their battles and their victories in Maryland. Lee could not leave the Capital with all his force so long as there was a semblance of an army threatening it.

As soon as it was discovered that Manassas was to be the real battle ground of the campaign, and Washington instead of Richmond the objective point, Lee lost no time in concentrating his army north of the Rappahannock. About the middle of August McLaws, with Kershaw's, Sumner's, Cobb's, and Barksdale's Brigades, with two brigades under Walker and the Hampton Legion Cavalry, turned their footsteps Northward, and bent all their energies to reach the scene of action before the culminating events above mentioned.

At Orange Court House, on the 26th, we hastened our march,

as news began to reach us of Jackson's extraordinary movements and the excitement in the Federal Army, occasioned by their ludicrous hunt for the "lost Confederate." Jackson's name had reached its meridian in the minds of the troops, and they were ever expecting to hear of some new achievement or brilliant victory by this strange, silent, and mysterious man. The very mystery of his movements, his unexplainable absence and sudden reappearance at unexpected points, his audacity in the face of the enemy, his seeming recklessness, gave unbounded confidence to the army. The men began to feel safe at the very idea of his disappearance and absence. While the thunder of his guns and those of Longstreet's were sounding along the valleys of Bull Run, and reverberating down to the Potomac or up to Washington, McLaws with his South Carolinians, Georgians, and Mississippians was swinging along with an elastic step between Orange Court House and Manassas.

McClellan himself had already reached Alexandria with the last of his troops, but by the acts of the ubiquitous Jackson his lines of communication were cut and the Federal commander had to grope his way in the dark for fear of running foul of his erratic enemy.

When we began nearing Manassas, we learned of the awful effect of the two preceding days' battle by meeting the wounded. They came singly and in groups, men marching with arms in slings, heads bandaged, or hopping along on improvised crutches, while the wagons and ambulances were laden with the severely wounded. In that barren country no hospital could be established, for it was as destitute of sustenance as the arid plains of the Arabian Desert when the great Napoleon undertook to cross it with his beaten army. All, with the exception of water; we had plenty of that.

Passing over a part of the battlefield about the 5th of September, the harrowing sights that were met with were in places too sickening to admit of description. The enemy's dead, in many places, had been left unburied, it being a veritable instance of "leaving the dead to bury the dead." Horses in a rapid state of decomposition literally covered the field. The air was so impregnated with the foul stench arising from the plains where the battle had raged fiercest, that the troops were forced to close their nostrils while passing. Here and there lay a dead enemy overlooked in the night of the general burial, stripped of his outer clothing, his blackened features and glassy eyes staring upturned to the hot September sun, while our soldiers hurried past, leaving them unburied and unnoticed. Some lay in the beaten track of our wagon trains, and had been run over ruthlessly by the teamsters, they not having the time, if the inclination, to remove them.

In the opening where the Washington Battalion of Artillery from New Orleans had played such havoc on the 30th with the enemy's retreating columns, it resembled some great railroad wreck—cannon and broken caissons piled in great heaps; horses lying swollen and stiff, some harnessed, others not; broken rammers, smashed wheels, dismounted pieces told of the desperate struggle that had taken place.

One of the strange features of a battlefield is the absence of the carrion crow or buzzard—it matters little as to the number of dead soldiers or horses, no vultures ever venture near—it being a fact that a buzzard was never seen in that part of Virginia during the war.

All was still, save the rumble of the wagon trains and the steady tread of the soldiers. Across Bull Run and out towards Washington McLaws followed with hasty step the track of Longstreet and Jackson.

On the 5th or 6th we rejoined at last, after a two months' separation from the other portion of the army. Lee was now preparing to invade Maryland and other States North, as the course of events dictated. Pope's Army had joined that of McClellan, and the authorities at Washington had to call on the latter to "save their Capital." When the troops began the crossing of the now classic Potomac, a name on every tongue since the commencement of hostilities, their enthusiasm knew no bounds. Bands played *Maryland, My Maryland,* men sang and cheered, hats filled the air, flags waved, and shouts from fifty thousand throats reverberated up and down the banks of the river, to be echoed back from the mountains and die away among the hills and highlands of Maryland. Men stopped midway in the stream and sang loudly the cheering strains of Randall's, *Maryland, My Maryland.*

We were overjoyed at rejoining the army, and the troops of Jackson, Longstreet, and the two Hills were proud to feel the elbow touch of such chivalrous spirits as McLaws, Kershaw, Hampton, and others in the conflicts that were soon to take place. Never before had an occurrence so excited and enlivened the spirits of the troops as the crossing of the Potomac into the land of our sister, Maryland. It is said the Crusaders, after months of toil, marching, and fighting, on their way through the plains of Asia Minor, wept when they saw the towering spires of Jerusalem, the Holy City, in the distance; and if ever Lee's troops could have wept for joy, it was at the crossing of the Potomac. But we paid dearly for this pleasure in the death of so many thousands of brave men and the loss of so many valuable officers. General Winder fell at Cedar Mountain, and Jackson's right hand, the brave Ewell, lost his leg at Manassas.

The army went into camp around Frederick City, Md. From here, on the 8th, Lee issued his celebrated address to the people of Maryland, and to those of the North generally, telling them of his entry into their country, its cause and purpose; that it was not as a conqueror, or an enemy, but to demand and enforce a peace between the two countries. He clothed his language in the most conservative and entreating terms, professing friendship for those who would assist him, and protection to life and the property of all. He enjoined the people, without regard to past differences, to flock to his standard and aid in the defeat of the party and people who were now drenching the country in blood and putting in mourning the people of two nations. The young men he asked to join his ranks as soldiers of a just and honorable cause. Of the old he asked their sympathies and prayers.

To the President of the Confederate States he also wrote a letter, proposing to him that he should head his armies, and, as the chieftain of the nation, propose a peace to the authorities at Washington from the very threshold of their Capital. But both failed of the desired effect. The people of the South had been led to believe that Maryland was anxious to cast her destinies with those of her sister States, that all her sympathies were with the people of the South, and that her young men were anxious and only awaiting the opportunity to join the ranks as soldiers under Lee. But these ideas and promises were all delusions, for the people we saw along the route remained passive spectators and disinterested witnesses to the great evolutions now taking place.

Chapter 5, Part 2

THE SIXTH WISCONSIN VOLUNTEERS

By Brevet Brigadier General Rufus R. Dawes, U. S. Volunteers

The sun rose clear on the morning of August 30th, 1862, and during the forenoon the troops of our army were moving quietly into position. From our hill we had an excellent view of the field. The whole of our army was spread before us, but intervening timber hid the enemy from our sight. The drift of talk was that the rebels were falling back. About three o'clock in the afternoon, we were ordered forward to "pursue the enemy." We marched on the Warrenton turnpike, perhaps half a mile, when our brigade was formed into two lines of battle in an open field on the right hand side. General Patrick's brigade was in front of us, formed also in two lines of battle. We had thus at our point of attack four lines of battle. Before us was woods, beyond which a railroad embankment. Behind this embankment quietly awaiting the attack were our antagonists at Gainesville, the veteran army corps of Stonewall Jackson. Just before we entered the edge of the woods, our brigade was changed to one line of battle with the Sixth Wisconsin on the right. As the troops entered the woods a very heavy artillery fire broke out upon our left (Longstreet's). Musketry opened in our front. Bullets, canister, shell, and the men said, "scraps of railroad iron," tore through the limbs and brush over us and around us. We pushed on, advancing as the lines in front of us advanced and lying down on the ground when they stopped.

There was no order to charge upon the enemy, and we wondered why such orders were not given. Thus we slowly advanced. Suddenly, the lines in our front broke and the men ran back in great disorder. The rebels raised a tremendous shout, and poured in a heavy fire of musketry. The sharp artillery fire of the enemy which enfiladed our line, added to the panic and confusion. Colonel Bragg shouted, "Sixth Wisconsin, kneel down! Captains, keep your men down! Let nobody tramp on them!" General Gibbon himself came running up on foot with his revolver drawn, shouting, "Stop those stragglers!—Make them fall in!—Shoot them if they don't!" It was a new experience, but we were not swept away. Our men were down with bayonets set, when the fugitives began to swarm upon them. All the officers were struggling to stop stragglers and force them to join our ranks. Many were held with us, but no Union troops were left in front of us. General Gibbon directed Colonel Bragg to throw forward a company as skirmishers. This was a fearful duty. Colonel Bragg called for my old company "K."

> "Who faltered or shivered?
> Who shunned battle stroke?
> Whose fire was uncertain?
> Whose battle line broke?
> Go ask it of history,
> Years from to-day,
> And the record shall tell you,
> Not 'company K.' "

The boys immediately sprang up under command of Captain David L. Quaw, and deployed forward upon a run. We could see them firing and dodging from tree to tree. They met a rebel skirmish line coming forward through the woods, and they drove it back upon the rebel line of battle. The spirit and conduct of company "K" was beyond praise. The panic and retreat of our own troops and the exultant shouts of thousands of rebel soldiers did not daunt these men. Captain Quaw says that "after the rebel skirmishers retreated, there arose up from behind a railroad bank, a mass of rebel soldiers several ranks deep. I shouted to my men to 'tree.' I jumped behind a small tree myself, where I must have shrunk to the dimensions of a wafer. A dozen bullets hit that tree. I did not wait for the rebels to fire again, but ordered the men back to the regiment."

All the troops that had been in the woods, except the Sixth Wisconsin, had now retreated and gone to the rear. Brigadier General John Gibbon, be it ever remembered to his honor, remained with our regiment. He said he had received no orders to retreat and he should stay until he got them. The regiment was now lying on the ground, subjected to a fire from rebel sharp-shooters and quite a number of our men were killed or wounded by them. A bullet would strike a man who would writhe, groan and die or spring up, throw away his impediments and start for the rear. Our men peered through the leaves, shooting at the puffs of powder smoke from the muskets of the rebels.

As I walked along the line, some men of company "I" said: "Major, don't go near that tree." I was not aware what tree, but had wit enough to jump away. Spat, went a bullet against a tree, cutting a corner from my haversack. They had noticed that the tree had been several times struck by the bullets of. a sharp-shooter. A soldier of a New York regiment lay wounded in front of our line. He begged piteously for water and for help. First Sergeant Charles Lampe, of company "F" went to give him a swallow from his canteen and was himself shot dead by the merciless bullet of the sharp-shooter. Private William Bickelhaupt, of company "F," had been shot through the body, and I heard the poor little boy, for such he was, in plaintive broken English telling his comrades what to write to his "Mutter."

It now being evident that no staff officer could bring us orders of any kind, General Gibbon directed Colonel Bragg to form a line of skirmishers to cover the retreat of the regiment, and to move to the rear. The skirmishers were quickly deployed and Colonel Bragg ordered the regiment to face about and march back. But the rebels redoubled their fire, killing and wounding quite a number of our men. Bragg immediately ordered the regiment to face to the front. Our skirmishers were hotly engaged with the enemy. By a slow backward step, we moved out of the woods. Upon reaching the open ground, Colonel Bragg faced the regiment by the rear rank and took a steady double quick. It was full three quarters of a mile over the open fields to the place where our new lines were forming. The Sixth Wisconsin regiment alone upon the plain, in full sight of both armies, marched this distance. General Rufus King in describing this scene says: "The Sixth Wisconsin, the very last to retire, marched slowly and steadily to the rear, with column formed and colors flying, faced the front as they reached their new position, and saluted the approaching enemy with three cheers and a rattling volley." General King is in error as to the volley. We should have killed our following skirmish line by such firing. The regiment was ordered into position in support of battery "B," 4th U. S. artillery. We were on a high point, commanding the Warrenton turnpike and the open fields over which we had retreated. Just as the line was being formed, a solid shot cut off the tail of a fine bay horse ridden by Lieutenant James Stewart, of battery "B." The shot gave the horse a deep cut across the rump, the scar of which lasted his life-time. The horse's tail flew into the faces of men of our regiment, switching them severely.

It was now late in the afternoon. The rebels (Longstreet's corps) directed a heavy fire of artillery on us, and began a general advance of their infantry toward our left. We could see regiment after regiment of the enemy moving in column by division, and forming into line of battle as they advanced upon our men. From the point where we lay upon the ground, the view of the battle was extensive. Our batteries were all actively firing upon the advancing columns of the enemy. Their artillery was also in action. The solid shot and shell struck around us and whizzed over us. Occasionally a horse would be killed by them, and one man's head was carried away entirely. Such sights very severely test one's nerves. A solid shot will plow into the ground, spitefully scattering the dirt, and bound a hundred feet into the air, looking as it flies swiftly away like an India rubber playing ball. We could see every movement of the left wing of our own army, and of the right wing of the rebel army. Our lines were in open fields in front of a strip of woods. The rebel musketry fire was pouring from the woods upon our men who were closing together and rallying under the attack. Regiments would sweep splendidly forward into the front line, fire a crashing volley into the woods and then work with great energy. But they quickly withered away until there would appear to be a mere company crowding around the colors. The open fields were covered with wounded and stragglers, going to the rear. The rebels charged up a ravine endeavoring to capture an Ohio battery upon our immediate left. The Second and Seventh Wisconsin had been consolidated and were under command of Lieutenant Colonel Lucius Fairchild. Colonel Fairchild had his men change front and attack the enemy, who were quickly driven back and the battery saved. We could now see that our troops upon the left were being driven back in confusion over the open fields. This outflanked our position, and it was evident that we must soon draw back our line. General Joseph Hooker, who was mounted on a white horse, rode up among the guns of our artillery and carefully noted the situation of affairs. He ordered batteries and infantry to retire. Regiments moved steadily by the right of companies to the rear, the batteries moved also in retreat. A rebel line in our front rose up from the ground and advanced slowly after us. It was a strange sight, our blue line slowly retreating, and the long gray line slowly and quietly following. When we halted and formed again, the rebels halted and lay down on the ground. It was growing dark. There was still a heavy roll of musketry to our left and some sharp firing on our right. By nine o'clock, all had died away. About ten o'clock, General Philip Kearny came up in rear of our regiment, which now lay across the Warrenton turnpike near the stone bridge over Bull Run. He informed us that our brigade was to be the rear guard of the army which was in full retreat. We had not before suspected the real extent of the disaster. General Kearny remained with us anxiously watching the front, and Colonel Bragg and I had much conversation with him. It was after midnight when we started for the rear. Mock camp fires had been built to deceive the enemy. We lay down to rest at a point three miles from the battlefield and on the early morning of August 31st, we drew back across Cub Run, forming a line of battle on the eastern bank. About noon of that day we marched from Cub Run to Centreville. We bivouacked near Centreville. Late at night, I was sent out to establish a line of pickets. Our men, after the privations, labor, and intense excitement of three successive days in battle, were unfitted for such duty. One man placed on picket post in the woods, in the bewilderment of his senses, got himself faced toward our camp instead of toward the enemy. When he was approached by his comrades to relieve him, he mistook them for the enemy and fired upon them and killed Rudolph Fine of Company "I."

On September 1st, 1862, we marched six miles toward Fairfax Court House. On the afternoon of this day occurred the battle of Chantilly, in which fell General Philip Kearny. We were in line of battle, but at some distance to the right of the troops engaged. A heavy storm was prevailing during this battle. The noise of the artillery and musketry intermingling with the roll of very sharp thunder produced a striking effect. The darkness incident to a sky overcast with heavy, rolling clouds, lighted up alternately by flashes of lightning and the flames of artillery, made a scene long to be remembered. Several wagon trains became jammed together on the turnpike and a great panic ensued. Wagons were two or three abreast, and the mules going at a full gallop. There came a sudden crash and a jam, and wild cursing and shouting by the drivers.

September 2nd, we marched twelve miles to Upton's Hill, within six miles of Washington and went into position. As the column approached Upton's Hill, the announcement was made that General George B. McClellan had been placed in command of all the troops. There was genuine enthusiasm at this news. General John P. Hatch who was commanding our division, swung his sword and called for cheers, which were given with an uproarious good will and repeated. Open sneering at General Pope was heard upon all sides. It began with the advent of the troops from the Army of the Potomac, and it spread through our whole body. General Pope made a grave blunder when he assailed the ingrained hero worship of General McClellan, which possessed our troops. The force of this feeling can be little understood now, because conditions akin to those which affected us have passed away. Such a feeling, as that for General McClellan, was never aroused for another leader in the war. An intense party spirit attended these conditions. The Army of the Potomac was smarting under criticism, and was disappointed at its own failure to meet the unduly elevated hopes and expectations of the people. Richmond had not been taken. Pope was now defeated, and there were those even in high position, who seemed to glory in the fact. Those were dark days for the administration of President Lincoln. He pursued the only course left to him, and he acted wisely in placing General Mc-Clellan again in command. The animadversions against the President himself, for what was called "interference" with the plans of his generals, were common and severe throughout the army.

Colonel Cutler had a curious experience in Washington, which well illustrates conditions in that city after the Pope campaign, and how they affected the temper of the great War Minister, Edwin M. Stanton. Colonel Cutler had bought a new uniform, and as soon as he could walk, he went with great difficulty, leaning on two canes, to pay his respects to the Honorable Secretary of War. The office of the Secretary was, as usual, crowded, and the Colonel patiently waited for his turn to be received. As the Colonel approached, the Secretary, with a glance at the new coat and bright brass buttons, blustered out as only Mr. Stanton could, "What in hell and damnation are you doing in Washington? Why don't you go to your regiment, where you are needed?" Colonel Cutler answered: "If I had not been shot and a fool, I would never have come here. Good day, Mr. Secretary."

6

THE MARYLAND CAMPAIGN AND
ANTIETAM CREEK

By Brigadier General Willard Webb, USAR

*Near where the stream called Antietam Creek flows into the
Potomac is the little Maryland town of Sharpsburg. In September,
1862, the Army of Northern Virginia took up a defensive position
along the stream at this point.*

*General Lee, for political reasons, as well as to provision his
armies outside the state of Virginia, invaded Maryland after his
resounding victory at Bull Run. In order to protect his lines of
communications, Lee sent a composite force to clear out the
Federal garrison at Harpers Ferry. The great military corridor of
the Shenandoah Valley was plugged by the Federal force at that
place. The Confederates disposition for the investment of Harpers
Ferry were good and the Federal garrison surrendered after no
great resistance. The division of A. P. Hill was left to parole the
prisoners and salvage the matériel of the garrison, while the rest of
the investing force returned to the main body at Sharpsburg. In
the meantime, McClellan again in command of the Federal forces,
had through fortuitous circumstances learned of Lee's dispositions,
which were admittably bad. Counting on McClellan's well known
indecisiveness, Lee had taken a position with the Potomac River
at his back and had badly dispersed the elements of his command.
While in this position, McClellan moved up to strike. In a series of
unimaginative heavy thrusts the Union forces first attacked the
Confederate left, then the center. Each of these was repulsed, be-*

99

*cause Lee could move his meager reserves to the point of impact.
But their repulses were costly for the Confederates and, when the
third and final attack came on the right, there was little left with
which to meet it. When the Confederate lines seemed broken and
the very existence of Lee's army in desperate jeopardy, Hill's
Division came onto the field at double time in a melodramatic* deus
ex machina, *which restored the lines and saved the day.*

*It seems not unreasonable to presume that had he been an
hour or even less, later the Army of Northern Virginia would have
suffered complete destruction. And without that army the Confederacy could not have long endured.*

*For two days the Confederates remained defiantly in their po-
sitions and then truculently withdrew across the Potomac.*

*Generally the battle of Antietam is conceded to be a draw. But
since it was at least not a defeat, President Lincoln seized on it as
an excuse for issuing the Proclamation of Emancipation, unquestionably the most crucial single event in the Civil War.*

The military geography of the American Civil War, in its eastern
theater, is very largely explained by rivers. The great corridor of
the Valley of the Shenandoah River and a series of streams running generally from northwest to southeast, largely shaped operations. The Valley and the Potomac are factors in the Maryland
Campaign. The army moved a few miles north from Ox Hill to
the Leesburg Pike. They bivouacked on September 3, 1862, at
Drainesville near the river and just above the fall line. When they
moved out, they kept the river a short distance to their right and
headed northwest. The next morning Hill was relieved of command as already discussed. They made twenty-eight miles to Leesburg that day.

Just north of Leesburg the Potomac makes one of its frequent
meanders and for a while runs from northeast to southwest. West
of the river the Bull Run Mountains run to a rugged termination.
The army, properly keeping the river on its flank, moved up this
corridor on the fairly good road to Point of Rocks. Half naked and
with much playing of *Maryland, My Maryland,* the Army crossed
the Potomac on September 5th and moved leisurely up to Fred-

erick, arriving on September 8th. There the Light Division went through the town and bivouacked on the Emmittsburg road. Maryland was mildly curious, but not enthusiastic, and any expectations of recruiting were quickly dissipated. Hill rode Champ at the rear of his division, while anger glinted in his nearly colorless eyes, and a hate smoldered in his heart which would only die when he did. Kyd Douglas has recorded that, even after Jackson's death, Hill spoke of him with distressing bitterness.

The army had taken 9,000 casualties in the Manassas Campaign; straggling, hard marching and lack of shoes had further greatly reduced its strength. General Lee and General Jackson had both been injured by their horses: Longstreet was crippled with a blistered heel. These injuries were inconvenient but in any case all three exercised considerable restraint in their social life. The Army of Northern Virginia's public relations were largely left in the extremely capable hands of General Stuart and of its junior officers. What Hill did is not a matter of record. He had had the indignity of being relieved of his command and put in arrest by his superior. Soldiers, however, are apt to respect the privacy of a comrade in disgrace. There is plenty of evidence that Hill did not lose the loyalty of his staff and subordinates because of his row with Jackson. Subsequent correspondence and reports chronicle their resentment of Hill's treatment.

The days of leisurely occupation and recuperation at Frederick were limited to four. General Lee conferred with his two wing commanders and General Walker. A plan of action was drawn up. The plan involved the use of three newly-joined divisions which partially made up the losses of the campaign just concluded. These were the divisions of D. H. Hill, Walker and McLaws, up from the James where troops were no longer needed to watch McClellan. Jackson's wing, plus these three divisions, would be used to take out Harpers Ferry, which was as an enemy strongpoint effectively plugging the Valley at its mouth. Until this was done Lee could not open a protracted axis of supply to support his operations north of the Potomac. East of the mountains that long supply line was too vulnerable. It must be moved across into the Valley. Longstreet opposed the plan to divide the army for accomplishing this and proposed that the whole army be used. This was sound and conventional tactics, but General Lee predicated his dispositions on his personal knowledge of McClellan's personality. As events turned out Longstreet was probably right but he was overruled and directed to move the remaining troops to Hagerstown. When Jackson had crossed the Potomac his instructions were to assume command of all troops north of the river: when Lee's headquarters followed, his staff assumed that Jackson's temporary command was terminated so far as D. H. Hill was concerned. In the meantime Jackson, McLaws and Walker were treated as separate commands until they should assemble at Harpers Ferry. When the junction was completed Jackson as the senior would take command of all troops present.

The whole army moved on September 10th, to the north and west except for Walker who went south, crossed the river and moved west to cover Harpers Ferry from the east.

At Middletown, Longstreet took his troops and with Army headquarters turned off to the right and headed for Hagerstown. McLaws turned to the left and headed almost south to cover Harpers Ferry from the north. Jackson went straight ahead. In a few miles his line of march crossed a little stream called Antietam Creek. On the eleventh, just beyond Williamsport, with his troops singing *Carry Me Back to Old Virginy,* he re-crossed the Potomac, where the river was only knee deep. Thence he struck south to Martinsburg. The garrison there retired before he reached the town. Here he turned east and came down on Harpers Ferry from the west. Thus the high ground on all sides of the Ferry was occupied by strong Confederate forces.

Even though there was no official communication with him, it was evident to Hill that a battle was imminent. He sent for Major Douglas of Jackson's staff and asked for his assistance. He asked Douglas, since he had brought the order for his arrest, to intercede with Jackson for his release. Hill asked only to be restored to command until the battle was over, at which time he would once more report himself in arrest. He had chosen a good advocate. Douglas dashed off and presented his proposal to Jackson, he says, as "forcefully as he could" and ventured to add that "no one could command the Light Division as well as Hill could." Jackson could not well refuse. Whatever his opinions of Hill's march discipline no one could question Hill's leadership and effectiveness in battle. Hill was perhaps the most experienced division commander in the army. Jackson restored him to duty and so notified Branch.

As will be shown subsequently, this offhand decision would save the Army of Northern Virginia from destruction, and may indeed have prolonged the life of the Confederacy by nineteen months. Hill quickly resumed his responsibilities. General Lee's attitude had been that "twere well if it were done quickly" and he had hoped that the investment of Harpers Ferry could be completed on September 12th. Jackson did not arrive until the 13th at about 11 A.M.

Bolivar Heights, the high ground west of Harpers Ferry, was crowned with works and appeared to be prepared to make a determined defense. Hill, after receiving orders to take the ridge, made a quick reconnaissance and saw its weak spot. In the night, his chief of artillery by great exertion moved guns into position, actually in rear of Federal lines, and was thus able to enfilade them. McLaws had trouble with Federal troops on his side of the river which delayed him somewhat. McLaws' assignment was not only to keep the Harpers Ferry garrison from escaping to the north, but also to serve as a sort of tactical connecting file between the forces now widely separated and on two sides of a river. Finally on the 14th all troops were in position and visual communication was established.

Harpers Ferry is a basin with high ground on all sides. When Jackson put six divisions and all of their artillery into position, it took only an hour's pounding with his guns and the threat of an infantry advance to bring about a surrender.

Federal fire dies away. There is a flash of some kind. Yes, it is white. Apparently someone carrying a white flag, a table cloth or a sheet. An officer seems to be waving it. Yes, they are surrendering. Hill sends Lieutenant Chamberlayne to investigate. Officially Chamberlayne is the first Confederate to enter the Federal lines. But individual Confederate troops have slipped in quickly and quietly.

Jackson sends Major Douglas. Yes, the Yankees wish to surrender. Hill rides forward to meet a handsomely mounted officer. His black horse is well groomed, his gauntlets are flawless. He is followed by a well-turned-out staff. Scarecrow rebel infantrymen stare in patronizing admiration. Chamberlayne introduces Brigadier General Julius White. The Federal general is a little self conscious about his resplendent appearance and apologizes to the somewhat worn and stained Hill. He had, he explains, expected to meet some of the high officials of the Confederacy. Hill strangely enough seems to have taken no offense. He could afford to abandon some of his old, almost neurotic sensitiveness.

The post is actually commanded by a Colonel Dixon S. Miles, White explains. The General is only there by accident, 'an unfortunate accident,' he adds dryly. He had just come to the command of the troops at Martinsburg when the Confederates approached and his superiors in Baltimore ordered him to fall back to Harpers Ferry. He had not thought it appropriate to exercise his seniority when Colonel Miles, an officer of forty years experience was receiving orders for withstanding the seige directly from Washington. Hill rides with White to Jackson. The conversation is amiable. White is complimentary concerning the skill and promptness with which the investment had been accomplished. Hill replies that he would rather take the place twenty times than to have to defend it once.

Jackson is unkempt and stern not for him amiable and trivial small talk. Decisions are brisk, orders laconic and incisive. No terms. Unconditional surrender. General Hill will handle the details of surrender: he is instructed to permit the prisoners to retain their private property, officers to retain their side arms, but no clemency for Confederate deserts found in the garrison. All other troops will prepare to move out by 3 P.M. In the meantime a few hours are permitted for troops to recoup from captured supplies and do a little sightseeing. A courier is dispatched to General Lee.

The booty was large. Eleven thousand, five hundred and eighty-three prisoners surrendered. 13,000 stacks of small arms, 73 cannon, 200 wagons and much quartermaster stores. There were mountains of rations and troops had sutler delicacies which they had not seen since Manassas. This time there was no relief column to be fended off. Hill's troops would be occupation troops, as it were, and according to other commands get more than their fair share of personal booty.

Hill found the garrison completely disorganized. Hill and White worked out the formal agreement of the terms of surrender. White spoke of the problem of officer's baggage and Hill agreed to lend him twenty-four wagons. Hill later complained that their return was long delayed. But the fault was not with White for the record contains this remarkable document.

> Annapolis, Maryland
> September 22, 1862

Colonel J. C. Kelton,
Assistant Adjutant General
Sir: I have received the following from Brigadier General White, and notified him that I refer this strange arrangement to headquarters. Shall the wagons be returned, and how?

General: I have the honor to state that, after capitulating at Harpers Ferry, I was allowed by General A. P. Hill, commanding, at that post, the forces of the enemy, some twenty-four wagons for the transportation of officers' baggage, after my pledge to return them to the enemy's lines. I respectfully request therefore, that the quartermaster be directed to forward them back.

> Very respectfully,
> Julius White
> Brigadier General
> Daniel Tyler
> Brigadier General

Jackson began to move the remaining troops off to join Lee. Hill was urged to show all expedition and follow as soon as possible. Each Federal regiment was formed, marched out to stack arms and be paroled. An Ohio colonel rebelled and sent a second in command. One of Pender's staff officers explained patiently that he had a choice of this or Libby Prison. The colonel gave in. The colonel of a New York regiment made a speech and, pointing contemptuously to the ragged staff officer accepting the paroles said, "We are not surrendering to that boy but to an act of God."

The men drew fresh underwear, good rifles and other badly needed items. It was a hectic time for Hill. Among the brigades surrendering was one composed of the 39th New York and 111th Massachusetts. Their commanding officer, Colonel Frederick G. D'Utassy, was in no way satisfied with the surrender anyhow. When he formed his regiments to parole the men, he and L. O'B. Branch bickered over the terms of the parole. Branch said it meant that the men could not be sent to drill or a camp of instruction. D'Utassy insisted that the men could be used against the Indians, "who like you are in insurrection against us," and since many were recruits it would be necesary to train them. Branch said he would have to ask Hill, and sent off a note. Come back at 9 o'clock. At 9 o'clock Branch told D'Utassy's adjutant that General Hill supported him, and the parole forbade training until exchanged. The Federal colonel said that he would not accept, that he would go to prison first. He ordered his men formed early the next morning. At 6 P.M. they turned out and the same adjutant, Lieutenant Charles G. Bacon, proceeded to Hill's office with the muster rolls and asked for passes for the two regiments. Hill asked if the troops had been paroled. Lieutenant Bacon replied "evasively" that he thought so. Hill wrote out the passes and two regiments, less their weapons, marched away with not an officer or man paroled. The commander had even hid the regimental flags in his personal baggage. The day of Branch's death had already dawned and if Hill ever knew of this dupeing there is no record that he ever mentioned it.

It was not yet quite 6:30 A.M. September 17, when a dusty courier on a sweat-stained horse drew to a plunging halt at Division Headquarters. There was about him an air of urgency. His message had an air of desperation. The veterans of the Light Division were needed—and at once.

The Army of Northern Virginia with its back to a river was facing desperate odds. Much of General Lee's planning was based on his estimate of the personality of his old adversary, General McClellan, now once more restored to command. But through one of those fatalistic horseshoe nails which divert the happenings of history, the usually cautious McClellan was boldly and vigorously following the Confederates. Because of the ambiguity of D. H.

Hill's status, orders were sent to him from Army Headquarters, and by Jackson. The copy sent by army, wrapped around the chronicled three cigars, was carelessly dropped in Frederick. Later it was picked up by a Federal soldier and put into channels. Thus McClellan was possessed of a detailed account of Lee's dispositions and intentions.

The courier brought urgent and galvanic instructions for the Light Division to rejoin the main body. There was a bustle of orders. The brigades fell in with a rattle of arms.

This division was to move with the utmost expedition: Thomas and his brigade was to remain to complete the details of paroling Yankee prisoners. "Fall in, fowa-a-rd, close up now—step out men—close up!" Jackson might rage and punish for lack of personal supervision on an administrative march but this was a tactical march—Hill was up and down his column. "Close up—step out. Eighteen miles to the staggering army—close up. Guns out ahead—close up!" The Division Commander was in his shirt-sleeves—his sword out. It was not the flat he was using this time, but the point. Literally he was goading his men forward. As the weaker fell out, he urged the rest on. Close up—step out! The pale eyes snapped—the fury of combat was on him—close up! By force of personality he carried them on. If one soldier—a whole company—a regiment had sunstroke, he would carry the rest on. Of Archer's four regiments only 340 men would still be with him when he arrived at the fight. This was the Light Division—his division—a thunderbolt on the Chickahominy—deciding factor at Cedar Mountain. The Army was in danger. Dilatory on the march? Here was no question of academic compliance with the precision of orders—no mere effecting of discipline. Orders from Lee were urgent—close up! The miles crawled by. Ahead the muttering of guns became louder and louder. Excitement spurred the pace as much as exortation of officers. Send the guns ahead—damn the dust—get the guns forward—tell General Lee I am coming—tell him where we are and that I have all my people except Thomas—move out—close up, men. And coming Hill was—hell for leather —coming at a pace that none but the toughest troops could stand. Ahead gleamed the Potomac. Jaded artillery horses had already been urged across with the frantic lashing of drivers. They hur-

ried down and splashed across Boetler's Ford. There was not even
time for the most Gideonlike to pause to scoop up water. The
sound of small arms was plain now—shifting smoke was visible.
They began to run into the backwash of battle—stragglers, walking wounded, sulkers, malingerers. Close up—close up—double
time there—close that gap—a frightened lieutenant cowering behind a tree—the grey horse swirled out of line—terrible in his
anger, Hill demanded the frightened man's sword and broke it
over his cowering back. Contemptuously Hill threw the broken
pieces away and surged along his panting column, then at a hard
run on ahead of his men so that he could learn the situation at
first hand.

On the firing line the situation was rapidly disintegrating. Mc-
Clellan had first struck the Confederate left, recoiled then, struck
the center, again was repulsed; and now at the end of the day
he was gaining success on the right. Confederate reserves were
completely used up in the first two attacks. There were none left
now. The force on the right was pitifully small. It had already sent
every unit that could be spared to the left where they had been
used up in repelling the earlier assaults. Now blue coats were
across the Antietam. Confederates were stubborn about their withdrawal, but they were withdrawing. The Confederate right bent
back—at an accelerated rate it folded more and more—there were
no reserves to stop this. The town of Sharpsburg was ablaze. A
little more and the Yankees would be in position to roll up the
whole army. The situation was desperate—if this army were destroyed it would end the Confederacy. General Lee watched anxiously down the road on which Hill was approaching. Some of his
artillery was already there and firing. McIntosh's battery was
whamming away with canister but their infantry was withdrawing
from around them. When the bluecoats were within sixty yards
the guns were abandoned and caissons and gunners got out just
ahead of capture. Hill was suddenly there, the dust cloud of his
troops not far behind. He reported himself to Lee. The relief of
that moment may have remained with Lee throughout all his subsequent problems with Hill. When he lay dying, almost his last
words were concerned with bringing A. P. Hill's troops forward. The terrible tension and great relief of this episode may

have been in his mind in his last delirium. Hill needed very little instruction to comprehend fully the situation. The battle was going to pieces before his eyes. A quick briefing by General D. R. Jones, the local commander and Hill whisked back to the head of his column. Deploy into line directly from the column. Pender, go in on the left of those troops—Breckenbrough, there to Pender's left.

Archer must get those guns back. What regiment is this? Twenty-eighth South Carolina. That cornfield is full of sharp-shooters. Clean them out—I will be responsible to your brigade commander.

His line sweeps forward, the screech of the Rebel yell pitched above the lower register of battle noises. Here the Army of North Virginia is at its most headlong combativeness. Hill's horse falters and sinks down, shot. Hill lands on his feet, without pause goes forward on foot, his sword out. It is a Slaughter Mountain on a larger scale. The Federal advance stumbles to a halt—recoils under the impetuous assault of Hill's troops. They begin to give ground—the tempo of their withdrawal increases. They are driven back across the river. The army is saved.

They could not have withstood much more of the mauling they took that day. But with that almost unreasonable pugnacity of which General Lee was capable, he elected to stand in his lines another twenty-four hours before pulling back across the Poto-mac. At bay, wounded, truculent, the Army of Northern Virginia snarled its unquavering defiance for another twenty-four hours.

This had been Hill's great moment. Never before, never again, did he show to such advantage. And here the probing curiosity of history finds him and remembers him. Silhouetted against the saffron flashes of guns which highlight the melodramatic red of his battle dress, a naked sword in his hand, on foot, combativeness incarnate, throwing himself in the blind madness of combat against a confident enemy. For the moment the smoke and dust of furious fighting clouds him into physical obscurity, but the white light of fame picks this out as his greatest hour.

7

BATTLE OF FREDERICKSBURG

By Lieutenant General Jubal Anderson Early

When the hectic fighting on Antietam Creek died down, Lee held his ground truculently for two more plays and then recrossed the Potomac into Virginia. The Federal Army followed but not with the aggressiveness which the Union Commander in Chief would like to have seen. Lee dispersed his forces leisurely not only with a view to the logistical requirements but also in such a manner that they could hastily be reassembled when the Northern intention was developed. Lincoln's patience with McClellan was finally exhausted and McClellan was relieved. General Burnside somewhat reluctantly accepted the command. He immediately thrust straight south. Lee preferred to make his stand on the North Anna but was overruled. He then took up a strong position on the high ground on the south side of the Rappahannock River—at the point of impact almost the west. Against this very strong position Burnside, on December 11, 1862, threw his divisions in an unimaginative assault and was bloodily repulsed. For the Confederates, it was an easy and fairly inexpensive victory. Had Burnside been more imaginative or had been willing to maneuver, the results might have been vastly different. Burnside's defeat must have effected Lincoln's decision to keep trying generals until he found one who could win.

The Confederate Army was conspicuous for its distinctive personalities. Not the least conspicuous among these, was Jubal Anderson Early. At Fredericksburg he commanded a Division of the Confederate Army. In after years he wrote a narrative of the war. Here is presented his first hand account of that battle.

Fredericksburg is located on the southern bank of the Rappan-hannock River at the head of tidewater, and the river is navigable to that point for steamboats and small vessels. On the northern bank, opposite, above and below Fredericksburg, are what are called the Stafford Heights, which are close to the river, and completely command the southern bank. Fredericksburg's exact location is on a narrow strip of low land between the river and a range of hills in the rear. These hills leaving the river opposite the small village of Falmouth, which is a short distance above Fredericksburg and on the northern bank, diverge from it below, and gradually declining, extend nearly to the Massaponix Creek, which empties into the river four or five miles below the town.

The river flats or bottoms immediately below Fredericksburg widen out considerably and continue to widen until they are from one and a half to two miles in width at the lower end of the range of hills, where they unite with similar but not so wide flats on the Massaponix, which extend back for some distance in rear of the range of hills mentioned. Below the mouth of the Massaponix there are other hills which approach near to the bank of the river, and extend down it for a considerable distance. Hazel Run, rising southeast of Fredericksburg, runs through the range of hills along a narrow valley, or ravine rather, and passing close on the east of the town, empties into the river. Deep Run rises below in the range of hills, and runs across the wide bottoms through a deep channel likewise into the river, something over a mile below the town. The hills just in rear of the town were, at the time of which I am speaking, nearly denuded of growing timber but below, to the end of the range, they were for the most part covered with woods. The bottoms were entirely cleared and in cultivation, furnishing several extensive farms, and up Deep Run to its sources is a valley making a large re-entering angle in the line of hills, which valley was then also cleared and in cultivation.

From the town a road, called the Telegraph Road, runs south, crossing Hazel Run and then ascending the hills passes towards

Richmond by the way of Hanover Junction. Another road called the Plank Road ascends the hills above Hazel Run and runs westward by Chancellorsville to Orange Court House. A third road, called the River Road, runs from the lower end of the town, crossing Hazel Run and Deep Run, and passing through the bottoms about half way from the river to the foot of the hills, in a direction very nearly parallel to the river, it crosses the Massaponix not far above its mouth, where it forks, one fork going to Port Royal below and the other by Bowling Green in the direction of Richmond. This is a wide road, and where it passes through the bottoms there were on both sides high, thick and firm embankments thrown up for fences or enclosures to the adjacent fields.

The Richmond, Fredericksburg & Potomac Railroad, leaving the Potomac at the mouth of Aquia Creek, crosses the river into Fredericksburg and then runs through the bottoms below the town between the river road and the hills, which latter it approaches closely at their lower end, and then passes around at their foot to take the direction to Richmond. Just at the rear of the foot of the lower end of the hills a country road, leading from the Telegraph Road and passing along the east of the ridge, crosses the railroad to get into the River Road; this is called "Hamilton's Crossing," from a gentleman of that name formerly residing near the place. A canal runs from the river along the foot of the hills above the town to the rear of it, for the purpose of supplying water to several mills and factories in it, and this canal connects by a drain ditch with Hazel Run, over which ditch the Plank Road crosses.

What is called Marye's Heights or Hill lies between Hazel Run and the Plank Road, and at the foot of it is a stone wall, behind which and next to the hill, the Telegraph Road runs. Above Marye's Hill on the east of the Plank Road are what are called respectively, Cemetery, Stansbury's and Taylor's Hills, all overlooking the canal. In rear of these hills and overlooking and commanding them are higher eminences. On the east of Hazel Run and the Telegraph Road is quite a high hill farther back than Marye's Hill and overlooking it and nearly the whole ground, to which the name of Lee's Hill has been given, because it was the position generally occupied by General Lee during the battle.

Burnside's army had taken position on and in rear of Stafford

Heights, and the heights themselves, from Falmouth to a point very nearly opposite the mouth of the Massaponix, were covered with numerous batteries of heavy guns, while the nature of the ground was such as to afford easy access to the river by his troops. Longstreet's corps occupied the hills in rear of Fredericksburg to Hamilton's Crossing, and positions for some distance above, while strong pickets were established in the town and on the river bank above and below to watch the enemy and impede a crossing.

It was impossible to resist successfully a crossing, as the river is only between two and three hundred yards wide, and the banks are so deep, and the river so accessible, on the north bank by means of ravines running into it, that our artillery, posted on the hills occupied by our troops, could not play upon the bridges either during the progress of the construction or afterwards, while the enemy's batteries were able, by a concentrated fire, to drive off the small bodies watching the river, or to prevent any aid being sent to them over the wide open plains formed by the bottoms. In addition to all this, the bottoms towards the lower end of our lines were so wide that we had no guns which would do effective firing across them, while the enemy's heavy guns from the north bank of the river completely swept the whole of our front, and reached over beyond our line.

On the morning of the 11th of December the enemy commenced his movement, and by the use of his artillery drove the regiments which were guarding the river from its banks after an obstinate resistance, and succeeded in laying down their pontoon bridges, one at the mouth of Deep Creek, and the other two at Fredericksburg. The first was laid early in the afternoon, but the latter two not until near night, and during night and the next day the enemy crossed in heavy force.

On the afternoon of the 12th I received an order from General Jackson to move at once to the vicinity of Hamilton's Crossing, which I did by marching nearly all night, and a short time before day I bivouacked some two miles in rear of the crossing where the division had a little time to rest. At light on the morning of the 13th I moved up to the crossing, and found our army in position confronting the enemy. Longstreet's line had been constructed from the right, and General A. P. Hill's division, which was much the largest in Jackson's corps, now occupied the right of the line which rested near the crossing. He was in the front skirts of the woods which covered the hills, and on his left was Hood's division.

On the right of Hill's line was a small hill cleared on the side next the enemy, on which were posted some fourteen pieces of artillery, under Lieutenant Colonel Walker, which were supported by Field's brigade, under Colonel Brockenborough, while Archer's brigade was on the left of the guns. On Archer's left there was an interval of several hundred yards in front of which was a low flat marshy piece of woodland extending across the railroad out into the bottom which was supposed to be impracticable, and was therefore not covered by any body of troops, but Gregg's brigade was posted in reserve in rear of this interval, without, however, being in the line of battle. On the left of the interval were the other three brigades of A. P. Hill's division, Lane's brigade being next to it, but in advance of the general line a considerable number of pieces of artillery were posted along the left of Hill's line, but they were on low and unfavorable ground, as there were no good positions for guns on that part of the line.

On my arrival, my division was posted on a second line several hundred yards in rear of A. P. Hill's, with Jackson's, now under Brigadier General Taliaferro, on my left. My right rested on the railroad at the crossing, and extended along the ridge road, which here crossed the railroad, for a short distance and then into the woods on my left. Hays' brigade was on my right, with Trimble's brigade under Colonel R. F. Hoke immediately in its rear, Lawton's brigade under Colonel N. N. Atkinson in the centre, and my own brigade under Colonel J. A. Walker on the left. In this position there was a thick woods intervening between my division and the enemy, and the consequence was that he was entirely excluded from our view as we were from his. D. H. Hill's division, which had followed mine from below, was posted in a third line in the open ground in my rear beyond the hills.

The weak point in our position was on our right, as there was the wide open plain in front of it extending to the river and perfectly covered and swept by the enemy's heavy batteries on the opposite heights, and to the right, extending around to our rear, were the open flats of the Massaponix, here quite wide and incapable of being covered by any position we could take. There was very great danger of our right being turned by the enemy's pushing a heavy column down the river across the Massaponix. The plains on that flank were watched by Stuart with two brigades of cavalry and his horse artillery.

A heavy fog had concealed the two armies from each other during the early morning, but about nine o'clock it began to rise, and then the artillery fire opened, which was just as my division was moving into position. The enemy's fire at first was not directed towards the place where my division was posted, but after a short interval the shells began to fall in our vicinity, and the division remained exposed to a random but quite galling cannonading for two or three hours.

Shortly after noon we heard in our front a very heavy musketry fire, and soon a courier from General Archer came to the rear in search of General A. P. Hill, stating that General Archer was very heavily pressed and wanted reinforcements. Just at that moment, a staff officer rode up with an order to me from General Jackson, to hold my division in readiness to move to the right promptly, as the enemy was making a demonstration in that direction. This caused me to hesitate about sending a brigade to Archer's assistance, but in order to be prepared to send it if necessary, I ordered Colonel Atkinson to get his brigade ready to advance: the order had been hardly given, before the adjutant of Walker's battalion of artillery came galloping to the rear with the information that the interval on Archer's left (an awful gulf as he designated it) had been penetrated by heavy columns of the enemy, and that Archer's brigade and all our batteries on the right would inevitably be captured unless there was instant relief. This was so serious an emergency that I determined to act upon it at once notwithstanding the previous directions from General Jackson to hold my division in readiness for another purpose. I accordingly ordered Atkinson to advance with his brigade.

I was then entirely unacquainted with the ground in front, having been able when I first got up to take only a hasty glance at the country to our right, and I asked Lieutenant Chamberlain, Walker's adjutant, to show the brigade the direction to advance. In reply he stated that the column of the enemy which had penetrated our line was immediately in front of the brigade I had ordered forward, and that by going right ahead there could be no mistake. The brigade, with the exception of one regiment, the 13th Georgia, which did not hear the order, accordingly moved off in handsome style through the woods, but as it did so Lieutenant Chamberlain informed me that it would not be sufficient to cover the entire gap in our line, and I ordered Colonel Walker to advance immediately with my own brigade on the left of Atkinson.

The enemy's column in penetrating the interval mentioned had turned Archer's left and Lane's right, while they were attacked in front, causing Archer's left and Lane's entire brigade to give way, and one column had encountered Gregg's brigade, which, being taken somewhat by surprise, was thrown into partial confusion, resulting in the death of General Gregg, but the brigade was rallied and maintained its ground. Lawton's brigade advancing rapidly and gallantly under Colonel Atkinson, encountered that column of the enemy which had turned Archer's left, in the woods on the hill in rear of the line, and by a brilliant charge drove it back down the hill, across the railroad, and out into the open plains beyond, advancing so far as to cause a portion of one of the enemy's batteries to be abandoned. The brigade, however, on getting out into the open plain came under the fire of the enemy's heavy guns, and the approach of a fresh and heavy column on its right rendered it necessary that it should retire, which it did under orders from Colonel Evans, who had succeeded to the command by reason of Atkinson's being severely wounded.

Two of Brockenborough's regiments from the right participated in the repulse of the enemy. Colonel Walker advanced, at a double quick, further to the left, encountering one of the columns which had penetrated the interval, and by a gallant and resolute charge he drove it back out of the woods across the railroad into the open plains beyond, when, seeing another column of the enemy crossing the railroad on his left, he fell back to the line of the road, and then deployed the 13th Virginia Regiment to the left, and ordered it to advance under cover of the timbers to attack the advancing column on its flank. This attack was promptly made and Thomas' brigade, attacking in front at the same time, the enemy was driven back with heavy loss.

As soon as Atkinson and Walker had been ordered forward, Hoke was ordered to move his brigade to the left of Hays, but before he got into position, I received a message stating that Archer's brigade was giving way and I ordered Hoke to move forward at once to Archer's support, obliquing to the right as he moved. Just as Hoke started, I received an order from General Jackson, by a member of his staff, to advance to the front with the whole division, and Hays' brigade was at once ordered forward in support of Hoke. The 13th Georgia Regiment which had been left behind on the advance of Lawton's brigade was ordered to follow Hoke's brigade and unite with it.

Hoke found a body of the enemy in the woods in rear of Archer's line on the left where the regiments on that flank, which had been attacked in rear, had given way, but Archer still held the right with great resolution, though his ammunition was exhausted. Upon a gallant charge, by the brigade under Hoke, the enemy was driven out of the woods upon his reserves posted on the railroad in front, and then by another charge, in which General Archer participated, the railroad was cleared and the enemy was pursued to a fence some distance beyond, leaving in our hands a number of prisoners, and a large number of small arms on the field.

The movements of the three brigades engaged have been described separately from the necessity of the case, but they were all engaged at the same time, though they went into action separately and in the order in which they have been mentioned, and Lawton's brigade had advanced further out into the plains than either of the others.

On the riding to the front, I directed Lawton's brigade, which was retiring, to be re-formed in the woods—Colonel Atkinson had been left in front severely wounded and he fell into the enemy's hands. Captain E. P. Lawton, Assistant Adjutant General of the brigade, a most gallant and efficient officer, had also been left in front at the extreme point to which the brigade advanced, mortally wounded, and he likewise fell into the enemy's hands.

I discovered that Hoke had got too far to the front where he was exposed to the enemy's artillery, and also to a flank movement on his right, and I sent an order for him to retire to the original line, which he did, anticipating the order by commencing to retire before it reached him. Two of his regiments and a small battalion were left to occupy the line of the railroad where there was cover for them and his other two regiments, along with the 13th Georgia, which had not been engaged, were put in the slight trenches previously occupied by Archer's brigade. Walker continued to hold the position on the railroad which he had taken after repulsing the enemy. Lawton's brigade was sent to the rear for the purpose of resting and replenishing its ammunition. Hays' brigade, which had advanced in rear of Hoke, had not become engaged, but in advancing to the front it had been exposed to a severe shelling which the enemy began, as his attacking columns were retiring in confusion before my advancing brigades. Hays was posted in rear of Hoke for the purpose of strengthening the right in the event of another advance.

When I had discovered Lawton's brigade retiring, I sent to General D. H. Hill for reinforcements for fear that the enemy might again pass through the unprotected interval, and he sent me two brigades, but before they arrived Brigadier General Paxton, who occupied the right of Taliaferro's line, had covered the interval by promptly moving his brigade into it.

The enemy was very severely punished for this attack, which was made by Franklin's grand division, and he made no further attack on our right. During this engagement and subsequently there were demonstrations against A. P. Hill's left and Hood's right which were repulsed without difficulty. Beginning in the forenoon and continuing until nearly dark, there were repeated and desperate assaults made by the enemy from Fredericksburg against the positions at Marye's Hill and the one to our right of it, but they were repulsed with terrible slaughter, mainly by the infantry from Longstreet's corps posted behind the stone wall at the foot of Marye's Hill, and the artillery on that, and on the neighboring heights. The loss to the enemy here was much heavier than that on our right, while our own loss at the same point was comparatively slight.

My two brigades, Trimble's under Hoke, and my own under Walker, and the 13th Georgia Regiment held their positions on the front until night, while Hays retained his position immediately in rear of Hoke, but there was no further attack made on that part of the line or on any part of Hill's front, except the demonstrations on his left which have been mentioned and which resulted in some skirmishing and artillery firing.

When my division was first put in position on the second line as described, having no use for my artillery, I ordered Captain J. W. Latimer, my acting chief of artillery, to report to Colonel Crutchfield, Chief of Artillery for the Corps, with six batteries attached to the division. Just before sunset of the day of the battle, after having seen that all was quiet in my front, I rode a little to the rear and discovered General D. H. Hill's division moving to the front through the woods.

On my inquiring the meaning of the movement, General Colquitt, in command of the front brigade, informed me that orders had been given for the advance of the whole line, and that Hill's division was ordered to advance in support. General D. H. Hill himself rode up in a few minutes, and confirmed the information. This was the first intimation I had received of the order, as it had not reached me. While General Hill and I were speaking of the matter, Lieutenant Morrison, aide-de-camp to General Jackson, rode up and stated that the General's orders were that I should hold my command in readiness to advance; and immediately afterwards one of my own staff officers came to me with the information that General Jackson wished me to take command of all the troops on the right and advance, regulating the distance to which I should go, by the effect produced on the enemy by our artillery which was to open.

I rode immediately to where Hoke's brigade was posted and found General Jackson himself, who repeated in person the orders to me, stating that I was to advance in support of some artillery which he was about to send forward. I informed him of the condition of my command, the separation of Walker from the rest, the fact of Lawton's brigade being in the rear, and that Hoke's and Hays' brigades and the 13th Georgia were the only troops immediately available. He told me to advance with the latter and that he would give me abundant support; I accordingly prepared to advance with Hoke's brigade and the 13th Georgia in front, followed by Hays' brigade. The program was that a number of pieces of artillery should be run out in front, and open on the enemy's infantry, when I was to advance and the artillery to be again moved forward, followed by my infantry.

The movement with the artillery was commenced, and as soon as it left the woods the enemy opened with numerous batteries from the plains and from behind the embankments on the river road. This fire was terrific and many shells went crashing past us into the woods in our rear, where D. H. Hill's division was massed. Our own guns opened and continued to fire for a brief space, and a part of Hoke's brigade advanced to the railroad, but General Jackson soon became satisfied that the advance must be attended with great difficulties and perhaps disastrous results, and abandoned it. It was well that he did. The enemy had very heavy forces massed behind the embankments on the river road, the one nearest us being pierced with embrasures for numerous pieces of artillery. We would have had to advance nearly a mile, over an entirely bare plain swept by all this artillery, as well as cannonaded by the heavy guns on Stafford Heights, and if we had been able to force back the bodies of infantry and the artillery occupying positions on the plain between us and the woods, still when we reached the road itself we would have found a vastly superior force behind a double line of very strong breastworks.

Nothing could have lived while passing over that plain under such circumstances, and I feel well assured that, while we were all ready to obey the orders of our heroic commander, there was not a man in the force ordered to advance, whether in the front or in support, who did not breathe freer when he heard the orders countermanding the movement.

I have subsequently examined this ground with great care, and this examination has strengthened the position first entertained. It may perhaps be asked why our troops had not occupied the line of this road, to which I will reply that the road and the embankments on each side of it were perfectly commanded by the batteries of Stafford Heights, which rendered the position untenable for us, and the retreat from it most hazardous, while it afforded safe protection to the enemy from our guns.

Shortly after the termination of this effort to advance, I received a notification from General Jackson to move my troops to the rear for the purpose of resting and getting provisions as soon as they should be relieved by the troops of A. P. Hill's division which had at first occupied the positions now held by me, but no troops came to my relief and I therefore remained in position. Orders were received during the night for Taliaferro to relieve Hill's troops in the front line beginning from the left, and for me to occupy the remainder of the line on the right which Taliaferro could not fill out. In accordance with these directions, before dawn on the 14th, Paxton relieved Walker, Hays took the position which Paxton vacated, Hoke remained stationary, Lawton's brigade under Colonel Evans was posted on Hoke's right, and Walker was moved from the left and placed in reserve behind Hoke. The evening before Carrington's battery had relieved Latimer's and Brown's on the left, and still remained in position, and on the morning of the 14th, Dement's battery relieved one of the batteries on the right which had been engaged the day before.

During the 14th the enemy remained in position on the plains and at Fredericksburg, an occasional shot being exchanged by the artillery and some firing from the skirmishers taking place on portions of the line, but none in my front.

Before light on the morning of the 15th, D. H. Hill's division relieved Taliaferro's and mine on the front line, and we moved to the rear in reserve, A. P. Hill's division occupying the second line.

There was quiet on the 15th, the enemy still retaining his position, but early on the morning of the 16th, as I was moving into position on the second line in accordance with previous orders, it was discovered that the enemy had re-crossed the river during the night, taking up his bridges, and I was ordered to move at once to the vicinity of Port Royal to guard against the possible contingency of the enemy's attempting to turn our right by crossing the river near that place; and I commenced the march immediately.

The loss in the division under my command in this battle was in killed 89 and wounded 639. General Lee's entire loss in the battle was in killed 458, and wounded, 3,743, to-wit: in Longstreet's corps, 130 killed, 1,276 wounded; in Jackson's corps, 328 killed and 2,454 wounded; and 13 wounded in Stuart's cavalry.

The enemy's loss was very much heavier, and over 900 prisoners, more than 9,000 stand of arms and a large quantity of ammunition fell into our hands.

The failure of General Lee to attempt to destroy the enemy's army after its repulse has been much criticised, and many speculations about the probable result of an attempt to drive the enemy into the river have been indulged in by a number of writers. In the first place, it must be recollected that no man was more anxious to inflict a decisive blow on the enemy than General Lee himself and none understood better the exact condition of things, and the likelihood of success in any attempt to press the enemy after his defeat on the 13th. That defeat was a repulse with very heavy loss, it is true, but it was not a rout of the enemy's army; and candid persons ought to presume that General Lee knew what he was about and had very good and sufficient reasons for not sallying from his line of defence, upon the exposed plains below, to make the attempt to convert the repulse into a rout.

If attention is given to the previous description of the ground on which the two armies were operating, it must be seen that an attempt to pass over the wide plain intervening between our line and the enemy's position below the town, while exposed to the fire of 150 heavy guns on the Stafford Heights and the numerous field pieces securely masked in the River road, would inevitably have resulted in diasaster, unless the enemy's forces had become so paralyzed as to be incapable of an effort at defence. Burnside's army was composed of about 150,000 men in the grand divisions under Sumner, Franklin and Hooker, respectively.

In none of the assaults on our lines were the whole of these grand divisions engaged, but when columns of attack were sent foward, there were always very heavy reserves for the attacking columns to fall back upon in case of repulse; Sumner's and Franklin's grand divisions had been mainly engaged and Hooker's scarcely at all. General Lee's army was not half as large as Burnside's and if he had at any time made an attempt to advance, any force that he could have massed for that purpose without abandoning his line of defence entirely would in all likelihood have still encountered a superior force of infantry behind a strong line of defence, in addition to the artillery.

As I have stated, General Jackson made the attempt to advance on the right late in the day on the 13th but he was compelled to desist, very fortunately, before any disaster happened. Above the town, the same canal, at the foot of the range of hills, which had furnished an insurmountable obstacle to any attack by the enemy on our extreme left, likewise furnished the same obstacle to an advance on our part. The only other quarter from which the advance could have been made was from the hills immediately in rear of the town upon the enemy in the town, and there the difficulties were greater even than below. Any attacking columns from that quarter must either have moved down the rugged face of the base hills, or by flank along the Telegraph and Plank roads, and then they would have been so much scattered by the artillery from the north bank, which would then have had a more effective range than even on the plains, that it would not have required the reserves, posted behind the houses and defences in the town, to complete the repulse and disaster.

As to a night attack, that is a very easy thing to talk about but a most hazardous experiment to try, especially on dark nights such as we then had. Such attacks cannot be ventured on with safety unless with the most thoroughly trained troops, and then not in large bodies, for fear of confusion and firing into each other, the very dread of which often paralyzes very brave troops.

It has been said that General Lee might have inflicted tremendous damage upon the enemy by forcing hot shot and shell into Fredericksburg while the enemy's troops were massed there. The heroic and patriotic people of that town, when it was threatened with a bombardment by Sumner, had not appealed to the commander of their country's army to cause the danger to be removed from them by not resisting its occupation by the enemy, but had exhibited most commendable unselfishness by, in most cases, abandoning their homes without a murmur, while there were some too poor to move elsewhere, and others who chose to remain and share all the dangers of the approaching struggle; it was not in the heart of the noble commander of the Army of Northern Virginia to doom, by his own act, the remaining few of that devoted people and the homes of the absent to destruction, for the sake of killing and wounding a few thousand of the enemy, and causing dismay among the remainder.

Is this forbearance one to be criticised with severity as a grievous military blunder?

It is probable that if General Lee had known that the enemy was evacuating the town, his artillery might have inflicted considerable damage, but the enemy had given no indication of such a purpose, and he took advantage of the darkness of the night and the prevalence of a storm and wind to make good his retreat, when the noise attending the movement could not be heard.

General Lee accomplished all that was possible with the means under his control except, indeed, the useless destruction of what the enemy had left of the town of Fredericksburg.

There was a ridiculous story about General Jackson, to which currency was given by the newspapers, which represented that, at a council of war called by General Lee on the night after the battle, General Jackson fell into a doze while the very grave question of what ought to be done under the circumstances was being discussed, and after all the rest had given their opinion, General Lee turned to General Jackson and asked, "Well, General, what is your opinion?" to which the latter, waking out of his nap, replied, "Drive 'em in the river, drive 'em in the river." This story is by no means creditable to General Jackson, yet it obtained a wide circulation, and the narrators of it seemed to think it was very characteristic.

General Jackson was a most able commander and heroic soldier, and it was not at all likely that he would have acted so much like a besotted member of a council of war called by his chief. I presume after the facts that I have before stated, it is not necessary to assert that no such incident occurred.

Had Burnside moved down the river to the Massaponix, after crossing, or had thrown other bridges across at or near the mouth of that stream and crossed one of his grand divisions there, he would inevitably have forced us to abandon our line of defence and fight him on other ground.

8

WOUNDING OF STONEWALL JACKSON AT CHANCELLORSVILLE

By Major Marcellus N. Moorman
Stuart Horse Artillery, Army of Northern Virginia

In the spring of 1862 the Army of the Potomac, augmented and reorganized, and under a new commander, again took up the mission of moving on to Richmond. The Confederate armies still occupied the general line of the Rappahannock River. Burnside having been unsuccessful in a frontal assault at Fredericksburg, General Joseph Hooker, his successor, decided to flank the fixed positions there by moving west on the north bank of the river and crossing higher up. This he did and plunged his army into the tangles of the Wilderness. The combination of enemy resistance and terrain slowed him down and caused him to take up positions with his own headquarters at the Chancellor mansion. While thus disposed in more or less of a line, General Lee took a large portion of his command and enveloped the Federal right flank and rolled it up badly.

Dr. Douglas S. Freeman has a chapter in his book "Robert E. Lee" which explains Gettysburg on the basis of the reorganization of the Confederate Army which followed the battle of Chancellorsville. Gettysburg is generally conceded to be the high water mark of the Confederacy and the turning point of the war. The reorganization which was effected in the Army of Northern Virginia, just before it moved into the Pennsylvania invasion, was necessitated by the death of Jackson. Until Jackson's death, the Army of Northern

Virginia was organized into two corps, one being commanded by Jackson. When Jackson was wounded at Chancellorsville, this necessitated the amputation of his left arm and General Lee is often quoted as saying that "Jackson has lost his left arm but I have lost my right arm." Certainly, neither the tactical genius of Stonewall Jackson nor his ability as an executive officer needs any elaboration. Second only to Lee, the reputation and performance of Thomas Jonathan Jackson make him the best known figure in the American Civil War.

At Chancellorsville, the Army of Northern Virginia really fought three battles. With a small force on his remote right flank, Lee held off Federal forces at Fredericksburg. With his main body, he faced vastly superior forces of Hooker's main body entangled in the gloomy region around the Chancellorsville plantation house. It was there that Lee, after consultation with Jackson, made the daring decision to take the bulk of his force and execute a wide single envelopment designed to roll up and destroy the Federal force. The execution of this hazardous maneuver was entrusted to Jackson. The right flank of the Federal forces had been discovered. Jackson and his troops, after a remarkably unimpeded and long march, placed themselves beyond the Federal flank and at right angles with it. Late in the afternoon, they moved forward in a column of divisions sweeping away the Federal forces before them in what by dark it had become virtually a rout. Success as well as failure has its confusions as in this case for, after dark came, Jackson riding forward to reconnoiter and try to straighten out his troop dispositions and prepare for the next morning's assault. In returning, as he rode into his own front lines, through a grievous error he was shot by his own men. A few days later he died of pneumonia as a result of his wounds. Jackson was only one of the thousands of casualties suffered at Chancellorsville but with his wounding the American Civil War reached one of its crucial points.

The afternoon of May 1st, 1863, my battery, of the Stuart Horse Artillery Battalion, was on the extreme left of our troops, then confronting Hooker's army, near the old Catherine Furnace. Late that afternoon we were ordered to shell a piece of woods in our

front. In order to do this we were turned into a very narrow old
road, through a dense forest which ran perpendicular to the woods
about to be shelled. The leading guns coming up, I at once rode
forward to find a position, as I was still so closely confined with the
scrub oak, that I could not unlimber. As I reached the guns in
front, the Federal artillery opened, apparently all over the woods.
Unable to move forward, I returned to my guns, where I found
Generals Jackson, Stuart and Wright shrapnel and canister raining
around them from the enemy's guns. Stuart remarked: "General
Jackson, we must move from here." But, before they could turn,
the gallant Channing Price, Stuart's Adjutant General, was mortally
wounded and died in a few hours. My battery lost six men without
being able to unlimber. We retired from this point and bivouacked
for the night.

By day the following morning I was ordered to move with General Fitz. Lee's Cavalry. On we pressed through byways and
highways, covering the troops of Jackson, until finally reaching the
plank road a halt was made, General Fitz. Lee being present.
In a short time General Jackson arrived at the head of his columns.
Some disposition of troops, both of cavalry and infantry, having
been made, General Lee remarked: "General Jackson, if you will
ride with me I can show you the enemy's right." They rode off in
the direction of Chancellorsville. Soon the order came to move
across to the old turnpike, which was done. There the head of the
column was turned to the right, and going possibly less than a mile
in the direction of Chancellorsville, I was halted, and unlimbered
one section—two guns—in the road. General Rodes, who was just
behind, was ordered to align his division upon my guns.

The two wings of Lee's army now occupied the same road; Lee
upon the east, fronting, and Jackson on the west, in rear of Hooker's
army. The cavalry having cleared the front, I was thinking it a little strange to receive no orders (my command being attached to
the cavalry) to retire with the cavalry, and seeing General Jackson
sitting near by, I approached him, saluted, and asked if I was expected to move with his line. "Yes, Captain," said he, "I will give
you the honor of going in with my troops." (Jackson had been my
old instructor at the Virginia Military Institute.) I remained talking with him during the formation of his lines; Rodes' division

leading, Colston's two hundred yards in their rear, and A. P. Hill only partially deployed, two hundred yards in rear of Colston.

Hearing such heavy artillery firing, just opposite, in the direction of Salem Church, I ventured to ask the General who it was. He asked, "How far do you suppose it is?" I replied, "Five or six miles." He then said, with characteristic sententiousness, "I suppose it is General Lee." He then asked me the time of day. "Five forty, General." "Thank you; time we were moving," was the General's laconic reply. I at once mounted and went to my guns. In a few minutes the clarion notes of the bugle from Major Blackford's skirmish line, some hundred and fifty yards in advance, rang out the command "Forward," when Jackson's twenty-five thousand veterans stepped forth into the dark shadows of the wilderness, in search of the right flank of Hooker's army; keeping two guns with the frontline of battle, and two with the second, alternating the sections as the leading guns would come into action. On we pressed through the carnage and destruction we had wrought, till a halt in the line was made.

It was now night, and dark, except the glimmer of the moon through the tangled woods. Being so ordered, I opened my guns down the road in the direction of Chancellorsville, which drew a rapid reply from a six gun battery. During this artillery duel, Rodes's and Colston's divisions, which had become intermingled during the constant fighting, were ordered to withdraw and reform, and A. P. Hill's division was sent to the front. General Lane, with the leading brigade of Hill's division, came up in rear of my guns and halted, withdrawing to the edge of the woods. General Hill seeing his brigades not moving, sent forward his Adjutant General, Lieutenant-Colonel Palmer, to know the cause of the delay. General Lane, in a letter to me, says: "In reaching the advance guns of Moorman's Battery, both sides opened their artillery and I ordered my command to lie down on the side of the road. General A. P. Hill sent his Adjutant General, Lieutenant Colonel Palmer, to know why I did not form my line of battle, and my reply was, because I do not wish to lose my command. I am unwilling to attempt to form my line in the dark, under such a fire and in such woods. Tell General Hill I believe the enemy is simply responding to our guns. If he will order our guns to cease firing the enemy will stop, and I will then form my line. The order was given through Colonel Palmer; your guns ceased firing and so did the enemy's, just as I expected, and I then formed my line. Two regiments on the right of the road, the Thirty-seventh and Seventh North Carolina, two on the left, the Eighteenth and Twenty-eighth North Carolina, with one, the Thirty-third North Carolina, were thrown well forward to the Van Wort house as skirmishers. My brigade were the only troops in line of battle at the time. Pender's and McGowan's brigades of A. P. Hill's division were in the road in rear of mine and it was there, while being carried to the rear, that Jackson gave his order, so often quoted, to Pender: 'Hold your ground, General Pender!' Pender did not form on the left of the road until after Jackson and A. P. Hill had been wounded and I had withdrawn the Eighteenth and Twenty-eighth North Carolina regiments and put them on my right, where they repulsed Sickles's formidable midnight attack and captured the colors of the Third Maine Regiment."

Just as Lane had established his line and came up to the pike in search of General Hill for orders, up rode General Jackson, who said to Lane: "Push ahead, General Lane," and passed on. Colonel Crutchfield, his chief of artillery, halted as they reached my guns, some fifty yards in advance of Lane's line, and said to me: "Captain, you can limber up and mount your men, and as soon as my guns arrive, which I have ordered in, you can retire and join your command."

It will be observed that there was an interval of many minutes between the withdrawal of Rodes and Colston and the establishment of Lane's brigade, during which there were no troops upon the firing line except my battery.

As General Jackson passed on, General Lane at once rode to the right of his brigade to move it forward. Colonel Hill, commanding the right regiment, the Seventh North Carolina, asked Lane to wait a few minutes, as he had heard a noise upon his right flank and must find out what it was. Lane said: "Send down and see." Colonel Hill at once sent Lieutenant Emack and four men in the direction of the noise. He had gone but a short distance through the woods when he walked right into the 128th Pennsylvania Regiment. Emack at once threw up his sword and said: "Men, Jackson has surrounded you; down with your guns, else we will shoot the last one of you." Down went the guns, and the lieutenant marched the captured regiment into his brigade.

Now, where was Jackson at this time? He had reached Lane's picket line and was talking with the officer in charge, awaiting Lane's advance, when some Federal soldier on horseback rode up in front of the picket line and asked for General Williams (of Hooker's Army.) The sergeant of the picket upon the right of the road, knowing him to be a Federal inquiring for a Federal General, responded by firing at him, which was taken up both right and left, until the entire picket line was blazing away in the darkness.

Now, Jackson turned to move back to his lines, being on the right of the road and the line of battle not coming forward as he had ordered. (Lane having been detained by the noise on his right and the capture of the Federal regiment.) Just at this moment Lane's regiments on the right of the road, the Thirty-seventh North Carolina and Seventh North Carolina opened one sheet of fire into the faces of my horses as they stood fronting the line, I having limbered up to move to the rear, being between the picket line and the battle line, was only awaiting the arrival of Crutchfield's guns; and I will say, just here, that not a gun of Crutchfield's had fired a shot or had arrived at the front, upon this road, up to the wounding of Jackson. My horses wheeled, breaking several poles. I at once rushed to the two regiments firing and asked: "What are you firing at? Are you trying to kill all my men in front of you? There are no Yankees here." The officer in charge gave the command to cease firing.

The firing having ceased I returned to my guns, thinking I had quieted the line. Jackson had, in the meantime, crossed to the left of the road, getting out of the line of fire of the two right regiments, the Seventh North Carolina and the Thirty-seventh North Carolina, and had nearly reached my guns, keeping on the edge of the woods, when Major John Barry, commanding the Eighteenth North Carolina, on the left of the road, for some reason, I know not what, ordered the Eighteenth North Carolina to fire. The Twenty-eighth North Carolina at once joined in the firing. It was this volley from the Eighteenth North Carolina that wounded Jackson. I say so for the reason that he was in front of the right of that regiment, which rested on the pike.

But censure not this gallant regiment, who would have laid down their lives for their beloved commander! Remember, we had been fighting for hours, when this new line deployed through a dense forest, and knowing nothing of Jackson's movements, believed they were firing upon the foe. My men informed me at once that General Jackson was wounded, just in the edge of the woods, and that one of my men, John Webb, had the General's little sorrel. A moment or two more, and the Federals opened upon us at least twenty, some say forty, guns, with shell, canister and solid shot, a most terrific fire, carrying a besom of destruction which seemed to sweep the very rocks from the old pike.

We, on our side, became quiet, the Yankees slowed down and soon ceased firing. I then replaced my poles and righted up my guns, except one caisson, and seeing Crutchfield's guns moving up, I withdrew some 150 or 200 yards to the rear and halted, sending back Dick Perkins with a pair of horses for the disabled caisson. As I halted, Major Rogers came up, wounded, was taken from his horse and placed in the ambulance. Then came up Colonel Crutchfield (an intimate friend of mine and schoolmate), and recognizing me, said: "Captain, please assist me to dismount." I asked: "How are you wounded, Colonel?" He replied: "My thigh is broken." I had him taken off and placed in the ambulance. Just as I turned to my horse a litter came up, borne by four men, several others following. Knowing that Jackson had been wounded, I asked: "Who have you there?" The General in his laconic style spoke up, "Tell him it is an officer." At once recognizing his voice, I said: "Hold the ambulance, men; take Major Rogers out and put General Jackson in with Colonel Crutchfield."

A few years ago, Major Hotchkiss asked me if it was my ambulance. My reply was, from the authority I was taking over it, I would suppose it was, but would not say with absolute certainty, for the question had never occurred to me. A few days after, meeting one of my old men, Lud. Hall, I asked him if he was with me at Chancellorsville when General Jackson was wounded, and he replied that he was. Then I made the inquiry, "what do you remember about it?" "Well," he said, "I remember that he was shot right by the battery, John Webb caught the horse, and we put him in *our* ambulance and sent him to the hospital."

Waiting a reasonable time for the disabled piece, I ordered a sergeant to ride back and ascertain why the caisson was not brought out. The reply was: "The Captain promised to send back a pair of horses, why doesn't he do that?" The sergeant replied: "He did send young Perkins with his team." "Well, he has gone somewhere else, or is killed. We are ready and waiting," was the response. The sergeant rode back, secured other horses and brought out the piece. Some eight months afterward, when Perkins returned to the battery, having been exchanged, I asked him how he was captured. He said: "Captain, I had almost reached our line of battle, when some one stepped out of the bushes and ordered me to halt. I replied: "Don't bother me, I am going after my piece." He sprung at me, seizing my horse, ran a pistol up into my face, saying: "Open your mouth and I will blow your head off." Thinking it prudent to see what this meant, I dismounted, when he took me by the arm, saying: "Take those reins in your hands and come along." We turned right back into the bushes, I leading the horses, and in a few minutes I found myself in the Yankee lines.

But to return, I retained the three horses—Jackson's, Crutchfield's and Rogers'—until we reached the vicinity of Orange Courthouse, some eight or ten days later, where I turned them over to General Stuart; Webb retaining the yellow nose-band from the bridle of the General's little sorrel, as a relic.

This is a plain statement of the facts, recorded in my memory, which passed under my personal observation, and they accord in all material points with the statements of General Lane and Major Hotchkiss.

No action during the war made as indellible an impression upon me as the work of that day and night, May 2, 1863, and I was in it from start to finish.

9

VICKSBURG AND THE OPENING
OF THE MISSISSIPPI

By Samuel M. Schmucker

The opening of the Mississippi River was a necessary requirement of Northern strategy. The operations to achieve this were rather consistently successful. But on the bluffs above Vicksburg stood a very strong work which could not be reduced by assault. It was eventually reduced at the end of long and complicated siege operations which brought about capitulation on July 4, 1863, the same day that victory at Gettysburg was announced.

The capture of Vicksburg was a protracted and demanding task. The technical complications and the discouragements were enormous. Fortunately for the Union cause the general who was made responsible for the action was, perhaps, the most tenacious and the most difficult to discourage that American arms have ever produced. His name was Ulysses S. Grant.

Here again, an account has been taken from Schmucker's very scarce book to describe the general picture of the seige. To this has been added an account by the son of General Grant who was present and gives a somewhat intimate picture of his father and others as well as the operation.

One of the most brilliant pages in the history of the war against Secession, is that which records the achievements of the champions of the Union on the Mississippi river. On the great "Father of Waters" defeats and disasters, though not wholly unknown, were unfamiliar things: triumph and supremacy were the prevalent features which marked the scene.

On the 6th of June, 1862, the fleet of Federal gunboats and rams commanded by Flag Officer C. H. Davis, comprising eight vessels, approached Fort Pillow, located on the banks of the Mississippi, in the vicinity of Memphis. It was the intention of the commodore to bombard the Rebel works, which were of considerable strength, mounting six one hundred-and-twenty-eight pounders and fifteen sixty-four pounders. But the enemy evacuated the place, together with Forts Randolph and Wright, rendering an attack unnecessary. These places were then occupied by a requisite number of Federal troops.

Commodore Davis then proceeded with his fleet toward Memphis. A formidable Rebel flotilla awaited his approach. It consisted of eight gunboats which respectively bore the names of the General Bragg, the Lovell, the Jeff Thompson, the Beauregard, General Van Dorn, the Sumter, General Price and the Little Rebel. They were commanded by Commodore Edward Montgomery. They had previously been coasting steamers, and had been converted into gunboats. They carried from two to twelve heavy guns each, which were worked *en barbette* on carriages. In the action which ensued the gunboats of Commodore Davis which were brought into action, were the flag ship Benton, the Louisville, Cairo, Saint Louis, and Carondelet. In addition to these there were four steam rams, commanded by Colonel Charles Ellet, named the Queen of the West, Monarch, Lancaster and Switzerland.

During the night preceding the battle, the Rebel fleet moved down the river toward Memphis. At that time Commodore Davis lay at anchor two miles above the city. When the morning of the 6th dawned, the Rebel fleet was seen steaming up in line of battle. They were soon met by the Federal vessels in gallant style opposite Memphis. The inhabitants of that city swarmed in multitudes upon the levee, the bluff, and the roofs of the houses adjacent to the river. The stores were closed and all business suspended, during a day which was destined to witness one of the most complete defeats to the Rebel arms which had yet overtaken them.

The engagement began at half-past-five in the morning. While the vessels were approaching each other Colonel Ellet ordered two rams, the Queen and the Monarch, to proceed down the river and pass between the Rebel boats and the shore. The current was strong, the river was narrow, and the enemy, from their position in fighting up stream, possessed the advantage of the steerage way.

The two rams having reached the desired position, rounded to and commenced the engagement. The Queen drove with prodigious force into the General Price, one of the Rebel rams, taking her wheel completely off; and after a short exchange of shots the latter sank. Soon afterward the Queen was herself run into by the Beauregard, and being struck on the wheelhouse with tremendous violence was severely disabled. The Monarch then approached the Beauregard, and saluted her with a ferocious butt in the bow, which completely disabled her. She subsequently sank; though her crew were rescued by the timely interposition of the Little Rebel.

The Benton and the Lovell then came into action. The fifty-pound Parrott guns of the former produced an immense effect on her antagonist. She was raked fore and aft, some of the shots penetrating her sides. In five minutes her boilers exploded, and the most horrible spectacle was presented to view. Her crew, scalded, suffocated, and suffering the intensest agonies, rushed upon deck and filled the air with their frantic screams, praying for help. The vessel immediately began to sink, and it was with difficulty that a yawl, sent from the Benton, was able to take off a few of the sufferers, before she went down in a hundred feet of water. Nearly all her crew were drowned; and their last exclamations of terror and despair mingled with the seething and bubbling sound of the waves, as she descended forever from view.

The remainder of the Rebel flotilla had thus far been engaged at long range. The Beauregard had been completely riddled with shot; was rapidly becoming unmanageable; was filling with water; and was drifting helplessly toward the shore. She eventually sank upon a shoal to her decks. The Little Rebel was struck by two shots upon her upper works; she was then run ashore by her commander, abreast of President's Island, and was eventually abandoned by her crew.

Disasters now came thickly upon the rest of the vessels of the enemy. By this time the Jeff Thompson was on fire; and the flames soon gained such headway that it was impossible to extinguish them. The fiery tongues of the destroying element ran hither and thither over her whole extent, enveloping every portion of it. Soon her wheel-houses disappeared, then her chimney fell overboard, tearing with it a portion of her deck; at length her magazine exploded. The concussion shook the earth, uprolled the tranquil bosom of the Mississippi in multitudinous billows, and filled the air with hundreds of flying shells. At last nothing remained of the once formidable vessel except a few blackened and charred timbers, which leisurely floated away in fragments on the surface of the river.

The Sumter now became disabled by the steady and destructive shot of the Federal boats, and was drifted ashore at the foot of President's Island. There she was abandoned. The General Bragg, unable any longer to continue the contest, retreated down the river, and was run ashore about three miles below Memphis. She was also abandoned by the Rebels. When the Federal victors from the Benton boarded her, they found twice the ordinary pressure of steam upon her boiler; thus proving the evident intention, on the part of her late occupants when leaving, to blow her to atoms. A prize crew was then placed on board, the stars and stripes were unfurled, and she was towed to an anchorage at Memphis. About the same time, a shot penetrated the boiler of the active and dauntless Little Rebel. It exploded, and she was at once completely disabled. She started to reach the Arkansas shore, but was overhauled and taken.

Thus the entire fleet of the enemy was either captured or destroyed, in an engagement which did not continue longer than an hour and a half, with the single exception of the flag-ship Van Dorn. This vessel, in consequence of her superior speed, being fleeter than the Federal gunboats, made her escape. She was pursued eight miles below Memphis, where the futile chase was relinquished.

A more complete and wholesale defeat could scarcely be imagined, than that which had thus overtaken this famous Mississippi flotilla. Its commander Commodore Montgomery, with most of his officers and some of his men, succeeded in making their escape to the forests on the Arkansas shore. Their loss in killed and wounded was heavy, probably not less than a hundred. The Federal loss was comparatively light. Commodore Ellet, the brave commander of the Union rams, was wounded during the action by a pistol shot in the leg. It was a singular fact that he alone, of all the Union soldiers in this engagement, should have been struck by the enemy; and that he should afterward expire from the combined effect of the wound, general exhaustion, and unskillful treatment.

Among the Federal vessels, the Queen of the West had been the most severely disabled. Her machinery was so terribly jarred by the vigorous butting of the Rebel rams, as to be unable to move, and she was towed to her anchorage after the termination of the battle.

Immediately after the engagement the victorious fleet steamed up to the landing at Memphis. Commodore Davis then dispatched a messenger to John Parke, the mayor of the city, informing him that he had taken possession of the place, that he would put it under military authority, and that he desired his coöperation in the preservation of order. To this communication Mayor Parke responded, that the municipal authorities of Memphis possessed no means of resistance, and that he would be happy to comply with the request of Commodore Davis, and assist him in the preservation of peace and order. A portion of the Federal troops were subsequently quartered in the city, the national colors were unfurled from the public buildings and the supremacy of the Federal Government again established in one of the chief marts of Tennessee.

The ultimate consequences of this victory were very important. It assisted materially in clearing the Mississippi of the presence and the power of the Rebel gunboats. With the single exception of Vicksburg, every other stronghold of the foe on that great river had now been removed; the conquest of Vicksburg alone was necessary to complete the triumph; and by this means one of the chief arteries of the body of the Rebel Confederacy would be effectually severed. It was confidently expected that that desirable result would be accomplished at an early period.

Other triumphs to the Federal arms occurred, nearly at the same time, on the soil of Tennessee. The Rebels had erected strong batteries at Chattanooga, a flourishing town in Hamilton county, a

hundred and forty miles southeast of Nashville. It was the eastern terminus of the railroad from the capital of the State and the
point of connection with the railways of Georgia. It was also a
valuable shipping point for middle and eastern Tennessee.

General Mitchell, appreciating the importance of the position,
determined to attack it with one of those brilliant and sudden assaults by which he had already distinguished himself. He entrusted
the execution of his enterprise on this occasion to General Negley.
Chattanooga being situated on the Tennessee river, at the head of
the light draught navigation, commanding the mountain region in
East Tennessee, being also a great railway centre, and being directly connected by them with Western Virginia and even with
Richmond, fully justified the risks which were run to attain its
possession, and to wrest it from the occupancy of the enemy.

Starting forth from the camp of General Mitchell at Huntsville
in Alabama, Colonel Hambright, under the orders of General Negley, rapidly approached Chattanooga, routing and dispersing on
his way a body of Rebel cavalry, commanded by General Adams.
On the 7th of June he commenced an attack on the batteries of
the enemy at that place. After a vigorous cannonading of three
hours duration they were silenced and evacuated. On the next
day the town was shelled. In six hours the Rebels were driven
from all their works, and were forced to evacuate the place entirely. As they retired they burned the railroad bridges, in order
to prevent the pursuit of the Federal victors. Eighty prisoners were
taken. A large number of horses and cattle, intended for the Rebel
service, were also captured. The Rebel works were completely
destroyed, and the place unfitted for future hostile operations.

This conquest relieved the loyal citizens of that vicinity from
the heavy yoke of the Rebel authorities which had so long galled
them, and confirmed their attachment to their legitimate government. It wrested from the enemy all the advantages which the
possession of the town had given them, from its peculiar position
as the great railroad centre, to which we have already referred.
After this achievement General Negley returned to camp with
the trophies of his victory. His loss was two killed, seven wounded,
three missing.

The advantages thus gained were increased in Tennessee on the

17th of June, when General Morgan advanced toward Cumberland Gap for the purpose of attacking and expelling the Rebel Generals Stevenson and Smith, who occupied it with 13,000 men.

This gap is a cleft in the Cumberland Mountains, which run from the northeast to the southwest through the State; and it is so deep and so narrow that there is room through the gap for only a single roadway. The Rebels had fortified it with great assiduity. Its importance as an entrance to Eastern Tennessee justified their efforts in reference to it. It was expected that they would defend its possession with the utmost tenacity. No such result followed.

When the Rebel leaders were informed of the approach of the Union force under General Morgan, they evacuated the place. They left several hundred tents standing, and they threw vast quantities of their projectiles over the cliffs into the yawning ravines below. Their mortar guns were spiked and their carriages mutilated. After thus rendering what they left behind them as useless as possible, the whole force retreated. The Gap was then occupied by the Federal troops, another avenue of communication was opened between the loyal citizens of eastern and western Tennessee, and another stronghold of the Rebels destroyed.

From these successes in the interior of the country, we turn to view the operations of the Federal arms on the Atlantic seaboard. There the tide of fortune turned against the Federal arms, and a disastrous defeat overtook them in the vicinity of the renowned hotbed of rebellion.

On the 16th of June General Benham, the second in command under General Hunter in the Department of the South, attacked the works which the Rebels had erected on James Island, in the neighborhood of Charleston; and was ignominiously repulsed with heavy losses.

The enemy had constructed a line of defenses running across this island, together with a fort and an observatory, in such a position as to enable them to overlook the operations of the Federal commanders. The purpose of General Benham was also to destroy a floating battery which had been anchored near Secessionville, and which, together with the works already named, presented serious obstacles to the further advance of the Federal forces toward Charleston and Fort Johnson.

Secessionville was a small village, the summer resort of a few of the planters who resided on James Island. Its location is on the eastern side of the island, on the high bank of a creek which passes through the marshes of James and Morris Islands, and empties into the Stone river near its mouth. Five hundred yards south of Secessionville Colonel Lamar had erected a battery, flanked on its sides by the marsh and the creek. The Rebel troops posted here consisted of several companies of the Charleston Light Infantry, and of the Charleston Battalion, with large detachments of the South Carolina volunteers, making in all about five thousand men.

The Federal force selected to assault the works consisted of three brigades commanded by Generals Stevens, Wright, and Williams, comprising about 3,500 men. The attack was commenced by General Stevens, whose troops consisted of the Michigan Eighth, the Connecticut Sixth and Seventh, and the Massachusetts Twenty-Eighth regiments, supported by a battery of four guns. The Michigan Eighth led the van, and suffered more severely than any of their associates.

The assault began at break of day. The Rebel pickets were driven in; and a rapid advance was then made toward the fort. In effecting this movement the Federals encountered an open battery of three guns, which were posted about a hundred yards in front of the entrenchments. The Rebels were driven from these pieces, which were captured. It was evident that the occupants of the entrenchments had been taken completely by surprise; but they were quickly aroused from their slumbers, and received the assailants with the utmost resolution.

In the engagement which ensued, General Wright's brigade supported General Stevens on the left, while General Williams was ordered to make a flank movement to the right, and from that quarter to join in the attack. As it was suspected that masked batteries were concealed in the woods in this direction, General Williams was advised to execute the movement with caution; but he ordered his men to advance rapidly without taking any measures against surprise. The result was that, as soon as his forces reached their desired position at the side of the fort, a powerful battery opened upon them from an opposite direction, which, together with the fire in their front, produced a deadly effect.

The fighting on both sides now became fierce and desperate. The works were surrounded by deep ditches, and surmounted by high parapets. The Eighth Michigan and New York Seventy-ninth assailed the fortifications in front with dauntless heroism. They succeeded in filling the ditch, and constructed a causeway at one point, under the close and heavy firing of the enemy. Repeated onsets were then made, and determined struggle took place to storm the works; but though often on the verge of success, the Federals were as often repulsed and driven back by the indomitable resistance of the enemy.

It is probable indeed, that if, at one time during the contest in front, a judicious and vigorous coöperative movement had been made on the flank, the assault might have been successful; but such was not the case. The Rebels were effectually aided in their defense by the firing from Fort Johnson, which was located at some distance to the right. Many of the gunners in the fort were killed; especially when, after being repulsed from the attack in front, the Federal troops drew off and renewed the assault on the right flank. There three regiments deployed in line of battle, and being partially protected by a growth of underbrush, poured into the fort a continuous and deadly fire, at the distance of 150 yards. Some of the gun-carriages in the entrenchments were perforated by their balls.

This assault might have proved more successful, had not the Louisiana battalion, commanded by McHenry, come to the rescue, formed on the right facing the marsh, and opened their fire upon their assailants with such effect that the latter were compelled to recede after suffering heavy losses. Another desperate attempt was made to carry the works by passing further out to the westward and attacking the fort directly in the rear. But this intention was also defeated by the stubborn and resolute resistance made by the Eutaw regiment.

At length it became evident that the assault was a total failure, and a general retreat was ordered. The Third New Hampshire troops were the last to leave the disastrous field, and narrowly escaped being captured by several regiments of South Carolina. Two Federal gunboats which then lay in the Stone River were unable to render much assistance, in consequence of their remote position; but during the retreat, in attempting to shell the pursuing Rebels, they did nearly as much damage to their allies as to their foes.

The entire enterprise was a most miserable disaster. Scarcely so great a military abortion had been perpetrated by any other Federal commander during the entire war. General Benham was afterward summoned to Washington to explain and justify his conduct.

The total loss of the Federal forces in killed, wounded, and missing, was 529. This large number demonstrated that the Federal soldiers had fought with the courage and determination which usually characterized them; and that their defeat was the result of causes which they could not possibly control, and for which they were not in the least degree responsible. In this action the Rebel Colonel Lamar was wounded. He had exhibited a degree of valor and skill which would have conferred honor upon a much nobler cause, than that in defense of which he had expended it.

The effect of this misfortune on the minds of the loyal community was extremely discouraging; inasmuch as they regarded Charleston and the Rebel works in its vicinity with peculiar repugnance, as being the real centre and effective source of a rebellion which had inflicted so many and such great calamities on the nation.

On the 12th of June an expedition was sent from Memphis under the orders of Colonel Fitch, for the purpose of sailing up the White River as far as Jacksonport, and conveying supplies and ammunition to the army of General Curtis. It was understood that the Rebels had placed obstructions in the stream, and that they had erected fortifications at St. Charles, an insignificant village about eighty-two miles above its junction with the Mississippi. The expedition consisted of four ironclad gunboats, namely: the flag-ship Mound City, the St. Louis, Lexington, and Conestoga, with the armed tug Spitfire, and three transports. The land force on board consisted of the Forty-sixth Indiana regiment. The first success of the expedition was the capture of a new and valuable Rebel steamer, the Clara Dolsen. The second and more important achievement was the attack and reduction of the works which had been constructed at St. Charles.

It was on the 17th of June that the fleet, having proceeded slowly about eighty miles up the White River, suddenly encountered the batteries which the enemy had erected. These were so concealed in the thick forest and brushwood on the Arkansas shore, that their position could only be conjectured from the direction of their shot. As the Union fleet approached, the Rebels commenced to fire upon them. Their guns were not very heavy, but they were aimed with more than ordinary precision. Two shots struck the casemates of the St. Louis. The Mound City, being in the lead up the stream, which at this point is narrow though deep, immediately returned the fire. She was soon followed by the St. Louis and Conestoga. As the works of the Rebels consisted of two distinct batteries, the Mound City proceeded past the first toward the second, half a mile distant. Both were situated on a high bluff. As the Mound City advanced the second battery opened its fire upon her, to which she promptly responded.

While the engagement was progressing between the gunboats and the forts, Colonel Fitch landed about five hundred men from the transports, on the southern shore of the river, for the purpose of attacking the works in the rear. Having reached the proper position, he signalled to the gunboats to suspend their fire, as it might injure his own men, and he felt able to take the forts by a land assault.

At that moment one of the most horrible catastrophes occurred which the mind of man can conceive, and to which few parallels can be found in the bloody annals of war. A ball from the enemy, cylindrical in shape, armed with iron flanges on each side, known as a "pigeon shot," struck the Mound City on the casemate on her port side, near the first gun. It came at an angle of ninety degrees. It passed through the casemate and severed the connecting pipe of the boilers. Instantly the steam rushed with the rapidity of lightning into every part of the vessel below, which was crowded with the crew, 175 in number, who had descended from the deck to avoid the shells of the enemy.

The horrors of the scene which immediately ensued transcended all powers of description. The hot vapor burnt and withered in a moment the mass of living victims, inflicting instant death upon some, and upon the rest, agonies far more terrible than death. Forty-five expired instantly. The remainder, scalded to a crimson hue, screamed and groaned, writhing with intense suffering. They rushed simultaneously toward the portholes. Maddened and frantic with their insupportable torments they threw themselves into the river. Soon seventy or eighty persons were struggling in the water.

At that awful moment, when common humanity would have dictated even among savages a cessation of the contest, the Rebels continued to fire upon the drowning wretches, as with desperation they strove to reach the land. Very few succeeded in doing so. Out of 175, who but a few moments before were in vigorous life, scarcely thirty escaped. Captain Fry, the commander of the Rebels, ordered his sharpshooters to distribute themselves along the shore, and to pick off the exhausted fugitives as they approached. This diabolical command was obeyed with an eagerness of cruelty such as would have disgraced a Fiji islander. The chief officer of the Conestoga promptly lowered his boats, and endeavored to rescue those who were yet alive. As soon as these emissaries of mercy came within range, they were also fired upon by the enemy. Both the gigs were struck, but fortunately were not sunk; and they succeeded in saving some from a watery grave.

In the meantime the Federal troops on shore had reached the Rebel works; and having witnessed the scene enacted upon the river, assaulted the enemy with a commendable and intensified degree of enthusiasm. They soon charged upon them with the bayonet. A brief but desperate resistance was made. In a short time, however, the two forts were carried and occupied by the Federals. The enemy then fled toward St. Charles. Their entire force consisted of five hundred men. Of these fifty were captured; about a hundred were killed and wounded; the rest escaped. Among the prisoners was Captain Fry, the commander of the Rebels, who had formerly been an officer in the Federal service. The indignation of the Union troops against him was so intense, that it was with difficulty that Colonel Fitch could preserve his life from their assaults, by extending to him a clemency and a protection which he did not deserve.

Except for the calamity on the Mound City, the expedition would have had unmixed success. In the end, nearly a hundred persons died in consequence of the terrible accident which had occurred. In a few days the Federal fleet resumed its progress up the White River; the obstructions in the stream were removed; and it eventually reached its destination without any further opposition or casualty.

The Federal commanders on the Mississippi continued their operations for the purpose of opening the navigation of that great commercial artery, with the most commendable energy and ability. Vicksburg now alone remained, throughout its whole extent, in the possession of the enemy. The situation of this city was remarkable. It is built on the eastern bank of the river, on a considerable elevation. Steep bluffs exist both above and below it, whose height above the level of the stream is nearly a hundred feet.

The Rebels had erected strong batteries in the vicinity of the town; and their position was such, that the guns of the besieging vessels could not be brought to bear with much effect upon them, while they, from their superior elevation, possessed every advantage. In other respects also the situation of the place was peculiar. At this point the Mississippi makes an abrupt bend, in shape not unlike a horseshoe, inclosing within its embrace a strip of land little more than half a mile in width. At the extremity of this bend the city is built.

These topographical oddities suggested to the minds of the Federal commanders, at a later period, the expedient of cutting a canal across this peninsula, thus opening a new channel for the river and setting back the city several miles from the margin of the stream which was the source of its opulence, the avenue of its commerce and the chief implement of its resistance to the Federal Government.

On the 21st of June Captain Porter, belonging to the fleet of Commodore Davis, who was then above Vicksburg, made a reconnaissance in the Octarora, for the purpose of ascertaining the best position at which his flotilla might be anchored. General Van Dorn commanded the Rebel forces at this place. These numbered 18,000 men. Having accomplished his purpose Captain Porter returned to his station. Commodore Davis then prepared to approach the city and commence the bombardment.

On Thursday, the 26th of June, a formidable fleet consisting of about forty vessels of all descriptions, including transports, appeared before Vicksburg. An attack was immediately commenced which was chiefly directed against the fortifications on the bluff below the town. The Rebel batteries responded with spirit. The firing continued during the whole day, and ceased only at the approach of night. On the next day it was resumed. In the afternoon the order was given to shell the town. Then the water batteries of the enemy responded, and the contest was kept up during the rest of the day. At night all the Federal captains of divisions were summoned to meet the commander on his flagship. They there received directions to resume the fire upon the city during that night, from all their mortars, and to continue the bombardment until further orders.

Accordingly, at the appointed moment the entire fleet of mortars, twenty in number, commenced the deadly music of their assault. The scene which ensued was extremely grand and imposing. The sound of the guns resembled a continuous peal of thunder; and the loud reverberations seemed to emulate the most furious discharges of heaven's artillery. The repeated explosions of the shells illuminated the midnight heavens far and near with incessant flashes of lurid light. The earth and river shook with the terrible concussions. The enormous shells, as they descended upon the doomed city, appeared like messengers of destruction from some distant and hostile sphere. Soon the city was in flames in various places, and after the lapse of an hour the order was given to suspend the bombardment.

On the next day Commodore Farragut, who lay five miles below Vicksburg with his fleet of wooden vessels, sent word to the commander of the mortars above, that if he would engage the forts on the following morning before daylight, he would attempt to pass the batteries on the bluff and unite their fleets. The suggestion was complied with, and his entire flotilla, consisting of three-men-of-war, two sloops-of-war, and three gunboats, succeeded in making the passage during the bombardment. The flagship of the commodore was struck twice in the hull, suffering some damage. The other vessels escaped serious injury. This action lasted an hour and thirty minutes. Its result convinced the Federal commanders that, however much their shot might injure the town, it would be impossible to capture or destroy the batteries which lined the bluffs, without the assistance of a land force. The entire fleet then proceeded a short distance above Vicksburg and anchored.

The mere destruction of the town alone would have been barren of results. Commodore Farragut therefore resolved to re-open the navigation of the Mississippi, which was the chief matter in dispute, by digging a new channel across the peninsula already described, named Cross-bend, thereby leaving Vicksburg at a harmless and impotent distance from the passing stream. Hundreds of negroes were immediately impressed from the adjoining plantations, and set to work in digging.

This novel undertaking would require to be half a mile in length, about fifty feet in width, and eight feet below the water level. The chief disadvantage which attended the enterprise was the fact that, at that period, the water of the river was falling instead of rising.

During the engagement before the town, and in the passage of the fleet of Commodore Farragut, the Federal loss was fifteen killed and thirty wounded. That of the Rebels was severe among the troops of Van Dorn, who then occupied Vicksburg.

Chapter 9, Part 2

WITH GRANT AT VICKSBURG

By Brigadier General Frederick Dent Grant,

U. S. Volunteers

I have always appreciated the good fortune which enabled me to be with my father and his able lieutenants in the field during our great struggle for national existence, and to see for myself the men and the events that made so famous the chapters of our history for the years from 1861 to 1865.

In March, 1863, while I was at school at Covington, Ky., my father gave his consent to my joining him at Young's Point, near Vicksburg.

Arriving at Young's Point, I found my father's headquarters on a steamboat at the levee. I also found my precious pony, had him saddled and bridled immediately, and joined my father on a trip of inspection to the canal. Here he found that the enemy was throwing up fortifications on the opposite side of the river, which so commanded the canal that its use would be impracticable. We returned to headquarters. Here I first saw General Sherman for whom my father had such unbounded admiration. Later, father went on board Admiral Porter's flagship, the Benton, for a consultation with his naval coadjutor. I accompanied him; but on board, the Admiral, doubtless remembering the old saying that "little pitchers have long ears," called a man to show me all over the ship—everywhere but in the cabin. Not then appreciating the reasons for this special courtesy, I enjoyed my explorations very much. It was during my absence that my father proposed the passage of the Vicksburg batteries.

The transports were protected with bales of hay packed around the boilers; calls were made for volunteers to man the boats; and the troops were reviewed. The call for boat crews was most eagerly responded to, especially by the men of General Logan's division. Some of the men advanced the most extraordinary reasons for being selected for the service, and their courage and persistency seemed truly marvelous to me.

On the 16th of April, 1863, General Grant and Admiral Porter held a final consultation. About 10 P.M. all lights were put out, and the fleet started down the river. Suddenly a rocket went up from the shore; a cannon blazed forth from Warrentown; and a shot passed directly in front of our boat. We stopped; a lurid flame sprang up from a house at De Soto, opposite Vicksburg, then another on the river front, and soon fires were burning along the whole front of the city, and the river was lighted as if by sunlight.

Six gunboats, looking like great black turtles, followed by three fragile transports, moved directly toward the Confederate batteries, which now opened fire. The Benton and the other gunboats responded, and, steaming up near the city, sent shot and shell pouring into Vicksburg. The transports kept over toward the Lousiana shore, and one—the Henry Clay—was set on fire by a red-hot shell, and burned to the water's edge.

The people of Vicksburg lined the hills, and manifested great excitement. On board our boat my father and I stood side by side on the hurricane deck. He was quietly smoking, but an intense light shone in his eyes.

As soon as our fleet passed the batteries, and firing had ceased, father's boat steamed back to Milliken's Bend. The first step of the great campaign had been successfully accomplished.

A few days later I accompanied my father, with eight officers of his staff and an escort of twenty cavalrymen, on a ride of thirty miles to visit McClernand at New Carthage. At the crossing of a slough, where there was but a narrow bridge, my father made one of his daring leaps putting his horse at the opposite bank, which he just managed to reach. The rest of us preferred to wait our turn at crossing by the bridge, over which a wagon train was slowly passing. The following day we returned to Milliken's Bend.

From there father moved to the head of the army, which now

had advanced to Hard Times. The problem now presented itself of getting the troops across the Mississippi River.

On the 29th of April our gunboats steamed down to Grand Gulf, and engaged the enemy's batteries for about five hours. Father was on board a little tug, which moved about amid the fleet. After a trip to the Lousiana shore we went on board the Benton, and, as we entered the porthole, I was sickened with the scenes of carnage. Admiral Porter had been struck on the back of the head with a fragment of shell, and his face showed the agony he was suffering, but he planned a renewal of the conflict for that night, in order to permit our transports to run past the Confederate batteries.

Our troops now moved down the western bank of the Mississippi, to De Shroon's plantation, where the negroes turned out to welcome us with great rejoicing, deeming us the messengers of the Lord bringing them freedom.

The following day, April 30, we went on board the General Price, formerly a Confederate ram, and moved down to where Bruinsburg had stood. Now not a house was to be seen; fire had destroyed the whole town. The crossing of the troops continued vigorously, and, tired of watching them, I fell asleep on deck. Awakening the next morning, I found that my father had gone to the front. General Lorenzo Thomas told me that father had given strict orders that I should not be allowed to go ashore, but he finally permitted me to join a party in chasing a rabbit on the land, and I took advantage of that permission to push my investigation over the hills. I fell in with a wagon train and secured a ride on a mule; and after going some distance in that way I joined a battery of artillery on its way to the front, and later followed a passing regiment—the Seventh Missouri—which was soon in battle. Presently my father appeared. My guilty conscience so troubled me that I hid from his sight behind a tree.

Within a short time a mighty shout announced the victory of our troops, and the horrors of a battlefield were brought vividly before me. I joined a detachment which was collecting the dead for burial. Sickening at the sights, I made my way with another detachment, which was gathering the wounded, to a log house which had been appropriated for a hospital. Here the scenes were so terrible that I became faint, and making my way to a tree, sat down, the most woebegone twelve-year-old lad in America.

Soon an approaching horseman hailed me, an orderly from my father's escort, and, dismounting, he proceeded to make me comfortable, putting down his saddle for a pillow, and advising me to go to sleep. This I did, but suddenly I heard the orderly cry out: "Your father has come." About fifty yards off sat my father, drinking coffee from a tin cup. I went to him, and was greeted with an exclamation of surprise, as he supposed I was still on board the boat. In after years he often told the story of my following him to the battle of Port Gibson.

The next morning, although horses were scarce, I succeeded in getting a mount. Two enormous white artillery horses had been captured the day before. I secured one of them, and Mr. Charles A. Dana, Assistant Secretary of War, the other. Mr. Dana, however, had the advantage of riding the horse with saddle and bridle; I had to content myself with improvising a harness made of a clothes-line and the tree of a side saddle without stirrups. At any rate, the sight of a small boy on the big white horse made some sport on the road for the soldiers I passed.

At Port Gibson General Logan came to see father, who complimented him highly on his operations of the previous day. On leaving, General Logan turned to me and said: "Come, my boy, and I will show you the prettiest fight you will ever see." We went down to the lower suspension bridge, to secure the crossing.

I returned to Port Gibson, and, finding that my father had left, I followed the troops which were crossing the bayou. I rode on quite a distance, and then, stopping at a house where some officers were sleeping on a porch, I crawled in for a nap between two of them. They awoke, and "said things," but when I mentioned my name, one of them—Colonel (afterward General) Sanborn—welcomed me kindly and lent me part of his overcoat for a pillow. Becoming very cold toward dawn, I went indoors, found a bed with two occupants, and crept in between them. I slept well, but by daylight I found that my bedfellows were two large negroes!

It was now the 3d of May, and I found my father at the North Fork, watching the crossing of the troops. Finding that I was lame from the falling of my horse the day before, father, who was ever kind and thoughtful, insisted that I should take his mount. All of his horses were at this time on the other side of the Mississippi. We moved toward Hankinson's Ferry. At the forks of the road it became necessary to clear away a body of the enemy's troops. With slight loss and the capture of some prisoners this was accomplished, and we moved into Grand Gulf.

Here we found our old friend the Benton, and the gallant Admiral, who welcomed us most cordially. He gave father a bundle of dispatches, including one from General Banks, who said that he could not reach Port Hudson as soon as he had expected, and that he would have fewer troops than he had counted upon. General Grant immediately began to write dispatches, a task at which he continued till two o'clock in the morning, when he borrowed a change of linen, ordered his horse, and started for McPherson's quarters. The next day Colonel Lagow, and I started on after father, and we overtook him at Rocky Springs. Near here, General Sherman, with the Fifteenth Corps, joined us.

From the 7th to the 12th of May General Grant was constantly in communication with Sherman, McPherson, and McClernand, riding around from one to the other. This made his headquarters so uncomfortable and his mess so irregular that I took my meals with the soldiers, who used to do a little foraging, and thereby set an infinitely better table than their commanding General. My father's table at this time was, I must frankly say, the worst I ever partook of.

On the 12th of May the Union army was pushed forward, and at Fourteen Mile Creek Osterhaus had a skirmish to clear the road. We heard the sounds of battle away off to the right, and later we learned that McPherson had won the day at Raymond.

We spent the night at Raymond, and then started for Jackson, the capital of Mississippi. While passing through a piece of dense woods on the way, the enemy's sharpshooters opened fire on us. One of the staff shouted to my father that they were aiming at him. His answer was to turn his horse and dash into the woods in the direction whence the bullets were coming. The escort and I followed, and in skirmishing fashion we advanced till we came to a large house, where we halted. Sherman's corps now came up, and

McPherson was already engaged. Generals Grant and Sherman were on the porch of the old house when our line was broken by artillery fire and our men began a retreat. The two generals immediately mounted, rode among the men, and reformed them. Meanwhile Tuttle's division had passed through the dense woods and had captured the enemy's breastworks, and, wheeling to the left, advanced up the line of intrenchments. Father accompanied them.

At this time I saw a mounted officer with a Union flag advancing toward the Capitol. I followed him into the building and entered the Governor's room, which had been hastily abandoned. Returning to the street, I saw the officer in the act of raising the Union flag over the building.

Father and his staff, advancing at the head of the army, soon reached the State House, where I joined them, and went with them to the Bowen House, the best hotel in Jackson, where we took the room in which General Joseph E. Johnston had slept the night before.

At Jackson we captured an important prisoner who was carrying dispatches from Johnston to Pemberton. The information gained from these dispatches caused activity at headquarters, and the next day—May 15—the army started off in the direction of Vicksburg.

That night Colonel Lagow announced the arrival of a messenger from McPherson, and father seemed surprised at the news he received. He gave orders for an early start in the morning, went back to bed, and was soon sleeping quietly again. After a light breakfast before daybreak, we moved rapidly to the front, General Grant keeping well ahead. At Champion's farm we came upon the enemy, and were soon in the midst of terrific firing. The staff officers were dispatched to various points, and very soon father and I were left alone. Our line broke, and was falling back, when father moved forward, rallied the men, and passed over from Hovey's division to McPherson's corps, putting the latter into action. There were now 15,000 men in our line, which was about three miles long, and the battle raged fiercely along its whole extent.

General Grant rode to all parts of the field, giving orders to the generals, and dispatching his staff in all directions. Suddenly hearty cheering was heard on the right of the line, and father moved over in that direction, to find 3,000 prisoners taken, with eighteen guns.

After the battle of Champion's Hill, while riding toward Edwards Station, father suddenly turned back, and I went on into a house filled with Confederate wounded. They were not feeling very friendly toward the Yankees, and they threatened to kill me. Further down the road, some of our own men, who did not know me, attempted to take me prisoner. Soon, however, an old soldier recognized me, and called for "Three cheers for young Grant," which were given with a will. About midnight I returned to the field, and reached a house in which I found my father and several of his staff officers. I slept in the room with my father that night; he, even after the great battle and victory of that day, and with the expectation of another battle on the morrow, was, as ever, most considerate of the comfort and welfare of his young son.

The next morning we made an early start, and moved toward the Big Black River.

Our troops were now moving on the enemy's line at a double quick, and I became enthused and galloped across a cotton-field, and went over the enemy's works with our men. Following the retreating Confederates to the Big Black, I was watching some of them swim the river, when a sharpshooter on the opposite bank fired at me and hit me in the leg. The wound was slight, but very painful; Colonel Lagow came dashing up and asked what was the matter. I promptly said, "I am killed." The Colonel presumed to doubt my word, and said, "Move your toes"—which I did with success. He then recommended our hasty retreat.

After the capture of the fortifications, May 17, our army bridged the Big Black and crossed during the night.

On May 18 we reached the summit of Walnut Hills, just behind Vicksburg, where Sherman had fought in December. Sherman was greatly elated over the success of the present campaign.

During the 19th father spent much of his time with McClernand on the extreme left. He feared lest Pemberton might make his escape through this thinly guarded part of our line. On the 22d, the great assault was made upon the fortifications. Early in the day General Grant had a narrow escape from a shell which was fired directly down a ravine which he had just entered. He was unhurt, however, but was covered with yellow dirt thrown up by the explosion.

On this day I saw a sight that will probably never again be witnessed in this country—an artillery duel extending over seven miles in length. Beneath the smoke of this cannonade the Army of the Tennessee could be seen moving to the assault upon the enemy's lines, which became a sheet of fire from the forts and rifle-pits. At one point our flag was planted right at the base of the enemy's parapet.

The wound I had received early in the campaign now began to trouble me very much, and, under Dr. Hewitt's expressed fears of having to amputate my leg, I remained much at headquarters. Because of this I saw a great deal of my father's methods, his marvelous attention to detail, and his cool self-possession. I also witnessed the devotion of his men to him, and the enthusiasm with which they greeted "the old man," as they called him, when he passed along the lines. Father was a splendid horseman, and visited many points of his army every day.

General Sherman commanded the Fifteenth Corps during part of the siege of Vicksburg, and the remainder of the time he had command of the troops placed from Haines's Bluff to the Big Black. His personality is too well known for me to describe it here, but it is a pleasure for me here to bear witness to my father's affection for Sherman, and his esteem for his soldierly qualities. Indeed, it gave General Grant more pleasure to see Sherman honored and rewarded than it did to receive such tributes himself. Sherman was impetuous in action, brilliant in conversation, and thoroughly versed in the art of war; but he was always thoroughly subordinate and ready to obey promptly any order given to him. Two hours' notice was amply sufficient for him to get under way to execute any desired movement. On the 15th of May he was at Jackson, Miss., and that night General Grant, desiring him to move to the front, sent him orders to that effect. On the afternoon of the 16th he arrived at Bolton with the head of his corps, having marched twenty-five or thirty miles that day; and he would have been in the battle of Champion's Hill had the enemy waited on the field a little longer.

The next officer in rank, the commander of the Seventeenth

Corps, was Major-General James B. McPherson, the Bayard of the Army of the Tennessee. Mounted on horseback, young and handsome, always splendidly dressed and most courtly in manner, he was the very impersonation of a knight. General Grant always regarded McPherson as the most promising officer of his age in the army, and on his death father said that he had lost one of his best friends and the country one of its ablest defenders. McPherson's troops loved him, and one needs hear but once the cheers given by the "Army of the Tennessee," whenever his name is mentioned in its presence, to appreciate the love and devotion with which his memory is still cherished. His very taking off was illustrative of the man. When ordered to surrender before Atlanta, he courteously lifted his hat, bowed low, wheeled his horse, and dashed into the woods. But the volley that instantly followed was but too well aimed, and he fell.

The siege of Vicksburg continued after the assaults of the 23d of May, without much excitement except such as was caused by reports, without foundation, however, that Johnston was about to attack our rear. The siege went on. Our parallels slowly but surely approached the doomed city. Deserters came in more frequently, and reported the desperate condition of the garrison. Rumors also came to us that Johnston was going to make a determined effort to relieve Pemberton. These reports led to another rumor that our troops would celebrate the Fourth of July by a grand storming of the works. Doubtless this rumor found its way into the beleaguered city, for on the morning of the 3d of July a flag of truce was announced. General Grant betrayed no excitement, but in the afternoon he rode out with his staff to a point opposite Fort Hill, I accompanying them. Soon a white flag appeared over the enemy's works, and a party of Confederates was seen approaching. Firing ceased, and, under an old tree, General Grant met his opponent.

The consultation of the commanding generals lasted a short while, and presently both parties retired to their own quarters. Father was immediately joined by the largest assemblage of general officers which I had ever seen—the heroes of this most brilliant campaign and siege—deciding upon and settling the fate of their foes. They had conquered and taken in their power the largest number of men, the greatest quantity of war material and spoils, ever surrendered in battle.

After conversation General Grant dispatched a note to the defender of Vicksburg, and the group of officers dispersed. I remained in the tent, and father sat at his table writing. Presently a messenger handed a note. He opened it, gave a sigh of relief, and said, calmly, "Vicksburg has surrendered." I was thus the first to hear officially announced the news of the fall of the Gibraltar of America, and I ran out to spread the glad tidings. Officers rapidly assembled, and there was a general rejoicing.

The next day, the glorious Fourth, as father was starting for the front on the Jackson road, the booming of guns was heard, apparently on our right. General Grant looked vexed, and was about to order the arrest of General Steele, whom he supposed to be responsible, saying that he "ought to know better than to allow any triumphing over conquered countrymen," when Steele himself rode up, the firing was definitely located on our left, and the salutes were stopped. Soon after, the Confederates were seen filing out of their works and stacking their arms—31,600 brave men surrendering 172 cannon and 60,000 muskets to the conquering but lenient Army of the Tennessee.

The arms being given up, the troops passed back into the city, and General Grant, at the head of the Army of the Tennessee, moved forward to take possession. His reception by General Pemberton was most frigid. With a group of Confederate officers, Pemberton was seated on the porch of a large house, but when father expressed a desire for a glass of water, he was allowed to go to hunt for it in the kitchen. This surly reception to the man who would not allow his men to celebrate their victory was deeply resented by the members of General Grant's staff, but father was satisfied with his success in capturing Vicksburg, and manifested no resentment.

The Confederate officers who thus received him gratefully appreciated, later on, the clemency they experienced at the fall of Vicksburg, and expressed this appreciation in the most touching manner during General Grant's last illness, at the time of his funeral, and at the dedication of his tomb.

Passing through the city, where the Union flag had already been hoisted over the courthouse, General Grant went on board the Benton, where Admiral Porter congratulated him upon the victory.

10

HIGH-WATER MARK—THE BATTLE OF GETTYSBURG

By Franklin A. Haskell

AT THE HEADQUARTERS, SECOND CORPS D'ARMÉE.
ARMY OF THE POTOMAC, NEAR HARPER'S FERRY,
JULY 16, 1863.

An analogy between chess and tactics is trite yet it is so often obviously comparable as to make it desirable. Nowhere is such an analogy better demonstrated than in the Confederate decision to invade the North for the second time. After Chancellorsville, Hooker's army was still intact, still superior to Lee's in numbers, and closer to Richmond than to Washington. They could not go after Lee's "king" while Lee was moving into position himself to effect a check against the Northern capital. If Lee moved up the Rook's Row, which lay along the Shenandoah Valley, then Hooker per-force had to conform despite his own temptation to continue towards Richmond. And so the Confederate Army did move north across Maryland and into Pennsylvania. Almost by chance, the two armies stumbled into each other at the obscure little village of Gettysburg. The first day's fighting was distantly a division commanders' fight, disjointed, uncoordinated, yet almost instinctively brilliant, and it was distinctly a Confederate victory. However, the Confederates unwittingly drove the Federals into an extremely strong position, stronger perhaps than either realized at the end of the first day of battle. The high ridge on which the Federal

*Army coiled itself could be taken only by frontal assault and it
was in an effort to break this line that there occurred, perhaps, the
most famous assault action in the history of American arms, the
so-called Charge of Pickett's Division at Gettysburg.*

*For nearly a century after the event, the battle of Gettysburg has
been studied and analyzed by uncounted soldiers and historians.
During the lifetime of the participants, there was lively contro-
versy over what caused the end of Lee's string of magnificent victories. Many reasons have been offered for his failure at Gettysburg. Longstreet and Stuart are the most frequently nominated
candidates for the villains in their lack of reconnaisance, inadequate range of artillery, inertia due to heat, and discouragement
over the outlook after seeing the vast and untouched resources of
Pennsylvania, are held by many to be the reasons. One significant
and frequently-neglected factor in the outcome of the Gettysburg
triumph was the magnificent and well-handled Federal army. Often
abused, improperly officered and inadequately used, it had steadily
improved in experience, equipment and strength. Its patient commander in chief in the White House constantly sought to remedy
its deficiencies in leadership. The Northern soldiers had more than
their just share of failures. The troops themselves were fine material, battle-hardened and rendered more determined by unde-
served defeat. They had needed only competent leadership to show
their real fighting ability. At last, the deficiencies of command were
not on the Federal side at Gettysburg. The mighty and disastrous
assault on the third day is comprehensible only in psychological—
not tactical—terms. The Confederates were not capable of accomplishing as much as they envisioned. The Federals were more
capable than past experience had led the Confederates to believe.
The Federal forces as it developed continued to improve and the
Confederates became progressively less effective.*

*The bronze book now records that the offensive spirit of the
Army of Northern Virginia reached its zenith on the slopes of
Gettysburg. Only a handful of men reached the Federal line at
the summit. This then was the ultimate peak as the surging wave
of high-water mark was reached. 15,000 men began that advance,
a pathetic few broke the Federal ranks to be inundated there by
swift, unexpected Federal counterattack. On that blood-stained*

Battle of Shiloh, 1862.

Charge on Plateau at Bull Run on the High Ground of Henry Hill.

Retreat of Confederate Forces from the Battle of Shiloh.

Charge and Check.

Salute of 100 Guns as part of Rebel Jubilation at Confederate Capital Richmond, Virginia, upon receiving the news of Confederate victory at Bull Run.

General Ambrose Everett Burnside's Division at the bridge during the Battle of Antietam in 1862.

The Loss of the Monitor, December 30, 1862.

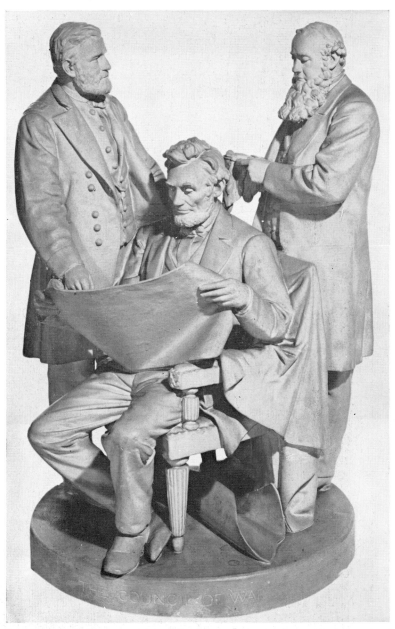

Council of War. President Lincoln, General U.S. Grant and Secretary of War Edwin McMasters Stanton.

The Wounded Scout (1862)   *Taking the Oath for Rations (1865)*

The Town Pump (1862)   *Union Refugees (1863)*

*slope, fifteen regiments of Virginians were destroyed in all the
horror and indignity of violent death. Pickett's Division was
wrecked beyond effective recuperation. At the top of the breaking
wave, in tragic anticlimax, the rivulet of broken men headed re-
sentfully down the ridge and back across the plain. The terrifying
Juggernaut of Lee's offensive was destined to roll no more. To be
sure, the keening shriek of the rebel yell would be heard again
but only in local offensives as part of overall defensive actions.
In recompense, one year and nine months would remain for Lee
to demonstrate his genius in defensive warfare. Perhaps the most
dramatic crucial moment of the Civil War was reached on the
slopes of Gettysburg.*

The great battle of Gettysburg is now an event of the past. The
composition and strength of the armies, their leaders, the strategy,
the tactics, the result, of that field are today by the side
of those of Waterloo,—matters of history. A few days ago these
things were otherwise. This great event did not so "cast its shadows before" as to moderate the hot sunshine that streamed upon
our preceding march, or to relieve our minds of all apprehension
of the result of the second great rebel invasion of the soil north of
the Potomac.

No,—not many days since, at times we were filled with fears
and forebodings. The people of the country, I suppose, shared the
anxieties of the army, somewhat in common with us, but they
could not have felt them as keenly as we did. We were upon the
immediate theater of events as they occurred from day to day,
and were of them. We were the army whose province it should
be to meet this invasion and repel it; on us was the responsibility
for results, most momentous for good or ill, but yet in the future.
And so in addition to the solicitude of all good patriots, we felt that
our own honor as men and as an army, as well as the safety of the
Capitol and the country, was at stake.

And what if that invasion should be successful, and in the coming battle the Army of the Potomac should be overpowered?
Would it not be? When our army was much larger than at present,
had rested all winter, and, nearly perfect in all its departments and

arrangements, was the most splendid army this continent ever saw, only a part of the rebel force, which it now had to contend with, had defeated it,—its leader, rather,—at Chancellorsville! Now the rebel had his whole force assembled; he was flushed with recent victory; was arrogant in his career of unopposed invasion; at a favorable season of the year, his daring plans, made by no unskilled head, to transfer the war from his own to his enemy's ground, were being successful; he had gone days' march from his front before Hooker moved or was aware of his departure. Then I believe the army in general, both officers and men, had no confidence in Hooker, either in his honesty or ability. Did they not charge him personally with the defeat at Chancellorsville? Were they not still burning with indignation against him for that disgrace? And now again under his leadership they were marching against the enemy! And they knew of nothing, short of the providence of God, that could or would remove him. For many reasons, during the marches prior to the battle, we were anxious and at times heavy at heart.

But the Army of the Potomac was no band of school girls. They were not the men likely to be crushed or utterly discouraged by any mere circumstances in which they might find themselves placed. They had lost some battles,—they had gained some. They knew what defeat was, and what was victory. But here is the greatest praise that I can bestow upon them, or upon any army; with the elation of victory, or the depression of defeat, amidst the hardest toils of the campaign, under unwelcome leadership, at all times and under all circumstances, they were a reliable army still. The Army of the Potomac would do as it was told, always.

Well clothed and well fed,—there never could be any ground of complaint on these heads,—but a mighty work was before them. Onward they moved,—night and day were blended,—over many a weary mile, through dust and through mud, in the broiling sunshine, in the flooding rain, over steeps, through defiles, across rivers, over last year's battlefields, where the skeletons of our dead brethren by hundreds lay bare and bleaching, weary, without sleep for days, tormented with the newspapers and their rumors that the enemy was in Philadelphia, in Baltimore, in all places where he was not,—yet these men could still be relied upon, I believed, when the day of conflict should come: *"Haec olim meminisse juvobit!"* We did not then know this. I mention them now that you may see that in these times we had several matters to think about, and to do, that were not so pleasant as sleeping upon a bank of violets in the shade.

In moving from near Falmouth, Va., the army was formed in several columns, and took several roads. The Second Corps, the rear of the whole, was the last to move, and left Falmouth at daybreak on the 15th of June, and pursued its march through Aquia, Dumfries, Wolf Run Shoals, Centerville, Gainesville, Thoroughfare Gap,—this last we left on the 25th, marching back to Haymarket, where we had a skirmish with the cavalry and horse artillery of the enemy,—Gum Spring, crossing the Potomac at Edward's Ferry, thence through Poolesville, Frederick, Liberty, and Uniontown. We marched from near Frederick to Uniontown, a distance of thirty-two miles, from eight o'clock A.M. on the 28th. I think this is the longest march accomplished in so short a time by a corps during the war. On the 28th, while we were near this latter place, we breathed a full breath of joy and of hope. The providence of God had been with us—we ought not to have doubted it—General Meade commanded the Army of the Potomac!

Not a favorable time, one would be apt to suppose, to change the general of a large army on the eve of battle, the result of which might be to destroy the government and the country. But it should have been done long before; at all events, any change could not have been for the worse, and the administration, therefore, hazarded little in making it now. From this moment my own mind was easy concerning results. I now felt that we had a clearheaded, honest soldier to command the army, who would do his best always,—that there would be no repetition of Chancellorsville. Meade was not as much known in the army as many of the other corps commanders, but the officers who knew, all thought highly of him; a man of great modesty, with none of those qualities which are noisy and assuming, and hankering for cheap newspaper fame,—not at all of the "gallant" Sickles stamp. I happened to know much of General Meade. He and General Gibbon have always been very intimate, and I had seen much of him. I think my own notions concerning General Meade at this time were shared quite generally by the army; at all events, all who knew him shared them.

By this time, by reports that were not mere rumors, we began to hear frequently of the enemy and of his proximity. His cavalry was all about us, making little raids here and there, capturing now and then a few of our wagons, and stealing a good many horses, but doing us really the least amount possible of harm, for we were not by these means impeded at all, and this cavalry gave no information at all to Lee, that he could rely upon, of the movements of the Army of the Potomac. The infantry of the enemy was at this time in the neighborhood of Hagerstown, Chambersburg, and some had been at Gettysburg, possibly were there now.

Gettysburg was a point of strategic importance; a great many roads, some ten or twelve at least, concentrated there, so the army could easily converge to, or, should a further march be necessary, diverge from, this point. General Meade, therefore, resolved to try to seize Gettysburg, and accordingly gave the necessary orders for the concentration of his different columns there. Under the new auspices the army brightened and moved on with a more majestic step toward the yet undefined field of conflict.

The First Corps, General Reynolds, already having the advance, was ordered to push forward rapidly, and take and hold the town, if he could; the rest of the army would assemble to his support. Buford's cavalry co-operated with this corps, and on the morning of the 1st of July found the enemy near Gettysburg and to the west, and promptly engaged him. The First Corps, having bivouacked the night before south of the town, came up rapidly to Buford's support, and immediately a sharp battle was opened with the advance of the enemy. The First Division, General Wadsworth, was the first of the infantry to become engaged; but the other two, commanded respectively by Generals Robinson and Doubleday, were close at hand, and forming the line of battle to the west and northwest of the town, at a mean distance of about a mile away. The battle continued for some hours with various success, which was on the whole with us until near noon. At this time a lull occurred, which was occupied by both sides in supervising and re-establishing the hastily formed lines of the morning.

New divisions of the enemy were constantly arriving and taking up positions, for this purpose marching in upon the various roads that terminate at the town, from the west and north. The position of the First Corps was then becoming perilous in the extreme, but it was improved at a little before noon by the arrival upon the field of two divisions of the Eleventh Corps, General Howard, these divisions commanded respectively by Generals Schurz and Barlow, who, by order, posted their commands to the right of the First Corps, with their right retired, forming an angle with the line of the First Corps.

Between three and four o'clock in the afternoon, the enemy, now in overwhelming force, resumed the battle with spirit. The portion of the Eleventh Corps, making ineffectual opposition to the advancing enemy, soon began to fall back. General Barlow was badly wounded, and their retreat soon became a disorderly rout and panic. They were hotly pursued in their flight through the town, and, owing to their disorganized condition, large numbers fell into the hands of the enemy.

The First Corps, deprived of this support, out-flanked upon either hand, and engaged in front, was compelled to yield the field. Making its last stand upon what is called "Seminary Ridge," not far from the town, it fell back in considerable confusion, through the southwest part of the town, making brave resistance, however, but with considerable loss. The enemy did not see fit to follow, or to attempt to, further than the town, and so the fight of the 1st of July closed here. I suppose our losses during the day would exceed five thousand, of whom a large number were prisoners. Such usually is the kind of loss sustained by the Eleventh Corps. You will remember that the old "Iron Brigade" is in the First Corps, and consequently shared this fight, and I hear their conduct praised on all hands.

In the Second Wisconsin, Colonel Fairchild lost his left arm; Lieutenant Colonel Stevens was mortally wounded, and Major Mansfield was wounded; Lieutenant Colonel Collis, of the Seventh Wisconsin, and Lieutenant Colonel Dudley, of the Nineteenth Indiana, were badly, dangerously wounded, the latter by the loss of his right leg above the knee.

I saw "John Burns," the only citizen of Gettysburg who fought

in the battle, and I asked him what troops he fought with. He said,
"Oh, I pitched in with them Wisconsin fellers." I asked what sort
of men they were, and he answered: "They fit terribly,—the
Rebs couldn't make anything of them fellers." And so the brave
compliment the brave. This man was touched by three bullets
from the enemy, but not seriously wounded.

But the loss of the enemy today was severe, also,—probably
in killed and wounded as heavy as our own, but not so great in
prisoners. Of these latter the "Iron Brigade" captured almost an
entire Mississippi brigade, however.

Of the events so far, of the 1st of July, I do not speak from personal knowledge. I shall now tell my introduction to these
events.

At eleven o'clock A.M., on that day, the Second Corps was
halted at Taneytown, which is thirteen miles from Gettysburg,
south; and there, awaiting orders, the men were allowed to make
coffee and rest. At between one and two o'clock in the afternoon,
a message was brought to General Gibbon requiring his immediate presence at the headquarters of General Hancock, who
commanded the corps. I went with General Gibbon, and we rode
at a rapid gallop to General Hancock. At General Hancock's headquarters the following was learned: the First Corps had met
the enemy at Gettysburg, and had possession of the town;
General Reynolds was badly, it was feared mortally, wounded; the
fight of the First Corps still continued. By General Meade's order,
General Hancock was to hurry forward and take command upon
the field of all troops there, or which should arrive there; the
Eleventh Corps was near Gettysburg when the messenger who
told of the fight left there, and the Third Corps was marching up,
by order, on the Emmitsburg Road. General Gibbon—he was not
the ranking officer of the Second Corps after Hancock—was ordered to assume the command of the Second Corps.

All this was sudden, and for that reason, at least, exciting; but
there were other elements in this information that aroused our
profoundest interest. The great battle that we had so anxiously
looked for during so many days had at length opened. It was a
relief, in some sense, to have these accidents of time and place es-

tablished. What would be the result? Might not the enemy fall upon and destroy the First Corps before succor could arrive?

General Hancock with his personal staff, at about two o'clock P.M., galloped off towards Gettysburg. General Gibbon took his place in command of the corps, appointing me his Acting Assistant Adjutant-General. The Second Corps took arms at once, and moved rapidly towards the field. It was not long before we began to hear the dull booming of the guns; and as we advanced, from many an eminence or opening among the trees we could look out upon the white battery smoke puffing up from the distant field of blood and drifting up to the clouds. At these sights and sounds the men looked more serious than before, and were more silent; but they marched faster, and straggled less.

At about five o'clock P.M., as we were riding along at the head of the column, we met an ambulance, accompanied by two or three wounded officers. We knew them to be staff officers of General Reynolds. Their faces told plainly enough what load the vehicle carried—it was the dead body of General Reynolds. Very early in the action, while seeing personally to the formation of the lines under fire, he was shot through the head by a musket or rifle bullet, and killed almost instantly. His death at this time affected us much, for he was one of the *soldier* generals of the army,—a man whose soul was in his country's work, which he did with a soldier's high honor and fidelity.

I remember seeing him after the first battle of Fredericksburg, —he then commanded the First Corps,—and while Meade's and Gibbon's divisions were assaulting the enemy's works; he was the very beau ideal of the gallant general. Mounted upon a superb black horse, with his head thrown back and his great black eyes flashing fire, he was everywhere upon the field, seeing all things and giving commands in person. He died as many a friend and many a foe to the country have died in this war.

Just as the dusk of evening fell, from General Meade the Second Corps have orders to halt where the head of the column then was, and to go into position for the night. The Second Division (Gibbon's) was accordingly put in position upon the left of the Taneytown road, its left near the southeastern base of "Round Top,"—

of which mountain more anon,—and the right near the road; the Third Division was posted upon the right of the road, abreast of the Second; and the First Division in rear of these two,—all facing towards Gettysburg. Arms were stacked and the men lay down to sleep,—alas! many of them their last but the great final sleep upon the earth.

Late in the afternoon, as we came near the field, from some slightly wounded men we met, and occasional stragglers from the scene of operations in front, we got many rumors, and much disjointed information, of battle, of lakes of blood, of rout and panic and indescribable disaster; from all of which the narrators were just fortunate enough to have barely escaped, the sole survivors. These stragglers are always terrible liars!

About nine o'clock in the evening, while I was yet engaged in showing the troops their positions, I met General Hancock, then on his way from the front to General Meade, who was back towards Taneytown; and he, for the purpose of having me advise General Gibbon, for his information, gave me a quite detailed account of the situation of matters at Gettysburg, and of what had transpired subsequently to his arrival there.

He had arrived and assumed command there, just when the troops of the First and Eleventh Corps, after their repulse, were coming in confusion through the town. Hancock is just the man for such an emergency as this. Upon horseback, I think he was the most magnificent looking general in the whole Army of the Potomac, at that time. With a large, well-shaped person, always dressed with elegance, even upon that field of confusion, he would look as if he was monarch of all he surveyed, and few of his subjects would dare to question his right to command, or do aught else but obey. His quick eye, in a flash, saw what was to be done, and his voice and his royal hand at once commenced to do it.

General Howard had put one of his divisions—Steinwher's— with some batteries, in position, upon a commanding eminence at the "Cemetery," which, as a reserve, had not participated in the fight of the day; and this division was now, of course, steady. Around this division the fugitives were stopped, and the shattered brigades and regiments, as they returned, were formed upon either flank, and faced toward the enemy again. A show of order, at least, speedily came from chaos. The rout was at an end; the First and Eleventh Corps were in line of battle again,—not very systematically formed, perhaps,—in a splendid position, and in a condition to offer resistance, should the enemy be willing to try them. These formations were all accomplished long before night. Then some considerable portion of the Third Corps—General Sickles—came up by the Emmitsburg road, and was formed to the left of the Taneytown road, on an extension of the line that I have mentioned; and all of the Twelfth Corps—General Slocum—arriving before night, the divisions were put in position, to the right of the troops already there, to the east of the Baltimore Pike. The enemy was in the town, and behind it, and to the east and west, and appeared to be in strong force, and was jubilant over his day's success.

Such was the posture of affairs as evening came on of the 1st of July. General Hancock was hopeful, and in the best of spirits; and from him I also learned that the reason of halting the Second Corps in its present position was, that it was not then known where, for the coming fight, the line of battle would be formed—up near the town, where the troops then were, or farther back towards Taneytown. He would give his views on this subject to General Meade, which were in favor of the line near the town,—the one that was subsequently adopted,—and General Meade would determine.

The night before a great pitched battle would not ordinarily, I suppose, be a time for much sleep to generals and their staff officers. We needed it enough, but there was work to be done. This war makes strange confusion of night and day! I did not sleep at all that night. It would perhaps be expected, on the eve of such great events, that one should have some peculiar sort of feelings, something extraordinary, some great arousing and excitement of the sensibilities and faculties, commensurate with the event itself; this certainly would be very poetical and pretty, but so far as I am concerned, and I think I can speak for the army in this matter, there was nothing of the kind. Men who have volunteered to fight the battles of the country, had met the enemy in many battles, and had been constantly before them, as have the Army of the Potomac, were too old soldiers, and long ago too well have weighed chances and probabilities, to be so disturbed now. No, I believe the army slept soundly that night, and well; and I am glad the men did, for they needed it.

At midnight General Meade and staff rode by General Gibbon's headquarters, on their way to the field; and in conversation with General Gibbon, General Meade announced that he had decided to assemble the whole army before Gettysburg, and offer the enemy battle there. The Second Corps would move at the earliest daylight, and take up its position.

At three o'clock A.M., of the 2d of July, the sleepy soldiers of the Second Corps were aroused; before six the corps was up to the field, and halted temporarily by the side of the Taneytown road upon which it had marched, while some movements of other troops were being made, to enable it to take position in the order of battle. The morning was thick and sultry, the sky overcast with low, vapory clouds. As we approached, all was astir upon the crests near the Cemetery, and the work of preparation was speedily going on. Men looked like giants there in the mist, and the guns of the frowning batteries so big that it was a relief to know that they were our friends.

Without a topographical map, some description of the ground and localities is necessary to a clear understanding of the battle. With the sketch that I have rudely drawn, without scale or compass, I hope you may understand my description. The line of battle, as it was established on the evening of the 1st, and morning of the 2d of July, was in the form of the letter "U," the troops facing outwards, and the Cemetery, which is at the point of the sharpest curvature of the line, being due south of the town of Gettysburg. Round Top, the extreme left of the line, is a small, woody, rocky elevation, a very little west of south of the town, and nearly two miles from it. The sides of this are in places very steep, and its rocky summit is almost inaccessible. A short distance north of this is a smaller elevation called "Little Round Top." On the very top of Little Round Top we had heavy rifled guns in position during the battle. Near the right of the line is a small woody eminence, named "Culp's Hill."

Three roads come up to the town from the south, which near the town are quite straight, and at the town the extreme ones unite, forming an angle of about sixty or more degrees. Of these the farthest to the east is the Baltimore Pike, which passes by the east entrance to the Cemetery; the farthest to the west is the Emmitsburg road, which is wholly outside of our line of battle, but near the Cemetery is within a hundred yards of it; the "Taneytown Road" is between these, running nearly due north and south, by the eastern base of Round Top, by the western side of the Cemetery, and uniting with the Emmitsburg road between the Cemetery and the town. High ground near the Cemetery is named "Cemetery Ridge."

The Eleventh Corps—General Howard—was posted at the Cemetery, some of its batteries and troops actually among the graves and monuments, which they used for shelter from the enemy's fire; its left resting upon the Taneytown road, and extending thence to the east, crossing the Baltimore Pike, and then bending backwards towards the southeast; on the right of the Eleventh came the First Corps, now, since the death of General Reynolds, commanded by General Newton, formed in a line curving still more to the south. The troops of these two corps were reformed on the morning of the 2d, in order that each might be by itself, and to correct some things not done well during the hasty formation here the day before. To the right of the First Corps, and on an extension of the same line, along the crest and down the southeastern slope of Culp's Hill, was posted the Twelfth Corps—General Slocum—its right, which was the extreme right of the line of the army, resting near a small stream called "Rock Run."

No changes that I am aware of occurred in the formation of this corps on the morning of the 2d. The Second Corps, after the brief halt that I have mentioned, moved up and took position, its right resting upon the Taneytown road, at the left of the Eleventh Corps, and extending the line thence, nearly half a mile, almost due south, towards Round Top, with its divisions in the following order, from right to left: the Third, General Alex. Hayes; the Second, (Gibbon's) General Harrow (temporarily); the First, General Caldwell. The formation was, in line by brigade in column, the brigades being in column by regiment, with forty paces interval between regimental lines, the Second and Third having each one, and the First Division two brigades. There were four brigades in the First, similarly formed, in reserve, one hundred and fifty paces in the rear of the line of their respective divisions. That is, the line of the corps, exclusive of its reserves, was the length of six regiments, deployed, and the intervals between them, some of which were left wide for the posting of the batteries, and consisted of four common deployed lines, each of two ranks of men; and a little more than one third was in reserve.

The five batteries, in all twenty-eight guns, were posted as follows: Woodruff's Regular, six twelve-pound Napoleons, brass, between the two brigades in line of the Third Division; Arnold's "A," First Rhode Island, six three-inch Parrotts, rifled, and Cushing's Regular, four three-inch ordnance, rifled, between the Third and Second Divisions; Hazard's (commanded during the battle by Lieutenant Brown), "B," First Rhode Island, and Rhorty's New York, each six twelve-pound Napoleons, brass, between the Second and First Divisions.

I have been thus specific in the description of the posting and formation of the Second Corps, because they were works that I assisted to perform; and also that the other corps were similarly posted with reference to the strength of the lines, and the intermixing of infantry and artillery. From this, you may get a notion of the whole.

The Third Corps—General Sickles—the remainder of it arriving upon the field this morning, was posted upon the left of the Second, extending the line still in the direction of Round Top, with its left resting near Little Round Top. The left of the Third Corps was the extreme left of the line of battle, until changes occurred which will be mentioned in the proper place. The Fifth Corps—General Sykes—arriving on the Baltimore Pike about this time, was massed there near the line of battle, and held in reserve until sometime in the afternoon, when it changed position, as I shall describe.

I cannot give a detailed account of the cavalry, for I saw but little of it. It was posted near the wings, and watched the roads and movements of the enemy upon the flanks of the army, but further than this participated but little in the battle. Some of it was also used for guarding the trains, which were far to the rear. The artillery reserve, which consisted of a good many batteries, though I cannot give the number, or the number of guns, was posted between the Baltimore Pike and the Taneytown Road, on very nearly the centre of a direct line passing through the extremities of the wings. Thus it could be readily sent to any part of the line. The Sixth Corps—General Sedgwick—did not arrive upon the field until sometime after noon; but it was now not very far away, and was coming up rapidly upon the Baltimore Pike. No fears were entertained that "Uncle John," as his men call General Sedgwick, would not be in the right place at the right time.

These dispositions were all made early, I think before eight o'clock in the morning; skirmishers were posted well out all around the line, and all put in readiness for battle. The enemy did not yet demonstrate himself. With a look at the ground now, I think you may understand the movements of the battle. From Round Top, by the line of battle, round to the extreme right, I suppose is about three miles. From this same eminence to the Cemetery extends a long ridge or hill—more resembling a great wave than a hill, however—with its crest, which was the line of battle, quite direct between the points mentioned. To the west of this, that is, towards the enemy, the ground falls away, by a very gradual descent, across the Emmitsburg Road, and then rises again, forming another ridge, nearly parallel to the first, but inferior in altitude, and something over a thousand yards away. A belt of woods extends partly along this second ridge, and partly farther to the west, at distances of from one thousand to thirteen hundred yards away from our line. Between these ridges, and along their slopes, that is, in front of the Second and Third Corps, the ground is cultivated, and is covered with fields of wheat, now nearly ripe, with grass and pastures, with some peach orchards, with fields of waving corn, and some farmhouses and their outbuildings along the Emmitsburg road.

There are very few places within the limits mentioned where troops or guns could move concealed. There are some oaks, of considerable growth, along the position of the right of the Second Corps,—a group of small trees, sassafras and oak, in front of the right of the Second Division of this corps, also; and considerable woods immediately in front of the left of the Third Corps, and also to the west of, and near Round Top.

At the Cemetery, where is Cemetery Ridge, to which the line of the Eleventh Corps conforms, is the highest point in our line, except Round Top. From this the ground falls quite abruptly to the town, the nearest point of which is some five hundred yards away from the line, and is cultivated, and checkered with stone fences. The same is the character of the ground occupied by, and in front of the left of the First Corps, which is also on a part of Cemetery Ridge. The right of this corps, and the whole of the Twelfth, are along Culp's Hill, and in woods, and the ground is very rocky, and in some places in front precipitous,—a most admirable position for defence from an attack in front, where, on account of the woods, no artillery could be used with effect by the enemy. Then these last three mentioned corps had, by taking rails, by appropriating stone fences, by felling trees, and digging the earth, during the night of the 1st of July, made for themselves excellent breastworks, which were a very good thing indeed. The position of the First and Twelfth Corps was admirably strong, therefore.

Within the line of battle is an irregular basin, somewhat wooded and rocky in places, but presenting few obstacles to the moving of troops and guns, from place to place along the lines, and also affording the advantage that all such movements, by reason of the surrounding crests, were out of view of the enemy. On the whole this was an admirable position to fight a defensive battle,—good enough, I thought, when I saw it first, and better, I believe, than could be found elsewhere in a circle of many miles. Evils, sometimes at least, are blessings in disguise, for repulse of our forces, and the death of Reynolds, on the 1st of July, with the opportune arrival of Hancock to arrest the tide of fugitives and fix it on these heights, gave us this position. Perhaps the position gave us the victory.

On arriving upon the field General Meade established his headquarters at a shabby little farmhouse on the left of the Taneytown Road, the house nearest the line and a little more than five hundred yards in rear of what became the centre of the position of the Second Corps,—a point where he could communicate readily and rapidly with all parts of the army. The advantages of this position, briefly, were these: the flanks were quite well protected by the natural defences there,—Round Top upon the left, and rocky, steep, untraversable ground upon the right. Our line was more elevated than that of the enemy, consequently our artillery had a greater range and power than theirs.

On account of the convexity of our line, every part of the line could be reinforced by troops having to move a shorter distance than if the line were straight; further, for the same reason, the line of the enemy must be concave and consequently longer, and, with an equal force, thinner, and so weaker, than ours. Upon those parts of our line which were wooded, neither we nor the enemy could use artillery; but they were so strong by nature, aided by art, as to be readily defended by a small against a very large body of infantry. Where the line was open, it had the advantage of having open country in front; consequently, the enemy could not surprise us; we were on a crest, which, besides the other advantages that I have named, had this: the enemy must advance to the attack up an ascent, and must therefore move slower, and be, before coming upon us, longer under our fire, as well as more exhausted. These and some other things rendered our position admirable for a defensive battle.

So, before a great battle, was ranged the Army of the Potomac. The day wore on, the weather still sultry, and the sky overcast, with a mizzling effort at rain. When the audience has all assembled, time seems long until the curtain rises: so to-day. "Will there be a battle to-day?" "Shall we attack the rebel?" "Will he attack us?" These and similar questions, later in the morning, were thought and asked a million times.

Meanwhile, on our part all was put in the best state of readiness for battle. Surgeons were busy riding about, selecting eligible places for hospitals, and hunting streams and springs and wells. Ambulances and ambulance men were brought up near the lines, and stretchers gotten ready for use. Who of us could tell but that he would be the first to need them? The Provost Guards were busy driving up all the stragglers and causing them to join their regiments. Ammunition wagons were driven to suitable places, and pack mules bearing boxes of cartridges, and the commands were informed where they might be found. Officers were sent to see that the men had each his hundred rounds of ammunition. Generals and their staffs were riding here and there among their commands to see that all was right. A staff officer or an orderly might be seen galloping furiously in the transmission of some order or message. All, all was ready, and yet the sound of no gun had disturbed the air or ear to-day.

Here let me state that according to the best information that I could get, I think a fair estimate of the rebel force engaged in this battle would be a little upwards of a hundred thousand men of all arms. Of course, we cannot now know, but there are reasonable data for this estimate. At all events there was no disparity of numbers in the two opposing armies. We thought the enemy to be somewhat more numerous than we, and he probably was. But if ninety-five men should fight with a hundred and five, the latter would not always be victorious, and slight numerical differences are of much less consequence in great bodies of men. Skilful generalship and good fighting are the jewels of war. These concurring are difficult to overcome; and these, not numbers, must determine this battle.

During all the morning, and the night, too, the skirmishers of the enemy had been confronting those of the Eleventh, First, and Twelfth Corps. At the time of the fight of the 1st he was seen in heavy force north of the town; he was believed to be now in the same neighborhood in full force. But from the woody character of the country, and thereby the careful concealment of troops, which the rebel is always sure to effect, during the early part of the morning almost nothing was actually seen by us of the invaders of the North. About nine o'clock in the morning, I should think, our glasses began to reveal them at the west and northwest of the town, a mile and a half away from our lines. They were moving toward our left, but the woods of Seminary Ridge so concealed them that we could not make out much of their movements.

About this time some rifled guns in the Cemetery at the left of the Eleventh Corps opened fire—almost the first shots of any kind this morning; and when it was found they were firing at a rebel line of skirmishers merely, that were advancing upon the left of that and the right of the Second Corps, the officer in charge of the guns was ordered to cease firing, and was rebuked for having fired at all. These skirmishers soon engaged those of the right of the Second Corps, who stood their ground and were reinforced to make the line entirely secure. The rebel skirmish line kept extending farther and farther to their right, towards our left; they would dash up close upon ours, and sometimes drive them back a short distance, in turn to be repulsed themselves: and so they continued to do until their right was opposite the extreme left of the Third Corps. By these means they had ascertained the position and extent of our line, but their own masses were still out of view.

From the time that the firing commenced, as I have mentioned, it was kept up by the skirmishers until quite noon, often briskly, but with no definite results further than those mentioned, and with no considerable show of infantry on the part of the enemy to support. There was a farmhouse and out-buildings in front of the Third Division of the Second Corps, at which the skirmishers of the enemy had made a dash and dislodged ours posted there; and from this their sharp-shooters began to annoy our line of skirmishers, and even the main line, with their long-range rifles. I was up to the line, and a bullet from one of the rascals hid there hissed by my cheek so close that I felt the movement of the air distinctly. And so I was not at all displeased when I saw one of our regiments go down and attack and capture the house and buildings and several prisoners, after a spirited little fight, and by General Hays' order, burn the buildings to the ground.

About noon the Signal Corps, from the top of Little Round Top, with their powerful glasses, and the cavalry at our extreme left, began to report the enemy in heavy force making dispositions of battle to the west of Round Top and opposite to the left of the Third Corps. Some few prisoners had been captured, some deserters from the enemy had come in, and from all sources by this time we had much important and reliable information of the enemy, of his dispositions and apparent purposes.

The rebel infantry consisted of three army corps, each consisting of three divisions. Longstreet, Ewell,—the same whose leg Gibbon's shell had knocked off at Gainesville on the 28th of August last year,—and A. P. Hill, each in the rebel service having the rank of lieutenant-general, were the commanders of these corps. Longstreet's division commanders were Hood, McLaws, and Pickett; Ewell's were Rhodes, Early, and Johnson; and Hill's were Pender, Heth, and Anderson. Stewart and Fitz Lee commanded divisions of the rebel cavalry. The rank of these division commands, I believe, was that of major general.

The rebel had about as much artillery as we did, but we never thought much of this arm in the hands of our adversaries. They have courage enough, but not the skill to handle it well. They generally fire too high, and their ammunition is assuredly of a very inferior quality. And of late we have begun to despise the enemy's cavalry, too; it used to have enterprise and dash, but in the late cavalry contests ours has always been victor, and so now we think that about all this chivalry is fit for is to steal a few of our mules occasionally and their negro drivers. The infantry of the rebel army, however, is good—to deny this is useless. I never had any desire to; and if one should count up, it would possibly be found that they have gained more victories over us than we have over them; and they will now, doubtless, fight well, even desperately. And it is not horses or cannon that will determine the result of this confronting of the two armies, but the men with the muskets must do it—the infantry must do the sharp work.

So we watched all this posting of forces as closely as possible, for it was a matter of vital interest to us, and all information relating to it was hurried to the commander of the army. The rebel line of battle was concave, bending around our own, with the extremities of the wings opposite to or a little outside of ours. Longstreet's Corps was upon their right, Hill's in the centre; these two rebel corps occupied the second or inferior ridge to the west of our position, as I have mentioned, with Hill's left bending towards and resting near the town, and Ewell's was upon their left, his troops being in and to the east of the town. This last corps confronted our Twelfth, First, and the right of the Eleventh Corps.

When I have said ours was a good defensive position, this is equivalent to saying that that of the enemy was not a good offensive one, for these are relative terms and cannot be both predicted of the respective positions of the two armies at the same time. The reasons that theirs was not a good offensive position are the same already stated of ours for defence. Excepting occasionally for a brief time during some movement of the troops, or when advancing to attack, their men and guns were kept constantly and carefully, by woods and inequalities of grounds, out of our view.

Noon is past, one o'clock is past, and, save the skirmishing that I have mentioned, and an occasional shot from our guns, at something or other of the nature of which the ones who fired it were ignorant, there was no fight yet. Our arms were still stacked, and the men were at ease.

As I looked upon those interminable rows of muskets along the crests, and saw how cool and good-spirited the men were, who were lounging about on the ground among them, I could not, and did not, have any fears as to the result of the battle. The storm was near, and we all knew it by this time, which was to rain death upon these crests and down these slopes, and yet the men who could not, and would not, escape it, were as calm and cheerful generally, as if nothing unusual were about to happen! You see, these men were veterans, and had been in such places so often that they were accustomed to them. But I was well pleased with the tone of the men to-day; I could almost see the foreshadowing of victory upon their faces, I thought.

And I thought, too, as I had seen the mighty preparations go on to completion for this great conflict, the marshalling of these two hundred thousand men and the guns, of the hosts that now but a narrow valley divided, that to have been in such a battle, and to survive on the side of the victors, would be glorious. Oh, the world is most unchristian yet!

Somewhat after one o'clock P.M.—the skirmish firing had nearly ceased now—a movement of the Third Corps occurred, which I shall describe. I cannot conjecture the reason of this movement. From the position of the Third Corps, as I have mentioned, to the second ridge west, the distance is about a thousand yards, and there the Emmitsburg road runs near the crest of the ridge. General Sickles commenced to advance his whole corps, from the general line, straight to the front, with a view to occupy this second ridge along and near the roads. What his purpose could have been is past conjecture. It was not ordered by General Meade, as I heard him say, and he disapproved of it as soon as it was made known to him. Generals Hancock and Gibbon, as they saw the move in progress, criticised its propriety sharply, as I know, and foretold quite accurately what would be the result. I suppose the truth probably is that General Sickles supposed he was doing for the best; but he was neither born nor bred a soldier. But this move of the Third Corps was an important one—it developed the battle; the results of the move to the corps itself we shall see. Oh, if this corps had kept its strong position upon the crest, and, supported by the rest of the army, had waited for the attack of the enemy!

It was magnificent to see these ten or twelve thousand men—they were good men—with their batteries, and some squadrons of cavalry upon the left flank, all in battle order, in several lines, with flags streaming, sweep steadily down the slope, across the valley, and up the next ascent, towards their destined position! From our position we could see it all. In advance Sickles pushed forward his heavy line of skirmishers, who drove back those of the enemy, across the Emmitsburg road, and thus cleared the way for the main body. The Third Corps now became the absorbing object of interest of all eyes. The Second Corps took arms; and the First Division of this corps was ordered to be in readiness to support the Third Corps, should circumstances render support necessary. As the Third Corps was the extreme left of our line, as it advanced, if the enemy was assembling to the west of Round Top with a view to turn our left, as we had heard, there would be nothing between the left flank of the corps and the enemy; and the enemy would be square upon its flank by the time it had attained the road.

So when this advance line came near the Emmitsburg road, and we saw the squadrons of cavalry mentioned come dashing back from their position as flankers, and the smoke of some guns, and we heard the reports, away to Sickles' left, anxiety became an element in our interest in these movements. The enemy opened slowly at first, and from long range; but he was square upon Sickles' left flank. General Caldwell was ordered at once to put his division—the First of the Second Corps, as mentioned—in motion, and to take post in the woods at the west slope of Round

Top, in such a manner as to resist the enemy should he attempt to come around Sickles' left and gain his rear. The division moved as ordered, and disappeared from view in the woods, towards the point indicated, at between two and three o'clock P.M., and the reserve brigade—the First, Colonel Heath temporarily commanding—of the Second Division was thereupon moved up, and occupied the position vacated by the Third Division. About the same time the Fifth Corps could be seen marching by the flank from its position on the Baltimore Pike, and in the opening of the woods heading for the same locality where the First Division of the Second Corps had gone. The Sixth Corps had now come up, and was halted upon the Baltimore Pike. So the plot thickened.

As the enemy opened up on Sickles with his batteries, some five or six in all, firing slowly, Sickles, with as many, replied, and with much more spirit. The artillery fire became quite animated, soon; but the enemy was forced to withdraw his guns farther and farther away, and ours advanced upon him. It was not long before the cannonade ceased altogether, the enemy having retired out of range, and Sickles, having temporarily halted his command, pending this, moved forward again to the position he desired, or nearly that.

It was now about five o'clock, and we shall soon see what Sickles gained by his move. First we have more artillery firing upon Sickles' left—the enemy seems to be opening again; and as we watched, the rebel batteries seem to be advancing there. The cannonade is soon opened again, and with great spirit upon both sides. The enemy's batteries press those of Sickles, and pound the shot upon them, and this time they in turn begin to retire to positions nearer the infantry. The enemy seems to be fearfully in earnest, this time. And what is more ominous than the thunder or the shot of his advancing guns, this time, in the intervals between his batteries, far to Sickles' left, appear the long lines and the columns of the rebel infantry, now unmistakably moving out to the attack. The position of the Third Corps became at once one of great peril, and it is probable that its commander by this time began to realize his true situation.

All was astir now on our crest. Generals and their staffs were galloping hither and thither; the men were all in their places, and you might have heard the rattle of ten thousand ramrods, as they drove home and "thugged" upon the little globes and cones of lead. As the enemy was advancing upon Sickles' flank, he commenced a change, or at least a partial one, of front, by swinging back his left and throwing forward his right, in order that his lines might be parallel to those of his adversary, his batteries meantime doing what they could to check the enemy's advance; but this movement was not completely executed before new rebel batteries opened upon Sickles' right flank—his former front—and in the same quarter appeared the rebel infantry also.

Now came the dreadful battle picture, of which we for a time could be but spectators. Upon the front and right flank of Sickles came sweeping the infantry of Longstreet and Hill. Hitherto there had been skirmishing and artillery practice—now the battle begins; for amid the heavier smokes and longer tongues of flame of the batteries, now began to appear the countless flashes, and the long, fiery sheets of the muskets, and the rattle of the volleys mingled with the thunder of the guns. We see the long gray lines come sweeping down upon Sickles' front, and mix with the battle smoke; now the same colors emerge from the bushes and orchards upon his right, and envelop his flank in the confusion of the conflict. Oh, the din and the roar, and these thirty thousand rebel wolf-cries! What a hell is there down that valley!

These ten or twelve thousand men of the Third Corps fight well, but it soon becomes apparent that they must be swept from the field, or perish there where they are doing so well, so thick and overwhelming a storm of rebel fire involves them. But these men, such as ever escape, must come from that conflict as best they can. To move down and support them there with other troops is out of the question, for this would be to do as Sickles did, to relinquish a good position, and advance to a bad one. There is no other alternative,—the Third Corps must fight itself out of its position of destruction! Why was it ever put there?

In the meantime some other dispositions must be made to meet the enemy, in the event that Sickles is overpowered. With this corps out of the way, the enemy would be in a position to advance upon the line of the Second Corps, not in a line parallel with its front, but they would come obliquely from the left. To meet this contingency the left of the Second Division of the Second Corps is thrown back slightly, and two regiments, the Fifteenth Massachusetts—Colonel Ward—and the Eighty-second New York—Lieutenant Colonel Horton—are advanced down to the Emmitsburg road, to a favorable position nearer us than the fight has yet come, and some new batteries from the artillery reserve are posted upon the crest near the left of the Second Corps. This was all General Gibbon could do. Other dispositions were made, or were now being made, upon the field, which I shall mention presently.

The enemy is still giving Sickles fierce battle,—or rather the Third Corps, for Sickles has been borne from the field minus one of his legs, and General Birney now commands,—and we of the Second Corps, a thousand yards away, with our guns and men, are, and must be, idle spectators of the fight. The rebel, as anticipated, tries to gain the left of the Third Corps, and for this purpose is now moving into the woods at the west of Round Top. We knew what he would find there. No sooner had the enemy got a considerable force into the woods mentioned, in the attempted execution of his purpose, than the roar of the conflict was heard there also. The Fifth Corps and the First Division of the Second were there at the right time, and promptly engaged him; and then, too, the battle soon became general and obstinate.

Now the roar of battle has become twice the volume that it was before, and it's rage extends over more than twice the space. The Third Corps has been pressed back considerably, and the wounded are streaming to the rear by hundreds, but still the battle there goes on, with no considerable abatement on our part. The field of actual conflict was now from a point to the front of the left of the Second Corps, away down to the front of Round Top, and the fight rages with the greatest fury. The fire of artillery and infantry and the yells of the rebels fill the air with a mixture of hideous sounds.

When the First Division of the Second Corps first engaged the enemy, for a time it was pressed back somewhat, but under the able and judicious management of General Caldwell, and the support of the Fifth Corps, it speedily ceased to retrograde, and stood its ground; and then there followed a time, after the Fifth Corps became well engaged, when from appearances we hoped the troops already engaged would be able to check entirely, or repulse, the further assault of the enemy. But fresh bodies of the rebels continued to advance out of the woods to the front of the position of the Third Corps, and to swell the numbers of the assailants of this already hard pressed command. The men there begin to show signs of exhaustion,—their ammunition must be nearly expended, —they have now been fighting more than an hour, and against greatly superior numbers.

From the sound of the fighting at the extreme left, and the place where the smoke rises above the tree-tops there, we know that the Fifth Corps is still steady, and holding its own there; and as we see the Sixth Corps now marching and near at hand to that point, we have no fears for the left,—we have more apparent reason to fear for ourselves. The Third Corps is being overpowered—here and there its lines begin to break,—the men begin to pour back to the rear in confusion,—the enemy are close upon them and among them,—organization is lost, to a great degree,— guns and caissons are abandoned and in the hands of the enemy, —the Third Corps, after a heroic, but unfortunate fight, is being literally swept from the field. That corps gone, what is there between the Second Corps and those yelling masses of the enemy? Do you not think that by this time we began to feel a personal interest in this fight? We did, indeed. We had been mere observers of all this,—the time was at hand when we must be actors in this drama.

Up to this hour General Gibbon had been in command of the Second Corps, since yesterday, but General Hancock, relieved of his duties elsewhere, now assumed command. Five or six hundred yards away the Third Corps was making its last opposition; and the enemy was hotly pressing his advantage there, and throwing in fresh troops whose line extended still more along our front, when Generals Hancock and Gibbon rode along the lines of their troops; and at once cheer after cheer—not rebel mongrel cries, but genuine cheers—rang out along the line, above the roar of battle, for "Hancock" and "Gibbon," and our "Generals." These were good. Had you heard their voices, you would have known these men would fight.

Just at this time we saw another thing that made us glad: we looked to our rear, and there, and all up the hillside, which was the rear of the Third Corps before it went forward, were rapidly advancing large bodies of men from the extreme right of our line of battle, coming to the support of the part now so hotly pressed. There was the whole Twelfth Corps, with the exception of about one brigade, that is, the larger portions of the divisions of Generals Williams and Geary, the Third Division of the First Corps—General Doubleday—and some other brigades from the same corps; and some of them were moving at the double quick. They formed lines of battle at the foot of the hill by the Taneytown road, and when the broken fragments of the Third Corps were swarming by them towards the rear, without haltering or wavering they came swiftly up, and with glorious old cheers, under fire, took their places on the crest in line of battle to the left of the Second Corps. Now Sickles' blunder is repaired. Now, rebel chief, hurl forward your howling lines and columns! Yell out your loudest and your last, for many of your host will never yell, or wave the spurious flag again!

The battle still rages all along the left, where the Fifth Corps is, and the west slope of Round Top is the scene of the conflict: and nearer us there was but short abatement as the last of the Third Corps retired from the field, for the enemy is flushed with his success,—he has been throwing forward brigade after brigade, and division after division, since the battle began, and his advancing line now extends almost as far to the right as the right of the Second Division of the Second Corps. The whole slope in our front is full of them; and in various formation, in line, in column, and in masses which were neither, with yells, and thick volleys, they are rushing towards our crest.

The Third Corps is out of the way. Now we are in for it. The battery men are ready by their loaded pieces. All along the crest is ready. Now Arnold and Brown—now Cushing and Woodruff and Rhorty! You three shall survive to-day! They drew the cords that move the friction primers, and gun after gun, along the batteries, in rapid succession, leaped where it stood, and bellowed its canister upon the enemy. The enemy still advance. The infantry open fire,—first the two advance regiments, the Fifteenth

Massachusetts and the Eighty-second New York, then here and there throughout the length of the long line at the points where the enemy comes nearest, and soon the whole crest, artillery and infantry, is one continued sheet of fire. From Round Top to near the Cemetery stretches an uninterrupted field of conflict. There is a great army upon each side, now hotly engaged.

To see the fight, while it went on in the valley below us, was terrible; what must it be now when we are in it, and it is all around us, in all its fury? All senses, for the time, are dead but the one of sight. The roar of the discharges and the yells of the enemy all pass unheeded; but the impassioned soul is all eyes, and sees all things that the smoke does not hide. How madly the battery men are driving the double charges of canister in those broad-mouthed Napoleons, whose fire seems almost to reach the enemy. How rapidly those long blue-coated lines of infantry deliver their file fire down the slope! But there is no faltering,—the men stand nobly to their work. Men are dropping, dead or wounded, on all sides, by scores and by hundreds; and the poor mutilated creatures, some with an arm dangling, some with a leg broken by a bullet, are limping and crawling towards the rear. They make no sound of complaint or pain, but are as silent as if dumb and mute.

A sublime heroism seems to pervade all, and the intuition that to lose that crest, all is lost. How our officers in the work of cheering on and directing the men are falling! We have heard that General Zook and Colonel Cross, in the First Division of our corps, are mortally wounded,—they both commanded brigades,—now near us Colonel Ward of the Fifteenth Massachusetts,—he lost a leg at Ball's Bluff,—and Lieutenant Colonel Horton of the Eighty-second New York, are mortally struck while trying to hold their commands, which are being forced back; Colonel Revere, Twentieth Massachusetts, grandson of old Paul Revere, of the Revolution, is killed, Lieutenant Colonel Max Thoman, commanding Fifty-ninth New York, is mortally wounded, and a host of others that I can not name. These were of Gibbon's division. Lieutenant Brown is wounded among his guns,—his position is a hundred yards in advance of the main line,—the enemy is upon his battery, and he escapes, but leaves three of his six guns in the hands of the enemy.

The fire all along our crest is terrific, and it is a wonder how anything human could have stood before it; and yet the madness of the enemy drove them on, clear up to the muzzles of the guns, clear up to the lines of our Infantry,—but the line stood right in their places. General Hancock with his aides rode up to Gibbon's division, under the smoke. General Gibbon, with myself, was near, and there was a flag dimly visible, coming towards us from the direction of the enemy. "Here, what are these men falling back for?" said Hancock. The flag was no more than fifty yards away, but it was the head of a rebel column, which at once opened fire with a volley. General Hancock, in the thick of it, told the First Minnesota, which was near, to drive these people away. That splendid regiment, the less than three hundred that are left out of fifteen hundred that it has had, swings around upon the enemy, gives them a volley in their faces, and advances upon them with the bayonet. The rebels fled in confusion; but Colonel Colville, Lieutenant Colonel Adams, and Major Downie are all badly, dangerously wounded, and many of the other officers and men will never fight again. More than two thirds fell.

Such fighting as this cannot last long; it is now near sundown, and the battle has gone on wondrously long already. But if we will stop to notice it, a change has occurred. The rebel cry has ceased, and the men of the Union begin to shout there, under the smoke, and their lines to advance. See, the rebels are breaking! They are in confusion in all our front! The wave has rolled upon the rock, and the rock has smashed it. Let us shout too!

First upon their extreme left the rebels broke, when they had almost pierced our lines; thence the repulse extended rapidly to their right; they hung longest about Round Top, where the Fifth Corps punished them; but in a space of time incredibly short, after they first gave signs of weakness, the whole force of the rebel assault, along the whole line, in spite of waving red flags, and yells, and the entreaties of officers, and the pride of the chivalry, fled like chaff before the whirlwind, back down the slope, over the valley, across the Emmitsburg road, shattered, without organization, in utter confusion, fugitive into the woods, and victory was with the arms of the Republic. The great rebel assault, the greatest ever made upon this continent, has been made and signally repulsed, and upon this part of the field the fight of today is now soon over. Pursuit was made as rapidly and as far as was practicable; but owing to the proximity of night, and the long distance which would have to be gone over before any of the enemy, where they would be likely to halt, could be overtaken, further success was not attainable today.

When the rebel rout first commenced, a large number of prisoners, some thousands at least, were captured; almost all their dead, and such of their wounded as could not themselves get to the rear, were within our lines; several of their flags were gathered up, and a good many thousand muskets, some nine or ten guns and some caissons lost by the Third Corps, and the three of Brown's battery —these last were in rebel hands but a few minutes—were all safe now with us, the enemy having had no time to take them off.

Not less, I estimate, than twenty thousand men were killed or wounded in this fight. Our own loss must have been nearly half this number,—about five thousand in the Third Corps, fully two thousand in the Second, and I think two thousand in the Fifth; and I think the losses of the First, Twelfth, and the little more than a brigade of the Sixth,—all of that corps which was actually engaged, —would reach nearly two thousand more. Of course, it will never be possible to know the numbers upon either side who fell in this particular part of the general battle, but from the position of the enemy, and his numbers, and the appearance of the field, his loss must have been as heavy as, I think much heavier, than our own; and my estimates are probably short of the actual loss.

The fight done, the sudden revulsions of sense and feeling follow, which more or less characterize all similar occasions. How strange the stillness seems! The whole air roared with the conflict but a moment since,—now all is silent; not a gunshot sound is heard, and the silence comes distinctly, almost painfully, to the senses. And the sun purples the clouds in the west, and the sultry evening steals on as if there had been no battle, and the furious shout and the cannon's roar had never shook the earth. And how look those fields—we may see them before dark—the ripening grain, the luxuriant corn, the orchards, the grassy meadows, and in their midst the rural cottage of brick or wood? They were beautiful this morning. They are desolate now,—trampled by the count-less feet of the combatants, plowed and scarred by the shot and shell, the orchards splintered, the fences prostrate, the harvests trodden in the mud. And more dreadful than the sight of all this, thickly strewn over all their length and breadth, are the habil-aments of the soldier,—the knapsacks, cast aside in the stress of the fight, or after the fatal lead has struck; haversacks, yawning with the rations the owner will never call for; canteens of cedar of the rebel men of Jackson, and of cloth-covered tin, of the men of the Union; blankets and trousers, overcoats and caps, and some are blue and some are gray; muskets and ramrods, and bayonets and swords, and scabbards and belts, some bent and cut by shot and shell; broken wheels, exploded caissons, and limber boxes, and dismantled guns; and all these were sprinkled with blood; horses, some dead, a mangled heap of carnage, some alive with a leg shot clean off, or other frightful wound, appealing to you with almost more than brute gaze as you pass; and last, but not least numerous, many thousands of men. And there was no rebellion here now,—the men of South Carolina were quiet by the side of those of Mas-sachusetts, some composed with upturned faces, sleeping the last sleep, some mutilated and frightful, some wretched, fallen, bathed in blood, survivors still, and unwilling witnesses of the rage of Gettysburg.

And yet with all this before them, as darkness came on, and the dispositions were made and the outposts thrown out for the night, the Army of the Potomac was quite mad with joy. No more light-hearted guests ever graced a banquet than were these men as they boiled their coffee and munched their soldier's supper to-night. Is it strange? Otherwise they would not have been soldiers. And such sights as all these will continue to be seen as long as war lasts in the world; and when war is done, then is the end, and the days of the millennium at hand.

The ambulances commenced their work as soon as the battle opened. The twinkling lanterns through the night, and the sun of tomorrow, saw them still with the same work unfinished.

I wish that I could write, that with the coming on of darkness ended the fight of today, but such was not the case. The armies have fought enough today, and ought to sleep tonight, one would think; but not so thought the rebel. Let us see what he gained by his opinion.

When the troops, including those of the Twelfth Corps, had been withdrawn from the extreme right of our line, in the afternoon, to support the left, as I have mentioned, thereby, of course, weakening that part of the line so left, the rebel Ewell, either becoming aware of the fact, or because he thought he could carry our right at all events, late in the afternoon commenced an assault upon that part of our line. His battle had been going on there simultaneously with the fight on the left. He had advanced his men through the woods, and in front of the formidable position lately held by the Twelfth Corps, cautiously, and to his surprise, I have no doubt, found our strong defenses upon the extreme right entirely abandoned. These he at once took possession of, and simultaneously made an attack upon our right flank, which was now near the summit of Culp's Hill, and upon the front of that part of the line. That small portion of the Twelfth Corps which had been left there, and some of the Eleventh Corps, sent to their assistance, did what they could to check the rebels; but could make but feeble resistance to the overwhelming forces of the enemy. Matters began to have a bad look in that part of the field; a portion of the First Division of the First Corps was sent them for support, the Sixth Wisconsin among them, and this improved matters. But still, as we had but a small number of men there, all told, the enemy, with their great numbers, were having there too much prospect of success; and it seems that probably, emboldened by this, Ewell had resolved upon a night attack, upon that wing of the army, and was making his disposition accordingly. The enemy had not at sundown actually carried any part of our rifle pits there, save the ones abandoned; but he was getting troops assembled upon our flank, and all together, with our weakness there at that time, matters did not look as we would like to have them.

Such was then the position of affairs, when the fight upon our left, that I have mentioned, was done. Under such circumstances it is not strange that the Twelfth Corps, as soon as its work was done upon the left, was quickly ordered back to the right, to its old position. There it arrived in good time; not soon enough, of course, to avoid the mortification of finding the enemy in the possession of a part of the works the men had labored so hard to construct, but in ample time before dark, to put the men well in the pits we already held, and to take up a strong defensible position, at right angles to and in rear of the main line, in order to resist these flanking dispositions of the enemy.

The army was secure again. The men in the works would be steady against all attacks in front, as long as they knew that their flank was safe. Until between ten and eleven o'clock at night, the woods upon the right resounded with the discharge of musketry. Shortly after, or about dark, the enemy made a dash upon the right of the Eleventh Corps. They crept up the windings of a valley, not in a very heavy force, but, from the peculiar manner in which this corps does outpost duty, quite unperceived in the dark until they were close upon the main line. It is said,—I do not know it to be true,—that they spiked two guns of one of the Eleventh Corps' batteries, and that the battery men had to drive them off with their sabres and rammers, and that there was some fearful Dutch swearing on the occasion,—*"donner wetter,"* among other similar impious oaths, having been freely used. The enemy here were finally repulsed by the assistance of Colonel Carroll's brigade of the Third Division of the Second Corps, and the One Hundred and Sixth Pennsylvania, from the Second Division of the same corps, was, by General Howard's request, sent there to do outpost duty.

It seems to have been a matter of utter madness and folly upon the part of the enemy to have continued their night attack as they did, upon the right. Our men were securely covered by ample works, and even in most places a log was placed a few inches above the top of the main breastwork, as a protection to the heads of the men as they thrust out the pieces beneath it to fire. Yet in the darkness the enemy would rush up, clambering over rocks and among trees, even to the front of the works, but only to leave their riddled bodies there upon the ground, or to be swiftly repulsed headlong into the woods again. In the darkness the enemy would climb trees close to the works, and endeavor to shoot our men by the light of the flashes. When discovered a thousand bullets would whistle after them in the dark, and some would hit, and then the rebel would make up his mind to come down.

Our loss was light, almost nothing, in this fight. The next morning the enemy's dead were thick all along this part of the line. Near eleven o'clock the enemy, wearied with his disastrous work, desisted; and thereafter until morning not a shot was heard in all the armies.

So much for the battle. There is another thing that I wish to mention, of the matters of the 2d of July. After evening came on, and from reports received, all was known to be going satisfactorily upon the right. General Meade summoned his corps commanders to his headquarters for consultation. A consultation is held upon matters of vast moment to the country, and that poor little farmhouse is honored with more distinguished guests than it ever had before, or than it will ever have again, probably. Do you expect to see a degree of ceremony and severe military aspect characterize this meeting, in accordance with strict military rules, and commensurate with the moment of the matters of their deliberation? Name it "Major General Meade, commander of the Army of the Potomac, with his corps generals, holding a council of war, upon the field of Gettysburg," and it would sound pretty well,—and that was what it was; and you might make a picture of it and hang it up by the side of "Napoleon and his Marshals," and "Washington and his Generals," may be, at some future time.

But for the artist to draw his picture from, I will tell how this council appeared. Meade, Sedgwick, Slocum, Howard, Hancock, Sykes, Newton, Pleasanton (commander of the cavalry), and Gibbon were the generals present. Hancock, now that Sickles is wounded, has charge of the Third Corps, and Gibbon again has the Second.

Meade is a tall, spare man, with full beard, which with his hair, originally brown, is quite thickly sprinkled with gray, has a Romanish face, very large nose, and a white large forehead, prominent and wide over the eyes, which are full and large, and quick in their movements, and he wears spectacles. His fibres are all of the long and sinewy kind. His habitual personal appearance is quite careless, and it would be rather difficult to make him look well dressed. Sedgwick is quite a heavy man,—short, thick-set, and muscular, with florid complexion, dark, calm, straight-looking eyes, rather full, heavyish features, which, with his eyes, have plenty of animation when he is aroused. He has a magnificent profile, well cut, with the nose and forehead forming almost a straight line, curly, short chestnut hair and full beard, cut short, with a little gray in it. He dresses carelessly, but can look magnificently when he is well dressed. Like Meade, he looks and is honest and modest. You might see at once why his men, because they love him, call him "Uncle John,"—not to his face of course, but among themselves. Slocum is small, rather spare, with black, straight hair and beard, which latter is unshaven and thin: large, full, quick, black eyes, white skin, sharp nose, wide cheek bones and hollow cheeks, and small chin. His movements are quick and angular, and he dresses with a sufficient degree of elegance. Howard is medium in size, has nothing marked about him, is the youngest of them all, I think; has lost an arm in the war, has straight brown hair and beard, shaves his short upper lip, over which his nose slants down, dim blue eyes, and on the whole appears a very pleasant, affable, well-dressed gentleman. Hancock is the tallest and most shapely, and in many respects is the best looking officer of them all. His hair is very light brown, straight and moist, and always looks well; his beard is of the same color, of which he wears the moustache and a tuft upon the chin; complexion ruddy, features neither large nor small, but well cut, with full jaw and chin, compressed mouth, straight nose, full, deep blue eyes, and a very mobile, emotional countenance. He always dresses remarkably well, and his manner is dignified, gentlemanly, and commanding. I think if he were in citizen's clothes and should give commands in the army to those who did not know him, he would be likely to be obeyed at once, and without any question as to his right to command. Sykes is a small, rather thin man, well dressed and gentlemanly, brown hair and beard which he wears full, with a red, pinched, rough-looking skin, feeble blue eyes, large nose, with the general air of one who is weary and a little ill-natured. Newton is a well-sized, shapely, muscular, well-dressed man, with brown hair, with a very ruddy, clean-shaved, full face, blue eyes, blunt, round features, walks very erect, curbs in his chin, and has somewhat of that smart sort of swagger, that people are apt to suppose characterizes soldiers. Pleasanton is quite a nice looking dandy, with brown hair and beard,—a straw hat with a little jockey rim, which he cocks upon one side of his head with an unsteady eye that looks slyly at you, and then dodges. Gibbon, the youngest of them all, save Howard, is about the same size as Slocum, Howard, Sykes, and Pleasanton, and there are none of these who will weigh one hundred and fifty pounds. He is compactly made, neither spare nor corpulent, with ruddy complexion, chestnut brown hair, with a clean-shaved face, except his moustache, which is decidedly reddish in color,—medium-sized, well-shaped head, sharp, moderately jutting brows, deep blue, calm eyes, sharp, slightly aquiline nose, compressed mouth, full jaws and chin, with an air of calm firmness in his manner. He always looks well dressed. I suppose Howard about thirty-five, and Meade about forty-five years of age; the rest are between these ages, but not many are under forty.

As they come to the council now there is the appearance of fatigue about them, which is not customary, but is only due to the hard labors of the past few days. They all wear clothes of dark blue, some have top boots and some not, and except the two-starred strap upon the shoulders of all save Gibbon, who has but one star, there was scarcely a piece of regulation uniform about them all. They wore their swords, of various patterns, but no sashes,—the army hat, but with the crown pinched into all sorts of shapes, and the rim slouched down and shorn of all its ornaments but the gilt band,—except Sykes, who wore a blue cap, and Pleasanton with his straw hat, with broad black band.

Then the mean little room where they met,—its only furniture consisted of a large, wide bed in one corner, a small pine table in the centre, upon which was a wooden pail of water, with a tin cup for drinking, and a candle, stuck to the table by putting the end in tallow melted down from the wick; and five or six straight-backed, rush-bottomed chairs. The generals came in; some sat, some kept walking or standing, two lounged upon the bed, some were constantly smoking cigars. And thus disposed, they deliberated, whether the army should fall back from its present position to one in rear which it was said was stronger; should attack the enemy on the morrow, wherever he could be found; or should stand there upon the horseshoe crest, still on the defensive, and await the further movements of the enemy. The latter proposition was unanimously agreed to. Their heads were sound. The Army of the Potomac would just halt right there, and allow the rebel to come up and smash his head against it, to any reasonable extent he desired,—as he had to-day. After some two hours this council dissolved, and the officers went their several ways.

Night, sultry and starless, droned on; and it was almost midnight that I found myself peering my way from the line of the Second Corps, back down to the general headquarters, which were an ambulance in the rear, in a little peach orchard. All was silent now but the sound of the ambulances as they were bringing off the wounded; and you could hear them rattle here and there about the field, and see their lanterns. I am weary and sleepy, almost to such an extent as not to be able to sit my horse. And my horse can hardly move,—the spur will not start him. What can be the reason? I know that he has been touched by two of their bullets to-day, but not to wound or lame him to speak of.

Then, in riding by a horse that is hitched, I get kicked. Had I not a very thick boot, the blow would have been likely to have broken my ankle; it did break my temper as it was, and, as if it would cure matters, I foolishly spurred my horse again. No use,— he would only walk. I dismounted; I could not lead him along at all, so, out of temper, I rode at the slowest possible walk to the headquarters, which I reached at last. Generals Hancock and Gibbon were asleep in the ambulance. With a light I found what was the matter with "Billy." A bullet had entered his chest just in front of my left leg as I was mounted, and the blood was running down all his side and leg, and the air from his lungs came out of the bullet-hole. I begged his pardon mentally for my cruelty in spurring him, and should have done so in words if he could have understood me. Kind treatment as is due to the wounded he could understand, and he had it. Poor Billy! He and I were first under fire together, and I rode him at the Second Bull Run, and the First and Second Fredericksburg, and at Antietam after brave "Joe" was killed; but I shall never mount him again. Billy's battles are over.

"George, make my bed here upon the ground, by the side of this ambulance. Pull off my sabre and my boots,—that will do!" Was ever princely couch, or softest down, so soft as those rough blankets, there upon the unroofed sod? At midnight they received me for four hours' delicious, dreamless oblivion of weariness and of battle. So, to me, ended the 2d of July.

At four o'clock on the morning of the 3d I was awakened by General Gibbons pulling me by the foot, and saying, "Come, don't you hear that?" I sprang to my feet. Where was I? A moment and my dead senses and memory were alive again, and the sound of brisk firing of musketry to the front and right of the Second Corps, and over at the extreme right of our line, where we heard it last in the night, brought all back to my memory. We surely were on the field of battle; and there were palpable evidences to my senses that today was to be another of blood. Oh, for a moment the thought of it was sickening to every sense and feeling! But the motion of my horse as I galloped over the crest a few minutes later, and the serene splendors of the morning now breaking through the rifted clouds and spreading over all the landscape soon reassured me. Come, day of battle! Up, rebel hosts, and thunder with your arms! We are all ready to do and to die for the Republic!

I found a sharp skirmish going on in front of the right of the Second Corps, between our outposts and those of the enemy; but save this—and none of the enemy but his outposts were in sight— all was quiet in all that part of the field. On the extreme right of the line the sound of musketry was quite heavy; and this I learned was brought on by the attack of the Second Division of the Twelfth Corps—General Geary—upon the enemy in order to drive him out of our works which he had sneaked into yesterday, as I have mentioned. The attack was made at the earliest moment of the morning when it was light enough to discern objects to fire at. The enemy could not use the works, but were confronting Geary in woods, and had the cover of many rocks and trees; so the fight was an irregular one, now breaking out and swelling to a vigorous fight, now subsiding to a few scattering shots; and so it continued by turns until the morning was well advanced, when the enemy was finally wholly repulsed and driven from the pits, and the right of our line was again re-established in the place it first occupied.

The heaviest losses the Twelfth Corps sustained in all the battle occurred during this attack; and they were here quite severe. I heard General Meade express dissatisfaction at General Geary for

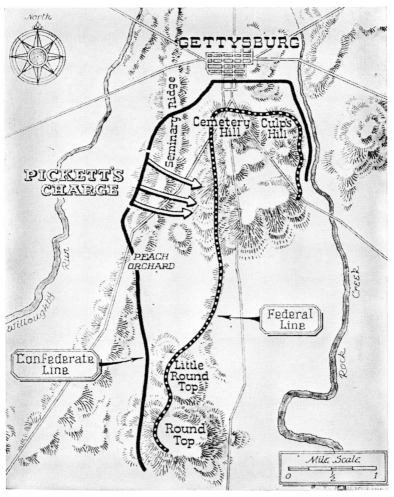

Map showing Gettysburg battle lines at the time of the charge of the Confederates under General George Edward Pickett, July 3, 1863. This resulted in the virtual annihilation of his division.

Union General George Gordon Meade presiding at the Council of War after the victory of the greatest battle of the Civil War at Gettysburg.

General Meade's Army crossing the Antietam in pursuit of General Lee, July 12, 1863.

Battle of the Wilderness. Attack near Spottsylvania Courthouse.

General Ulysses Simpson Grant, 1822-1885.

The Second Michigan raising the stars and stripes over the custom house after the capture of Petersburg, Virginia, April 3, 1865.

*The Confederate flight from Richmond as seen in a contemporary **Currier** and Ives print. The city burned when fires, meant to destroy valuable tobacco, got out of control.*

Photograph taken by Matthew B. Brady and Alexander Gardner of the ruins of Richmond the day after its evacuation in 1865.

Confederate General Ambrose P. Hill (1825-65). A West Pointer, he was in the Peninsular Campaign. His division was heavily engaged in the Seven Days Battles, Second Bull Run and the Antietam Campaign. Hill was wounded at Chancellorsville after assuming command from General Stonewall Jackson who had been mortally wounded. In the assault which finally broke Lee's lines at Petersburg, Virginia, on April 2, 1865, he went out with characteristic impulsiveness to rally his troops and was killed.

General Robert E. Lee signing the document of surrender in the humble parlor of the house of Wilmer McLean on April 9, 1865, in the presence of General Grant.

making this attack, as a thing not ordered and not necessary, as the works of ours were of no intrinsic importance, and had not been captured from us by a fight, and Geary's position was just as good where he was during the night. And I heard General Meade say that he sent an order to have the fight stopped; but I believe the order was not communicated to Geary until after the repulse of the enemy.

Later in the forenoon the enemy again tried to carry our right by storm. We heard that old rebel Ewell had sworn an oath that he would break our right. He had Stonewall Jackson's corps, and possibly imagined himself another Stonewall; but he certainly hankered after the right of our line, and so up through the woods, and over the rocks, and up the steeps, he sent his storming parties. Our men could see them now in the daytime. But all the rebel's efforts were fruitless, save in one thing—slaughter to his own men. These assaults were made with spirit and determination, but as the enemy would come up, our men, lying behind their secure defences, would just singe them with a blaze of their muskets, and riddle them, as a hailstorm the tender blades of corn. The rebel oath was not kept any more than his former one to support the Constitution of the United States. The rebel loss was very heavy indeed, here, ours but trifling.

I regret that I cannot give more of the details of this fighting upon the right; it was so determined upon the part of the enemy, both last night and this morning,—so successful to us. About all that I actually saw of it during its progress was the smoke, and I heard the discharges. My information is derived from officers who were personally in it. Some of our heavier artillery assisted our infantry in this by-firing, with the pieces elevated, far from the rear, over the heads of our men, at a distance from the enemy of two miles, I suppose. Of course, they could have done no great damage. It was nearly eleven o'clock that the battle in this part of the field subsided, not to be again renewed. All the morning we felt no apprehension for this part of the line; for we knew its strength, and that our troops engaged, the Twelfth Corps and the First Division, Wadsworth's, of the First, could be trusted.

For the sake of telling one thing at a time, I have anticipated events somewhat, in writing of this fight upon the right. I shall now go back to the starting point,—four o'clock this morning, and, as other events occurred during the day second to none in the battle in importance, which I think I saw as much of as any man living, I will tell you something of them, and what I saw, and how the time moved on.

The outpost skirmish that I have mentioned soon subsided. I suppose it was the natural escape of the wrath which the men had during the night hoarded up against each other and which, as soon as they could see in the morning, they could no longer contain, but must let it off through their musket barrels at their adversaries. At the commencement of the war such firing would have awakened the whole army, and roused it to its feet and to arms; not so now.

The men upon the crest lay snoring in their blankets, even though some of the enemy's bullets dropped among them, as if bullets were harmless as the drops of dew around them. As the sun arose today the clouds became broken, and we had once more glimpses of sky and fits of sunshine—a rarity—to cheer us. From the crest, save to the right of the Second Corps, no enemy, not even his outposts, could be discovered along all the position where he so thronged upon the Third Corps yesterday. All was silent there. The wounded horses were limping about the fields; the ravages of the conflict were still perfectly visible,—the scattered arms and the ground thickly dotted with the dead,—but no hostile foe. The men were roused early, in order that their morning meal might be out of the way in time for whatever should occur. Then ensued the hum of an army, not in ranks, chatting in low tones, and running about and jostling among each other, rolling and packing their blankets and tents. They looked like an army of rag-gatherers while shaking these very useful articles of the soldier's outfit, for you must know that rain and mud in conjunction have not had the effect to make them very clean, and the wear and tear of service have not left them entirely whole. But one could not have told by the appearance of the men that they were in battle yesterday and were likely to be again today. They packed their knapsacks, boiled their coffee, and munched their hard bread, just as usual,—just like old soldiers, who know what campaigning is; and their talk is far more concerning their present employment—some joke or drollery—than concerning what they saw or did yesterday.

As early as practicable the lines all along the left are revised and
re-formed, this having been rendered necessary by yesterday's
battle, and also by what is anticipated to-day. It is the opinion of
many of our generals that the rebel will not give us battle today,
that he had enough yesterday; that he will be heading towards the
Potomac at the earliest practicable moment, if he has not already
done so. But the better and controlling judgment is, that he will
make another grand effort to pierce or turn our lines; that he will
either mass and attack the left again, as yesterday, or direct his
operations against the left of our centre, the position of the Second
Corps, and try to sever our line. I infer that General Meade was
of the opinion that the attack today would be upon the left,—this
from the disposition he had ordered. I know that General Hancock
anticipated the attack upon the centre.

The dispositions today upon the left are as follows: The Second
and Third Divisions of the Second Corps are in the positions of
yesterday; then on the left came Doubleday's—the Third Division
and Colonel Stannard's Brigade of the First Corps; then Caldwell's,
—the First Division of the Second Corps; then the Third Corps,
temporarily under the command of Hancock, since Sickles' wound.
The Third Corps is upon the same ground in part, and on the
identical line where it first formed yesterday morning, and where,
had it stayed instead of moving out to the front, we should have
many more men today, and should not have been upon the brink
of destruction yesterday. On the left of the Third is the Fifth Corps,
with a short front and deep line; then comes the Sixth Corps, all
but one brigade, which is sent over to the Twelfth. The Sixth, a
splendid corps, almost intact in the fight of yesterday, is the extreme left of our line, which terminates to the south of Round Top,
and runs along its western base, in the woods, and thence to the
Cemetery. This corps is burning to pay off scores made on the
fourth of May, then back of Fredericksburg.

Note well the position of the Second and Third Divisions of the
Second Corps,—it will become important. There are nearly six
thousand men and officers in these two divisions here upon the
field. The losses were quite heavy yesterday,—some regiments
are detached to other parts of the field,—so all told there are less
than six thousand men now in the two divisions, who occupy a line

of about a thousand yards. The most of the way along this line upon the crest was a stone fence, constructed from small rough stones, a good deal of the way badly fallen down; but the men had improved it and patched it with rails from the neighboring fences, and with earth, so as to render it in many places a very passable breastwork against musketry and flying fragments of shells. These works are so low as to compel the men to kneel or lie down generally to obtain cover. Near the right of the Second Division, and just by the little group of trees that I have mentioned there, this stone fence made a right angle, and extended thence to the front, about twenty or thirty yards, where with another less than a right angle it followed along the crest again. (Thus⌐|___.) The lines were conformed to these breastworks and to the nature of the ground upon the crest, so as to occupy the most favorable places,—to be covered, and still be able to deliver effective fire upon the enemy should he come there. In some places a second line was so posted as to be able to deliver its fire over the heads of the first line behind the works; but such formation was not practicable all of the way. But all the force of these two divisions was in line, in position, without reserves, and in such a manner that every man of them could have fired his piece at the same instant.

The division flags—that of the Second Division being a white trefoil upon a square blue field—waved behind the divisions at the points where the generals of divisions were supposed to be; the brigade flags, similar to these but with a triangular field, were behind the brigades; and the national flags of the regiments were in the lines of the regiments.

To the left of the Second Division, and advanced something over a hundred yards, were posted a part of Stannard's brigade, two regiments or more, behind a small bush-crowned crest that ran in a direction oblique to the general line. These were well covered by the crest, and wholly concealed by the bushes, so that an advancing enemy would be close upon them before they could be seen. Other troops of Doubleday's division were strongly posted in rear of these in the general line.

I could not help wishing all the morning that this line of the divisions of the Second Corps were stronger; it was, so far as numbers constitute strength, the weakest part of our whole line of battle.

What if, I thought, the enemy should make an assault here to-day, with two or three heavy lines,—a great overwhelming mass,—would he not sweep through that thin six thousand? But I was not General Meade, who alone had power to send other troops there; and he was satisfied with that part of the line as it was.

He was early on horseback this morning, and rode along the whole line, looking to it himself, and with glass in hand sweeping the woods and fields in the direction of the enemy, to see if aught of him could be discovered. His manner was calm and serious, but earnest. There was no arrogance of hope, or timidity of fear, discernible in his face; but you would have supposed he would do his duty conscientiously and well, and would be willing to abide the result. You would have seen this in his face. He was well pleased with the left of the line to-day, it was so strong with good troops. He had no apprehension for the right where the fight was now going on, on account of the admirable position of our forces there. He was not of the opinion that the enemy would attack the centre, our artillery had such sweep there, and this was not a favorite point of attack with the rebel; besides, should he attack the centre, the general thought he could reinforce it in good season. I heard General Meade speak of these matters to Hancock and some others, at about nine o'clock in the morning, while they were up by the line, near the Second Corps.

No further changes of importance, except those mentioned, were made in the disposition of the troops this morning, except to replace some of the batteries that were disabled yesterday, by others from the artillery reserve, and to brace up the lines well with guns, wherever there were eligible places, from the same source. The line is all in good order again, and we are ready for general battle.

Save the operations upon the right, the enemy, so far as we could see, was very quiet all the morning. Occasionally the outposts would fire a little, and then cease. Movements would be discovered which would indicate the attempt on the part of the enemy to post a battery; our Parrotts would send a few shells to the spot, then silence would follow. At one of these times a painful accident happened to us, this morning. First Lieutenant Henry Ropes, Twentieth Massachusetts, in General Gibbon's division, a most estimable gentleman and officer, intelligent, educated, refined, one of the noble souls that came to the country's defence, while lying at his post with his regiment, in front of one of the batteries, which fired over the infantry, was instantly killed by a badly made shell, which, or some portion of it, fell but a few yards in front of the muzzle of the gun. The same accident killed or wounded several others.

Between ten and eleven o'clock, over in a peach orchard in front of the position of Sickles yesterday, some little show of the enemy's infantry was discovered. A few shells scattered the graybacks; they again appeared, and it becoming apparent that they were only posting a skirmish line, no further molestation was offered them. A little after this some of the enemy's flags could be discerned over near the same quarter, above the top, and behind a small crest of a ridge. There seemed to be two or three of them —possibly they were guidons,—and they moved too fast to be carried on foot. Possibly, we thought, the enemy is posting some batteries there. We knew in about two hours from this time better about the matter. Eleven o'clock came. The noise of battle has ceased upon the right; not a sound of a gun or musket can be heard on all the field. The sky is bright with only the white fleecy clouds floating over from the west; the July sun streams down its fire upon the bright iron of the muskets in stacks upon the crest, and the dazzling brass of the Napoleons. The army lolls and longs for the shade, of which some get a hand's breadth from a shelter tent stuck upon a ramrod. The silence and sultriness of a July noon are supreme.

Now it so happened that just about this time of day a very original and interesting thought occurred to General Gibbon and several of his staff: that it would be a very good thing, and a very good time, to have something to eat. When I announce to you that I had not tasted a mouthful of food since yesterday noon, and that all I had had to drink since that time, but the most miserable, muddy, warm water, was a little drink of whiskey that Major Biddle, General Meade's aid-de-camp, gave me last evening, and a cup of strong coffee that I gulped down as I was first mounting this morning, and further, that, save the four or five hours in the night, there was scarcely a moment since that time but that I was in the saddle, you may have some notion of the reason of my assent to this extraordinary proposition. Nor will I mention the doubts I had as to the feasibility of the execution of this very novel proposal, except to say that I knew this morning that our larder was low; not to put too fine a point upon it, that we had nothing but some potatoes and sugar and coffee in the world. And I may as well say here, that of such, in scant proportions, would have been our repast, had it not been for the riding of miles by two persons, one an officer, to procure supplies; and they only succeeded in getting some few chickens, some butter, and one huge loaf of bread, which last was bought of a soldier, because he had grown faint in carrying it, and was afterwards rescued with much difficulty, after a long race, from a four-footed hog which had got hold of and had actually eaten a part of it. "There is a divinity," etc.

Suffice it, this very ingenious and unheard of contemplated proceeding, first announced by the general, was accepted, and at once undertaken by his staff. Of the absolute quality of what we had to eat, I could not pretend to judge, but I think an unprejudiced person would have said of the bread, that it was good; so of the potatoes, before they were boiled. Of the chickens, he would have questioned their age, but these were large and in good running order. The toast was good, and the butter,—there were those who, when coffee was given them, called for tea, and vice versa, and were so ungracious as to suggest that the water that was used in both might have come from near a barn. Of course, it did not.

We all came down to the little peach orchard where we had stayed last night, and, wonderful to see and tell, ever mindful of our needs, had it all ready, had our faithful John. There was an enormous pan of stewed chickens, and the potatoes and toast, all hot, and the bread and the butter, and tea and coffee. There was satisfaction derived from just naming them all over. We called John an angel, and he snickered and said he "knowed" we'd come. General Hancock is, of course, invited to partake, and without delay we commenced operations. Stools are not very numerous,—two in all,—and these the two generals have by common consent. Our table was the top of the mess chest. By this the generals sat; the rest of us sat upon the ground, cross-legged like the picture of a smoking Turk, and held our plates upon our laps. How delicious was the stewed chicken! I had a cucumber pickle in my saddlebags, the last of a lunch left there two or three days ago, which George brought, and I had half of it.

We were just well at it, when General Meade rode down to us from the line, accompanied by his staff, and by General Gibbon's invitation they dismounted and joined us. For the general commanding the Army of the Potomac, George, by an effort worthy of the person and the occasion, finds an empty cracker-box for a seat. The staff officer must sit upon the ground with the rest of us. Soon Generals Newton and Pleasanton, each with an aide, arrive. By an almost superhuman effort a roll of blankets is found, which, upon a pinch, is long enough to seat these generals both, and room is made for them. The aides sit with us. And, fortunate to relate, there was enough cooked for us all, and from General Meade to the youngest second lieutenant we all had a most hearty and well-relished dinner.

The generals ate and, after, lighted cigars, and under the flickering shade of a very small tree discoursed of the incidents of yesterday's battle, and of the probabilities of today. General Newton humorously spoke of General Gibbon as "this young North Carolinian," and how he was becoming arrogant and above his position because he had commanded a corps. General Gibbon retorted by saying that General Newton had not been long enough in such a command, only since yesterday, to enable him to judge of such things.

General Meade still thought that the enemy would attack his left again today, towards evening; but he was ready for them. General Hancock believed that the attack would be upon the position of the Second Corps. It was mentioned that General Hancock would again resume command of the Second Corps from that time, so that General Gibbon would again return to the Second Division. General Meade spoke of the Provost Guards,—that they were good men, and that it would be better today to have them in the ranks than to stop stragglers and skulkers, as these latter would be good for but little even in the ranks; and so he gave the order that all the Provost Guards should at once temporarily rejoin their regiments. Then General Gibbon called up Captain Farrell, First Minnesota, who commanded the Provost Guard of his division, and directed him for that day to join the regiment. "Very well, sir," said the captain, as he touched his hat and turned away. He was a quiet, excellent gentleman, and thorough soldier. I knew him well, and esteemed him. I never saw him again. He was killed in two or three hours from that time, and over half of his splendid company were either killed or wounded.

And so the time passed on, each general now and then dispatching some order or message by an officer or orderly, until about half past twelve, when all the generals, one by one, first General Meade, rode off their several ways; and General Gibbon and his staff alone remained. We dozed in the heat, and lolled upon the ground, with half open eyes. Our horses were hitched to the trees, munching some oats. A great lull rests upon all the field. Time was heavy, and for want of something better to do, I yawned and looked at my watch; it was five minutes before one o'clock. I returned my watch to its pocket, and thought possibly that I might go to sleep, and stretched myself upon the ground accordingly. My attitude and purpose were those of the general and the rest of the staff.

What sound was that? There was no mistaking it! The distinct, sharp echo of one of the enemy's guns, square over to the front, caused us to open our eyes and turn them in that direction, when we saw directly above the crest the smoke of the bursting shell, and heard its noise. In an instant, before a word was spoken, as if that was the signal gun for general work, loud, startling, booming, the report of gun after gun, in rapid succession, smote our ears, and their shells plunged down and exploded all around us. We sprang to our feet. In briefest time the whole rebel line to the west was pouring out its thunder and its iron upon our devoted crest. The wildest confusion for a few moments obtained among us. The shells came bursting all about. The servants ran terror-stricken for dear life, and disappeared. The horses hitched to the trees, or held by the slack hands of orderlies, neighed out in fright, and broke away and plunged riderless through the fields. The general at the first had snatched his sword, and started on foot to the front. I called for my horse; nobody responded. I found him tied to a tree near by, eating oats, with an air of the greatest composure, which under the circumstances, even then struck me as exceedingly ridiculous. He alone, of all beasts or men near, was cool. I am not sure but that

I learned a lesson then from a horse. Anxious alone for his oats, while I put on the bridle and adjusted the halter, he delayed me by keeping his head down, so I had time to see one of the horses of our mess wagon struck and torn by a shell. The pair plunge,—the driver has lost the rein; horses, driver, and wagon go into a heap by a tree. Two mules close at hand, packed with boxes of ammunition, are knocked all to pieces by a shell.

General Gibbon's groom has just mounted his horse, and is starting to take the general's to him, when the flying iron meets him and tears open his breast; he drops dead, and the horses gallop away. No more than a minute since the first shot was fired, and I am mounted and riding after the general.

The mighty din that now rises to heaven and shakes the earth is not all of it the voice of the rebellion; for our guns, the guardian lions of the crest, quick to awake when danger comes, have opened their fiery jaws and begun to roar,—the great hoarse roar of battle. I overtook the general half way up to the line. Before we reach the crest his horse is brought by an orderly. Leaving our horses just behind a sharp declivity of the ridge, on foot we go up among the batteries. How the long streams of fire spout from the guns! how the rifled shells hiss! how the smoke deepens and rolls! But where is the infantry? Has it vanished in smoke? Is this a nightmare or a juggler's devilish trick? All too real. The men of the infantry have seized their arms, and behind their works, behind every rock, in every ditch, wherever there is any shelter, they hug the ground, silent, quiet, unterrified, little harmed.

The enemy's guns, now in action, are in position at their front of the woods, along the second ridge that I have before mentioned and towards their right, behind a small crest in the open field, where we saw the flags this morning. Their line is some two miles long, concave on the side toward us, and their range is from 1000 to 1800 yards. 125 rebel guns, we estimate, are now active, firing twenty-four-pound, twenty, twelve, and ten-pound projectiles, solid shot and shells, spherical, conical, spiral. The enemy's fire is chiefly concentrated upon the position of the Second Corps. From the Cemetery to Round Top, with over a hundred guns, and to all parts of the enemy's line, our batteries reply, of twenty and ten-pound Parrotts, ten-pound rifled ordnance, and twelve-pound

Napoleons, using projectiles as various in shape and name as those of the enemy. Captain Hazard, commanding the Artillery Brigade of the Second Corps, was vigilant among the batteries of his command, and they were all doing well.

All was going on satisfactorily. We had nothing to do, therefore, but to be observers of the grand spectacle of battle. Captain Wessels, Judge Advocate of the division, now joined us, and we sat down just behind the crest, close to the left of Cushing's battery, to bide our time, to see, to be ready to act when the time should come, which might be at any moment. Who can describe such a conflict as is raging around us? To say that it was like a summer storm, with the crash of thunder, the glare of lightning, the shrieking of the wind, and the clatter of hailstones, would be weak. The thunder and lightning of these 250 guns, and their shells, when smoke darkens the sky, are incessant, all-pervading, in the air above our heads, on the ground at our feet, remote, near, deafening, ear-piercing, astounding; and these hailstones are massy iron charged with exploding fire. And there is little of human interest in a storm; it is an absorbing element of this. You may see flame and smoke, and hurrying men, and human passion, at a great conflagration; but they are all earthly, and nothing more. Those guns are great infuriate demons, not of the earth, whose mouths blaze with snaky tongues of living fire, and whose murky breath, sulphur-laden, rolls around them and along the ground, the smoke of Hades. These grimy men, rushing, shouting, their souls in frenzy, plying the dusky globes and the igniting spark, are in their league, and but their willing ministers. We thought that at the Second Bull Run, at the Antietam, and at Fredericksburg on the 11th of December, we had heard heavy cannonading; they were but holiday salutes compared with this.

Besides the great ceaseless roar of the guns, which was but the background of the others, a million various minor sounds engaged the ear. The projectiles shriek long and sharp. They hiss, they scream, they growl, they sputter,—all sounds of life and rage; and each has its different note, and all are discordant. Was ever such a chaos of sound before? We note the effect of the enemy's fire among the batteries and along the crest. We see the solid shot strike axle, or pole, or wheel, and the tough iron and heart of oak snap and fly like straws. The great oaks there by Woodruff's guns heave down their massy branches with a crash, as if the lightning had smote them. The shells swoop down among the battery horses, standing there apart; a half dozen horses start, they tremble, their legs stiffen, their vitals and blood smear the ground.

And these shot and shells have no respect for men either. We see the poor fellows hobbling back from the crest, or unable to do so, pale and weak, lying on the ground, with the mangled stump of an arm or leg dripping their life-blood away, or with a cheek torn open or a shoulder smashed. And many, alas! hear not the roar as they stretch upon the ground with upturned faces and open eyes, though a shell should burst at their very ears. We saw them but a moment since, there among the flame, with brawny arms and muscles of iron, wielding the rammer and pushing home the cannon's plethoric load.

Strange freaks these round shot play! We saw a man coming up from the rear with his full knapsack on, and some canteens of water held by the straps in his hands. He was walking slowly, and with apparent unconcern, though the iron hailed around him. A shot struck the knapsack, and it and its contents flew thirty yards in every direction; the knapsack disappeared like an egg thrown spitefully against the rock. The soldier stopped, and turned about in puzzled surprise, put up one hand to his back to assure himself that the knapsack was not there, and then walked slowly on again unharmed, with not even his coat torn. Near us was a man crouching behind a small disintegrated stone, which was about the size of a common water-bucket. He was bent up, with his face to the ground, in the attitude of a pagan worshiper before his idol. It looked so absurd to see him thus, that I went and said to him: "Do not lie there like a toad,—why not go to your regiment and be a man?" He turned up his face with a stupid, terrified look upon me, and then without a word turned his nose again to the ground. An orderly that was with me at the time told me a few moments later, that a shot struck the stone, smashing it in a thousand fragments, but did not touch the man, though his head was not six inches from the stone.

All the projectiles that came near us were not so harmless. Not ten yards away from us a shell burst among some small bushes, where sat three or four orderlies, holding horses. Two of the men and one horse were killed. Only a few yards off a shell exploded over an open limber box in Cushing's battery, and almost at the same instant another shell over a neighboring box. In both the boxes the ammunition blew up with an explosion that shook the ground, throwing fire and splinters and shells far into the air and all around, and destroying several men. We watched the shells bursting in the air, as they came hissing in all directions. Their flash was a bright gleam of lightning radiating from a point, giving place in a thousandth part of a second to a small, white, puffy cloud, like a fleece of the lightest, whitest wool. These clouds were very numerous. We could not often see the shell before it burst, but sometimes, as we faced towards the enemy, and looked above our heads, the approach would be heralded by a prolonged hiss, which always seemed to me to be a line of something tangible, terminating in a black globe, distinct to the eye, as the sound had been to the ear. The shell would seem to stop, and hang suspended in the air an instant, and then vanish in fire and smoke and noise. We saw the missiles tear and plow the ground. All in rear of the crest for a thousand yards, as well as among the batteries, was the field of their blind fury.

Ambulances passing down the Taneytown road with wounded men were struck. The hospitals near this road were riddled. The house which was General Meade's headquarters was shot through several times, and a good many horses of officers and orderlies were lying dead around it. Riderless horses, galloping madly through the fields, were brought up, or down rather, by these invisible horse-tamers, and they would not run any more. Mules with ammunition, pigs wallowing about, cows in the pastures, whatever was animate or inanimate, in all this broad range, were no exception to their blind havoc. The percussion shells would strike and thunder, and scatter the earth, and their whistling fragments, the Whitworth bolts, would pound and ricochet, and bowl far away sputtering, with the sound of a mass of hot iron plunged in water; and the great solid shot would smite the unresisting earth with a sounding thud, as the strong boxer crashes his iron fist into the jaws of his unguarded adversary.

Such were some of the sights and sounds of this great iron battle of missiles. Our artillery men upon the crest budged not an inch, nor intermitted; but, though caisson and limber were smashed, and guns dismantled, and men and horses killed, there, amidst smoke and sweat, they gave back without grudge or loss of time in the sending, in kind whatever the enemy sent,—globe and cone and bolt, hollow or solid,—an iron greeting to the rebellion, the compliments of the wrathful Republic.

An hour has droned its flight since first the roar began. There is no sign of weariness or abatement on either side. So long it seemed, that the din and crashing around began to appear the normal condition of nature there, and fighting man's element. The general proposed to go among the men, and over to the front of the batteries; so at about two o'clock he and I started. We went along the lines of the infantry as they lay there flat upon the earth a little to the front of the batteries. They were suffering little, and were quiet and cool. How glad we were that the enemy were no better gunners, and that they cut the shell fuses too long. To the question asked the men: "What do you think of this?" the replies would be, "Oh, this is bully"; "We are getting to like it"; "Oh, we don't mind this." And so they lay under the heaviest cannonade that ever shook the continent, and among them a thousand times more jokes than heads were cracked. We went down in front of the line some two hundred yards, and as the smoke had a tendency to settle upon a higher plane than where we were, we could see near the ground distinctly all over the field, as well back to the crest where were our own guns, as to the opposite ridge where were those of the enemy. No infantry was in sight save the skirmishers, and they stood silent and motionless,—a row of gray posts through the field on one side, confronted by another of blue.

Under the grateful shade of some elm trees, where we could see much of the field, we made seats of the ground and sat down. Here all the more repulsive features of the fight were unseen by reason of the smoke. Man had arranged the scenes, and for a time had taken part in the great drama; but at last, as the plot thickened, conscious of his littleness, and inadequacy to the mighty part, he had stepped aside and given place to more powerful actors. So it seemed; for we could see no men about the batteries. On either crest we could see the great flaky streams of fire, and they seemed numberless, of the opposing guns, and their white banks of swift convolving smoke; but the sound of the discharges was drowned in the universal ocean of sound. Over all the valley, the smoke a sulphur arch, stretched its lurid space; and through it always, shrieking on their unseen courses, thickly flew a myriad of iron deaths. With our grim horizon on all sides round, toothed thick with battery flame, under that dissonant canopy of warring shells, we sat, and saw, and heard in silence. What other expression had we that was not mean, for such an awful universe of battle?

A shell struck our breastwork of rails up in sight of us, and a moment afterwards we saw the men bearing some of their wounded companions away from the same spot; and directly two men from there came down toward where we were, and sought to get shelter in an excavation near by, where many dead horses, killed in yesterday's fight, had been thrown. General Gibbon said to these men, more in a tone of kindly expostulation than of command: "My men do not leave your ranks to try to get shelter here. All these matters are in the hands of God, and nothing that you can do will make you safer in one place than another." The men went quietly back to the line at once. The general then said to me: "I am not a member of any church, but I have always had a strong religious feeling; and so, in all these battles, I have always believed that I was in the hands of God, and that I should be unharmed or not, according to his will. For this reason, I think it is, I am always ready to go where duty calls, no matter how great the danger."

Half-past two o'clock, an hour and a half since the commencement, and still the cannonade did not in the least abate; but soon thereafter some signs of weariness and a little slacking of fire began to be apparent upon both sides. First we saw Brown's battery retire from the line, too feeble for further battle. Its position was a little to the front of the line. Its commander was wounded, and many of its men were so, or worse; some of its guns had been disabled, many of its horses killed; its ammunition was nearly expended. Other batteries in similar cases had been withdrawn before, to be replaced by fresh ones, and some were withdrawn afterwards. Soon after the battery named had gone, the general started to return, passing towards the left of the division, and crossing the ground where the guns had stood. The stricken horses were numerous, and the dead and wounded men lay about, and as we passed these latter, their low, piteous call for water would invariably come to us, if they had yet any voice left. I found canteens of water near—no difficult matter where a battle has been—and held them to livid lips; and even in the faintness of death the eagerness to drink told of the terrible torture of thirst.

But we must pass on. Our infantry was still unshaken, and in all the cannonade suffered very little. The batteries had been handled much more severely. I am unable to give any figures. A great number of horses have been killed,—in some batteries more than half of all. Guns had been dismounted, a great many caissons, limbers, and carriages had been destroyed, and usually from ten to twenty-five men to each battery had been struck, at least along our part of the crest. Altogether the fire of the enemy had injured as much, both in the modes that I have stated, and also by exhausting our ammunition and fouling our guns, so as to render our batteries unfit for further immediate use. The scenes that met our eyes on all hands among the batteries were fearful. All things must end, and the great cannonade was no exception to the general law of earth. In the number of guns active at one time, and in the duration and rapidity of their fire, this artillery engagement up to this time must stand alone and pre-eminent in this war. It has not been often, or many times, surpassed in the battles of the world. 250 guns, at least, rapidly fired for two mortal hours! Cipher out the number of tons of gunpowder and iron that made these two hours hideous.

Of the injury of our fire upon the enemy, except the facts that ours was the superior position, if not better served and constructed artillery, and that the enemy's artillery hereafter during the battle was almost silent, we knew little. Of course, during the fight we often saw the enemy's caissons explode, and the trees, rent by our shot, crashing about his ears; but we can from them alone infer but little of general results. At three o'clock, almost precisely, the last shot hummed and bounded and fell, and the cannonade was over. The purpose of General Lee in all this fire of his guns—we know it now, we did not at the time so well—was to disable our artillery and break up our infantry upon the position of the Second Corps, so as to render them less an impediment to the sweep of his own brigades and divisions over our crest and through our lines. He probably supposed our infantry was massed behind the crest and the batteries; and hence his fire was so high and the fuses to his shells were cut so long, too long. The rebel general failed in some of his plans in this behalf as many generals have failed before, and will again.

The artillery fight over, men began to breathe more freely, and to ask: "What next, I wonder?" The battery men were among their guns, some leaning to rest and wipe the sweat from their sooty faces; some were handling ammunition boxes and replenishing those that were empty. Some batteries from the artillery reserve were moving up to take the places of the disabled ones; the smoke was clearing from the crest. There was a pause between acts, with the curtain down, soon rise upon the great final act and catastrophe of Gettysburg. We had passed by the left of the Second Division coming from the front; when we crossed the crest, the enemy was not in sight, and all was still. We walked slowly along in rear of the troops, by the ridge, cut off now from a view of the enemy or his position, and were returning to the spot where we had left our horses. General Gibbon had just said that he inclined to the belief that the enemy was falling back, and that the cannonade was only one of his noisy modes of covering the movement. I said that I thought that fifteen minutes would show that, by all his bowling, the rebel did not mean retreat. We were near our horses when we noticed Brigadier General Hunt, Chief of Artillery of the army, near Woodruff's battery, swiftly moving about on horseback, and apparently in a rapid manner giving some orders about the guns. Thought we, what could this mean? In a moment afterwards we met Captain Wessels, and the orderlies who had our horses; they were on foot leading the horses. Captain Wessels was pale, and he said, excited: "General, they say the enemy's infantry is advancing." We sprang into our saddles; a score of bounds brought us upon the all-seeing crest. To say that none grew pale and held their breath at what we and they then saw, would not be true. Might not six thousand men be brave and without shade of fear, and yet, before a hostile eighteen thousand, armed, and not five minutes' march away, turn ashy white?

None on that crest need now be told that the enemy is advancing! Every eye could see his legions, an overwhelming, resistless tide of an ocean of armed men, sweeping upon us! Regiment after regiment, and brigade after brigade, move from the woods and rapidly take their places in the lines forming the assault. Pickett's proud division, with some additional troops, holds their right; Pettigrew's (Heth's) their left. The first line, at short intervals, is followed by a second, and that a third succeeds; and columns between support the lines. More than half a mile their front extends; more than a thousand yards the dull gray masses deploy, man touching man, rank pressing rank, and line supporting line. Their red flags wave; their horsemen gallop up and down; the arms of eighteen thousand men, barrel and bayonet, gleam in the sun,—a sloping forest of flashing steel. Right on they move, as with one soul, in perfect order, without impediment of ditch or wall or stream, over ridge and slope, through orchard and meadow and cornfield, magnificent, grim, irresistible. All was orderly and still upon the crest; no noise and no confusion. The men had little need of commands; for the survivors of a dozen battles knew well enough what this array in front portended, and, already in their places, they would be prepared to act when the right time should come. The click of the locks as each man raised the hammer to feel with his finger that the cap was on the nipple; the sharp jar as a musket touched a stone upon the wall when thrust, in aiming, over it; and the clinking of the iron axles, as the guns were rolled up by hand a little further to the front, were quite all the sounds that could be heard. Cap boxes were slid around to the front of the body; cartridge boxes opened; officers opened their pistol holsters. Such preparation, little more, was needed.

The trefoil flags, colors of the brigade and divisions, moved to their places in rear; but along the lines in front, the grand old ensign that first waved in battle at Saratoga, in 1777, and which these people coming would rob of half its stars, stood up, and the west wind kissed it as the sergeants sloped its lance towards the enemy. I believe that not one above whom it then waved but blessed his God that he was loyal to it, and whose heart did not swell with pride towards it, as the emblem of the Republic, before that treason's flouting rag in front.

General Gibbon rode down the lines, cool and calm, and in an unimpassioned voice he said to the men: "Do not hurry, men, and fire too fast; let them come up close before you fire, and then aim low and steadily." The coolness of their general was reflected in the faces of his men.

Five minutes had elapsed since first the enemy had emerged from the woods,—no great space of time, surely, if measured by the usual standards by which men estimate duration,—but it was long enough for us to note and weigh some of the elements of mighty moment that surrounded us: the disparity of numbers between the assailants and the assailed; that, few as were our numbers, we could not be supported or reinforced until support would not be needed, or would be too late; that upon the ability of the two trefoil divisions to hold the crest, and repel the assault, depended not only their own safety or destruction, but also the honor of the Army of the Potomac and defeat or victory at Gettysburg. Should these advancing men pierce our line, and become the entering wedge, driven home, that would sever our army asunder, what hope would there be afterwards, and where the blood-earned fruits of yesterday? It was long enough for the rebel storm to drift across more than half the space that had first separated it from us. None, or all, of these considerations either depressed or elevated us. They might have done the former, had we been timid; the latter, had we been confident and vain. But we were there waiting and ready to do our duty; that done, results could not dishonor us.

Our skirmishers open a spattering fire along the front, and, fighting, retire upon the main line—the first drops, the heralds of the storm, sounding upon our windows. Then the thunders of our guns, first Arnold's, then Cushing's and Woodruff's and the rest, shake and reverberate through the air, and their sounding shells smite the enemy. The general said I had better go and tell General Meade of this advance. To gallop to General Meade's headquarters, to learn there that he had changed them to another part of the field, to despatch to him by the Signal Corps, in General Gibbon's name, the message, "The enemy is advancing his infantry in force upon my front," and to be again upon the crest, were but the work of a minute.

All our available guns are now active, and from the fire of shells as the range grows shorter and shorter, they change to shrapnel, and from shrapnel to canister; but in spite of shells and shrapnel

and canister, without wavering or halt, the hardy lines of the enemy
continue to move on. The rebel guns make no reply to ours, and no
charging shout rings out today, as is the rebel wont; but the courage of these silent men amid our shot seems not to need the
stimulus of other noise. The enemy's right flank sweeps near Stannard's bushy crest, and his concealed Vermonters rake it with a
well-delivered fire of musketry. The gray lines do not halt or reply,
but withdrawing a little from that extreme they still move on. And
so across all that broad, open ground they have come, nearer and
nearer, nearly half the way, with our guns bellowing in their faces,
until now a hundred yards, no more, divide our ready left from
their advancing right. The eager men there are anxious to begin.
Let them. First Harrow's breastworks flame, then Hall's, then
Webb's. As if our bullets were the fire coals that touched off their
muskets, the enemy in front halts and his countless level barrels
blaze back upon us. The Second Division is struggling in battle.
The rattling storm soon spreads to the right, and the blue trefoils
are vying with the white.

All along each hostile front, a thousand yards, with narrowest
space between, the volleys blaze and roll; as thick the sound as
when a summer hailstorm pelts the city roofs; as thick the fire as
when the incessant lightning fringes a summer cloud. When the
rebel infantry had opened fire our batteries soon became silent,
and this without their fault, for they were foul by long previous
use. They were the targets of the concentrated rebel bullets, and
some of them had expended all their canister; but they were not
silent before Rhorty was killed, Woodruff had fallen mortally
wounded, and Cushing, firing almost his last canister, had
dropped dead among his guns, shot through the head by a bullet.
The conflict is left to the infantry alone.

Unable to find my general when I had returned to the crest after
transmitting his message to General Meade, and while riding in the
search, having witnessed the development of the fight from the first
fire upon the left by the main lines, until all of the two divisions
were furiously engaged, I gave up hunting as useless,—I was convinced General Gibbon could not be on the field; I left him
mounted; I could easily have found him now had he so remained,
but now, save myself, there was not a mounted officer near the

engaged lines,—and was riding towards the right of the Second Division, with purpose to stop there, as the most eligible position to watch the further progress of the battle, then to be ready to take part, according to my own notions, wherever and whenever occasion was presented. The conflict was tremendous, but I had seen no wavering in all our line.

Wondering how long the rebel ranks, deep though they were, could stand our sheltered volleys, I had come near my destination, when—great heaven! were my senses mad?—the larger portion of Webb's brigade.—my God, it was true,—there by the group of trees and the angles of the wall, was breaking from the cover of the works, and without order or reason, with no hand uplifted to check them, was falling back, a fear-stricken flock of confusion! The fate of Gettysburg hung upon a spider's single thread! A great, magnificent passion came on me at the instant; not one that overpowers and confounds, but one that blanches the face and sublimes every sense and faculty. My sword that had always hung idle by my side, the sign of rank only, in every battle, I drew, bright and gleaming, the symbol of command. Was not that a fit occasion and those fugitives the men on whom to try the temper of the Solingen steel? All rules and properties were forgotten, all considerations of person and danger and safety despised; for, as I met the tide of those rabbits, the damned red flags of the rebellion began to thicken and flaunt along the wall they had just deserted, and one was already waving over the guns of the dead Cushing. I ordered those men to "halt," and "face about," and "fire" and they heard my voice, and gathered my meaning, and obeyed my commands. On some unpatriotic backs, of those not quick of comprehension, the flat of my sabre fell, not lightly; and at its touch their love of country returned, and with a look at me as if I were the destroying angel, as I might have become theirs, they again faced the enemy.

General Webb soon came to my assistance. He was on foot, but he was active, and did all that one could do to repair the breach or to avert its calamity. The men that had fallen back, facing the enemy, soon regained confidence and became steady. This portion of the wall was lost to us, and the enemy have gained the cover of the reverse side, where he now stormed with fire. But Webb's men, with their bodies in part protected by the abruptness of the crest, now sent back in the enemy's faces as fierce a storm. Some scores of venturesome rebels that, in their first push at the wall, had dared to cross at the further angle, and those that had desecrated Cushing's guns, were promptly shot down, and speedy death met him who should raise his body to cross it again.

At this point little could be seen of the enemy, by reason of his cover and the smoke, except the flash of his muskets and his waving flags. Those red flags were accumulating at the wall every moment, and they maddened us as the same color does the bull. Webb's men were falling fast, and he is among them to direct and encourage; but, however well they may now do, with that walled enemy in front, with more than a dozen flags to Webb's three, it soon becomes apparent that in not many minutes they will be overpowered, or that there will be none alive for the enemy to overpower. Webb has but three regiments, all small,—the Sixty-ninth, Seventy-first, and Seventy-second Pennsylvania;—the One Hundred and Sixth Pennsylvania, except two companies, is not here today,—and he must have speedy assistance, or this crest will be lost. Oh! where is Gibbon,—where is Hancock,—some general, anybody, with the power and the will to support this wasting, melting line? No general came, and no succor! I thought of Hayes upon the right; but from the smoke and roar along his front, it was evident he had enough upon his hands, if he stayed the inrolling tide of the rebels there. Doubleday upon the left was too far off, and too slow, and on another occasion I had begged him to send his idle regiments to support another line, battling with thrice its numbers, and this "Old Sumter Hero" had declined.

As a last resort I resolved to see if Hall and Harrow could not send some of their commands to reinforce Webb. I galloped to the left in the execution of my purpose, and as I attained the rear of Hall's line, from the nature of the ground there, and the position of the enemy, it was easy to discover the reason and the manner of this gathering of rebel flags in front of Webb. The enemy, emboldened by his success in gaining our line by the group of trees and the angle of the wall, was concentrating all his right against, and was further pressing, that point. There was the stress of his assault,—there would he drive his fiery wedge to split our line. In front of Harrow's and Hall's brigades he had been able to advance no nearer than when he first halted to deliver fire; and these commands had not yielded an inch. To effect the concentration before Webb, the enemy would march the regiment on his extreme right of each of his lines, by the left flank, to the rear of the troops, still halted and facing to the front, and so continuing to draw in his right. When they were all massed in the position desired, he would again face them to the front, and advance to the storming. This was the way he made the wall before Webb's line blaze with his battle flags, and such was the purpose then of his thick-crowding battalions. Not a moment must be lost.

Colonel Hall I found just in rear of his line, sword in hand, cool, vigilant, noting all that passed, and directing the battle of his brigade. The fire was constantly diminishing now in his front, in the manner, by the movement of the enemy, that I have mentioned, drifting to the right. "How is it going?" Colonel Hall asked me as I rode up. "Well, but Webb is hotly pressed, and must have support, or he will be overpowered. Can you assist him?" "Yes." "You cannot be too quick." "I will move my brigade at once." "Good." He gave the order, and in briefest time I saw five friendly colors hurrying to the aid of the imperiled three; and each color represented true, battle-tried men, that had not turned back from rebel fire that day or yesterday, though their ranks were sadly thinned. To Webb's brigade, pressed back as it had been from the wall, the distance was not great from Hall's right. The regiments marched by the right flank. Colonel Hall superintended the movement in person. Colonel Devereaux coolly commanded the Nineteenth Massachusetts,—his major, Rice, had already been wounded and carried off. Lieutenant Colonel Macy, of the Twentieth Massachusetts, had just had his left hand shot off, and so Captain Abbott gallantly led over this fine regiment; the Forty-second New York followed their excellent colonel, Mallon. Lieutenant Colonel Steele, Seventh Michigan, had just been killed, and this regiment, and the handful of Fifty-ninth New York, followed their colors. The movement, as it did, attracting the enemy's fire, and executed in haste, as it must be, was difficult; but in reasonable time, and in order that is serviceable, if not regular, Hall's men are fighting gallantly side by side with Webb's, before the all-important point.

I did not stop to see all this movement of Hall's, but from him I

went further to the left, to the First Brigade. General Harrow I did
not see, but his fighting men would answer my purpose as well.
The Nineteenth Maine, the Fifteenth Massachusetts, the Eighty-
second New York, and the shattered old thunderbolt, the First
Minnesota—poor Farrell was dying then upon the ground where
he had fallen—all men that I could find, I took over to the right at
the double quick. As we were moving to, and near, the other brigades of the division, from my position on horseback I could see
that the enemy's right, under Hall's fire, was beginning to stagger
and to break. "See," I said to the men, "see the 'chivalry,' see the
gray-backs run!" The men saw, and as they swept to their places
by the side of Hall's and opened fire, they roared, and this is a
manner that said more plainly than words,—for the deaf could
have seen it in their faces, and the blind could have heard it in
their voices,—the crest is safe!

The whole division concentrated, and changes of position, and
new phases, as well on our part as on that of the enemy, having, as
indicated, occurred, for the purpose of showing the exact present
posture of affairs some further description is necessary. Before
the Second Division the enemy is massed, the main bulk of his
force covered by the ground that slopes to his rear, with his front
at the stone wall. Between his front and us extends the very apex
of the crest. All there are left of the White Trefoil Division—yesterday morning there were 3800; this morning there were less than
3000 at this moment there are somewhat over 2000,—twelve regiments in three brigades, are below, or behind the crest, in such a
position that by the exposure of the head and upper part of the
body above the crest they can deliver their fire in the enemy's
faces along the top of the wall.

By reason of the disorganization incidental, in Webb's brigade,
to his men having broken and fallen back, as mentioned: in the
two other brigades to their rapid and difficult change of position
under fire; and in all the division, in part, to severe and continuous
battle; formation of companies and regiments in regular ranks is
lost. But commands, companies, regiments, and brigades are
blinded and intermixed,—an irregular, extended mass,—men
enough, if in order, to form a line of four or five ranks along the
whole front of the division. The twelve flags of the regiments wave

defiantly at intervals along the front. At the stone wall, at unequal distances from ours of forty, fifty or sixty yards, stream nearly double this number of battle flags of the enemy.

These changes accomplished on either side, and the concentration complete—although no cessation or abatement of the general din of conflict since the commencement had at any time been appreciable—now it was as if a new battle, deadlier, stormier than before, had sprung from the body of the old; a young phœnix of combat, whose eyes stream lightning, shaking his arrowy wings over the yet glowing ashes of his progenitor. The jostling, swaying lines on either side boil and roar and dash their foamy spray, two hostile billows of a fiery ocean. Thick flashes stream from the wall; thick volleys answer from the crest. No threats or expostulation now; only example and encouragement. All depths of passion are stirred, and all combative fire, down to their deep foundations. Individuality is drowned in a sea of clamor; and timid men, breathing the breath of the multitude, are brave. The frequent dead and wounded lie where they stagger and fall; there is no humanity for them now, and none can be spared to care for them. The men do not cheer, or shout—they growl; and over that uneasy sea, heard with the roar of musketry, sweeps the muttered thunder of a storm of growls.

Webb, Hall, Devereux, Mallon, Abbott, among the men where all are heroes, are doing deeds of note. Now the loyal wave rolls up as if it would overleap its barrier, the crest; pistols flash with the muskets. My "Forward to the wall!" is answered by the rebel counter-command, "Steady, men," and the wave swings back. Again it surges, and again it sinks. These men of Pennsylvania, on the soil of their own homesteads, the first and only ones to flee the wall, must be the first to storm it. "Major, lead, lead your men over the crest,—they will follow!" "By the tactics, I understand my place is in the rear of the men." "Your pardon, sir; I see your place is in rear of the men. I thought you were fit to lead. Captain Suplee, come on with your men." "Let me first stop this fire in the rear, or we shall be hit by our own men." "Never mind the fire in the rear; let us take care of this in front first." "Sergeant, forward with your color. Let the rebels see it close to their eyes once more before they die."

The color sergeant of the Seventy-second Pennsylvania, grasping the stump of the severed lance in both his hands, waved the flag above his head, and rushed toward the wall. "Will you see your color storm the wall alone?" One man only started to follow. Almost half way to the wall, down go color bearer and color to the ground,—the gallant sergeant is dead. The line springs; the crest of the solid ground, with a great roar, heaves forward its maddened load,—men, arms, smoke, fire, a fighting mass; it rolls to the wall; flash meets flash; the wall is crossed; a moment ensues of thrusts, yells, blows, shots, an undistinguished conflict, followed by a shout, universal, that makes the welkin ring again; and the last and bloodiest fight of the great battle of Gettysburg is ended and won.

Many things cannot be described by pen or pencil; such a fight is one. Some hints and incidents may be given, but a description or picture, never. From what is told, the imagination may for itself construct the scene; otherwise he who never saw, can have no adequate idea of what such a battle is.

When the vortex of battle passion had subsided, hopes, fears, rage, joy, of which the maddest and the noisiest was the last, and we were calm enough to look about us, we saw that, as with us, the fight with the Third Division was ended; and that in that division was a repetition of the scenes immediately about us. In that moment the judgment almost refused to credit the senses. Are these abject wretches about us, whom our men are now disarming, and driving together in flocks, the jaunty men of Pickett's Division, whose steady lines and flashing arms, but a few moments since, were sweeping up the slope to destroy us? Are these red cloths that our men toss about in derision the "fiery Southern crosses," thrice ardent, the battle-flags of the rebellion that waved defiance at the wall? We know, but so sudden has been the transition we yet can scarce believe.

Just as the fight was over, and the first outburst of victory had a little subsided, when all in front of the crest was noise and confusion, prisoners being collected, small parties in pursuit of them far down into the field, flags waving, officers giving quick, sharp commands to their men, I stood apart for a few moments upon the crest, by that group of trees which ought to be historic forever, a spectator of the thrilling scenes around. Some few musket shots were still heard in the Third Division; and the enemy's guns, almost silent since the advance of his infantry, until the moment of his defeat, were dropping a few sullen shells among friend and foe upon the crest,—rebellion fosters such humanity.

Near me, saddest sight of the many of such a field, and not in keeping with all this noise, were mingled, alone, the thick dead of Maine, and Minnesota, and Michigan, and Massachusetts, and the Empire and Keystone States, who, not yet cold, with the blood still oozing from their death wounds, had given their lives to the country upon that stormy field. So mingled upon that crest let their honored graves be. Look, with me, about us. These dead have been avenged already. Where the long lines of the enemy's thousands so proudly advanced, see now how thick the silent men of gray are scattered. It is not an hour since those legions were sweeping along so grandly,—now sixteen hundred of their fiery mass are strewn among the trampled grass, dead as the clods they load; more than seven thousand, probably eight thousand, are wounded, some there with the dead in our hands, some fugitive far towards the woods, among them Generals Pettigrew, Garnett, Kemper and Armistead, the last three mortally, and the last one in our hands,— "Tell General Hancock," he said to Lieutenant Mitchell, Hancock's aide-de-camp, to whom he handed his watch, "that I know I did my country a great wrong when I took up arms against her, for which I am sorry, but for which I cannot live to atone."

Four thousand not wounded are prisoners of war; more in number of the captured than the captors. Our men are still gathering them in. Some hold up their hands, or a handkerchief, in sign of submission; some have hugged the ground to escape our bullets, and so are taken; few made resistance after the first moment of our crossing the wall; some yield submissively with good grace, some with grim, dogged aspect, showing that, but for the other alternative, they would not submit to this. Colonels, and all less grades of officers, in the usual proportions, are among them, and all are being stripped of their arms. Such of them as escaped wounds and capture are fleeing, routed and panic-stricken, and disappearing in the woods.

Small arms, more thousands than we can count, are in our hands, scattered over the field. And these defiant battle-flags, some inscribed with "First Manassas," "South Mountain," "Sharpsburg" (our Antietam), "Fredericksburg," "Chancellorsville," and many more names, our men have, and are showing about—over thirty of them.

Such was really the closing scene of the grand drama of Gettysburg. After repeated assaults upon the right and the left, where, and in all of which, repulse had been his only success, this persistent and presuming enemy forms his chosen troops, the flower of his army, for a grand assault upon our center. The manner and the result of such assault have been told,—a loss to the enemy of from 12,000 to 14,000 killed, wounded and prisoners, and of over thirty battle-flags. This was accomplished by not over 6000 men, with a loss on our part of not over 2,500 killed and wounded.

Would to Heaven Generals Hancock and Gibbon could have stood there where I did, and have looked upon that field! It would have done two men, to whom the country owes much, good to have been with their men in that moment of victory, to have seen the results of those dispositions which they had made, and of that splendid fighting which men schooled by their discipline had executed. But they are both severely wounded, and have been carried from the field. One person did come that I was glad to see there; and he was no less than Major General Meade, whom the Army of the Potomac was fortunate enough to have at that time to command it. See how a great general looked upon the field, and what he said and did, at the moment, and when he learned of his great victory.

To appreciate the incident I give, it should be borne in mind that one coming up from the rear of the line, as did General Meade, could have seen very little of our own men, who had now crossed the crest, and although he could have heard the noise he could not have told its occasion, or by whom made, until he had actually attained the crest. One who did not know results, so coming, would have been quite as likely to have supposed that our line there had been carried and captured by the enemy, so many gray rebels were on the crest, as to have discovered the real truth. Such mistake was really made by one of our own officers as I shall relate.

General Meade rode up, accompanied alone by his son, who is his aide-de-camp,—an escort, if select, not large for a commander of such an army. The principal horseman was no bedizened hero of some holiday review, but he was a plain man, dressed in a serviceable summer suit of dark blue cloth, without badge or ornament, save the shoulder straps of his grade, and a light, straight sword of a general, or general staff officer. He wore heavy high top boots and buff gauntlets, and his soft black felt hat was slouched down over his eyes. His face was very white, not pale, and the lines were marked and earnest, and full of care. As he arrived near me, coming up the hill, he asked in a sharp, eager voice, "How is it going here?" "I believe, General, the army is repulsed," I answered. Still approaching, and a new light began to come upon his face, of gratified surprise, with a touch of incredulity, of which his voice was also the medium, he further asked, "What! is the assault entirely repulsed?" his voice quicker and more eager than before. "It is, sir," I replied.

By this time he was on the crest, and when his eye had for an instant swept over the field, taking in just a glance of the whole,— the masses of prisoners, the numerous captured flags, which the men were derisively flaunting about, the fugitives of the routed enemy disappearing with the speed of terror in the woods,—partly at what I had told him, partly at what he saw, he said impressively, and his face was lighted, "Thank God." And then his right hand moved as if he would have caught off his hat and waved it; but this gesture he suppressed, and instead he waved his hand, and said "Hur–rah!" The son, with more youth in his blood, and less rank upon his shoulders, snatched off his cap and roared out his three "hurrahs" right heartily. The general then surveyed the field some minutes in silence. He at length asked who was in command. He had heard that Hancock and Gibbon were wounded, and I told him that General Caldwell was the senior officer of the corps, and General Harrow of the division. He asked where they were, but before I had time to answer that I did not know, he resumed. "No matter; I will give my orders to you, and you will see them executed." He then gave directions that the troops should be re-formed as soon as practicable, and kept in their places, as the enemy might be mad enough to attack again; he also gave directions concerning the posting of some reinforcements, which he said would soon be there, adding, "If the enemy does attack, charge him in the flanks and sweep him from the field,—do you understand?" The general, then a gratified man, galloped in the direction of his headquarters.

Then the work of the field went on. First the prisoners were collected and sent to the rear. "There go the men," the rebels were heard to say by some of our surgeons who were in Gettysburg, at the time Pickett's division marched out to take position—"there go the men that will go through your damned Yankee lines for you." A good many of them did "go through our lines for us," but in a very different way from the one they intended,—not impetuous victors, sweeping away our thin line with ball and bayonet, but crestfallen captives, without arms, guarded by the truce bayonets of the Union, with the cheers of their conquerors ringing in their ears. There was a grain of truth, after all, in this rebel remark. Collected, the prisoners began their dreary march, a miserable, melancholy stream of dirty gray to pour over the crest to our rear. Many of their officers were well dressed, fine, proud gentlemen, such men as it would be a pleasure to meet when the war is over. I had no desire to exult over them, and pity and sympathy were the general feelings of us all over the occasion. The cheering of our men, and the unceremonious handling of the captive flags, were probably not gratifying to the prisoners, but not intended for taunt or insult to the men; they could take no exception to such practices.

When the prisoners were turned to the rear and were crossing the crest, Lieutenant-Colonel Morgan, General Hancock's chief of staff, was conducting a battery from the artillery reserve towards the Second Corps. As he saw the men in gray coming over the hill, he said to the officer in command of the battery, "See up there; the enemy has carried the crest. See them come pouring over. The old Second Corps has gone, and you had better get your battery away from here as quickly as possible, or it will be captured." The officer was actually giving the order to his men to move back, when closer observation discovered that the graybacks that were coming had no arms, and then the truth flashed upon the minds of the observers. The same mistake was made by others.

In view of the results there that day,—the successes of the arms of the country,—would not the people of the whole country, standing then upon the crest with General Meade, have said with him, "Thank God"?

I have no knowledge, and little notion, of how long a time elapsed from the moment the fire of the infantry commenced until the enemy was entirely repulsed in this his grand assault. I judge, from the amount of fighting, that probably the fight was of nearly an hour's duration, but I cannot tell, and I have seen none who knew. The time seemed but a very few minutes when the battle was over.

When the prisoners were cleared away, and order was again established upon the crest, where the conflict had impaired it, until between five and six o'clock, I remained upon the field directing troops to their positions, in conformity to the orders of General Meade. The enemy appeared no more in front of the Second Corps; but while I was engaged as I have mentioned, further to our left some considerable force of the enemy moved out and made a show of attack. Our artillery, now in good order again, in due time opened fire, and the shells scattered the "Butternuts," as clubs do the gray snow-birds of winter, before they came within range of our infantry. This, save unimportant outpost firing, was the last of the battle.

Of the pursuit of the enemy, and the movements of the army subsequent to the battle, until the crossing of the Potomac by Lee, and the closing of the campaign, it is not my purpose to write. Suffice it, that on the night of the 3d of July the enemy withdrew his left, Ewell's corps, from our front, and on the morning of the 4th we again occupied the village of Gettysburg, and on that national day victory was proclaimed to the country; that floods of rain on that day prevented army movement of any considerable magnitude, the day being passed by our army in position upon the field, in burying our dead and some of those of the enemy, and in making the movements already indicated; that on the 5th the pursuit of the enemy was commenced, his dead were buried by us, and the corps of our army, upon various roads, moved from the battlefield.

With a statement of some of the results of the battle, as to losses and captures, and of what I saw in riding over the field when the army was gone, my account is done.

Our own losses in "killed, wounded, and missing" I estimate at 23,000. Of the "missing" the larger proportion were prisoners lost on the 1st of July. Our loss in prisoners, not wounded, probably was 4,000. The losses were distributed among the different army corps about as follows: In the Second Corps, which sustained the heaviest loss of any corps, a little over 4,500, of whom the "missing" were a mere nominal number; in the First Corps, a little over 4,000, of whom a good many were "missing"; in the Third Corps, 4,000, of whom some were "missing"; in the Eleventh Corps, 4,000, of whom the most were "missing"; and the rest of the loss, to make the aggregate mentioned, were shared by the Fifth, Sixth and Twelfth Corps and the cavalry. Among these the "missing" were few, and the losses of the Sixth Corps and the cavalry were light. I do not think the official reports will show my estimate of our losses to be far from correct, for I have taken great pains to question staff officers upon the subject, and have learned approximate numbers from them. We lost no gun or flag, that I have heard of, in all the battle. Some small arms, I suppose, were lost on the 1st of July.

The enemy's loss in killed, wounded, and prisoners I estimate at 40,000, and from the following data, and for the following reasons: so far as I can learn we took 10,000 prisoners, who were not wounded,—many more than these were captured, but several thousands of them were wounded. I have, so far as practicable, ascertained the number of dead the enemy left upon the field, approximately, by getting the reports of different burying parties. I think the dead upon the field were 5,000, almost all of whom, save those killed on the 1st of July, were buried by us, the enemy not having them in their possession. In looking at a great number of tables of killed and wounded in battles, I have found that the proportion of the killed to the wounded is as one to five, or more than five; rarely less than five. So with the killed at the number stated, 25,000 would probably be wounded; hence the aggregate that I have mentioned. I think 14,000 of the enemy, wounded and unwounded, fell into our hands. Great numbers of his small arms, two or three guns, and forty or more—was there ever such bannered harvest?—of his regimental battleflags, were captured by us. Some day, possibly, we may learn the enemy's loss, but I doubt if he will ever tell truly how many flags he did not take home with him. I have great confidence, however, in my estimates, for they have been carefully made, and after much inquiry, and with no desire or motive to overestimate the enemy's loss.

The magnitude of the armies engaged, the number of the casualties, the object sought by the rebel, the result, will all contribute to give Gettysburg a place among the great historic battles of the world. That General Meade's concentration was rapid,—over thirty miles a day were marched by several of the corps,—that his position was skilfully selected, and his dispositions good, that he fought the battle hard and well, that his victory was brilliant and complete, I think all should admit. I cannot but regard it as highly fortunate to us, and commendable in General Meade, that the enemy was allowed the initiative, the offensive in the main battle; that it was much better to allow the rebel, for his own destruction, to come up and smash his lines and columns upon the defensive solidity of our position, than it would have been to hunt him, for the same purpose, in the woods, or to unearth him from his rifle-pits. In this manner our losses were lighter, and his heavier, than if the case had been reversed. And whatever the books may say of troops fighting the better who make the attack, I am satisfied that in this war, Americans, the rebels as well as ourselves, are best on the defensive. The proposition is deducible from the battles of the war, I think, and my observation confirms it.

But men there are who think that nothing was gained or done well in this battle, because some other general did not have the command, or because any portion of the army of the enemy was permitted to escape capture or destruction. As if one army of a hundred thousand men could encounter another of the same number, of as good troops, and annihilate it! Military men do not claim or expect this; but the sensational paragraphers do; the doughty knights of purchasable newspaper quills; the formidable warriors from the brothels of politics; men of much warlike experience against—honesty and honor; of profound attainments in—ignorance; who have the maxims of Napoleon, whose spirit they as little understand as they do most things, to quote to prove all things; but who, unfortunately, have much influence in the country and with the government, and so over the army. It is very pleasant for these people, no doubt, at safe distances from guns, in the enjoyment of a lucrative office, or of a fraudulently obtained government contract, surrounded by the luxuries of their own firesides, where mud and flooding storms and utter weariness never penetrate, to discourse of battles, and how campaigns should be conducted, and armies of the enemy should be destroyed.

But it should be enough, perhaps, to say that men here or elsewhere, who have knowledge enough of military affairs to entitle them to express an opinion on such matters, and accurate information enough to realize the nature and the means of this desired destruction of Lee's army, before it crossed the Potomac into Virginia, will be most likely to vindicate the Pennsylvania campaign of General Meade, and to see that he accomplished all that could have been reasonably expected of any general, of any army. Complaint has been, and is, made specifically against Meade, that he did not attack Lee near Williamsport, before he had time to withdraw across the river. These were the facts concerning the matter:

The 13th of July was the earliest day when such an attack, if practicable at all, could have been made. The time before this, since the battle, had been spent in moving the army from the vicinity of the field, finding something of the enemy, and concentrating before him. On that day the army was concentrated, and in order of battle, near the turnpike that leads from Sharpsburg to Hagarstown, Md., the right resting at or near the latter place, the left near Jones's Cross-roads, some six miles in the direction of Sharpsburg, and in the following order from left to right: the Twelfth Corps, the Second, the Fifth, the Sixth, the First, the Eleventh,—the Third being in reserve behind the Second.

The mean distance to the Potomac was some six miles, and the enemy was between Meade and the river. The Potomac, swelled by the recent rain, was boiling and swift and deep, a magnificent place to have drowned all this rebel crew. I have not the least doubt but that General Meade would have liked to drown them all, if he could, but they were unwilling to be drowned, and would fight first. To drive them into the river, then, they must first be routed.

General Meade, I believe, favored an attack upon the enemy at this time, and he summoned his corps commanders to a council upon the subject. The First Corps was represented by Wadsworth; the Second by William Hays; the Third by French; the Fifth by Sykes; the Sixth by Sedgwick; the Eleventh by Howard; the Twelfth by Slocum; and the cavalry by Pleasanton. Of the eight generals, three, Wadsworth, Howard and Pleasanton, were in favor of immediate attack; and five, Hays, French, Sykes, Sedgwick, and Slocum, were not in favor of attack until better information was obtained of the position and situation of the enemy. Of the pros, Wadsworth only temporarily represented the First Corps, in the brief absence of Newton, who, had a battle occurred, would have commanded; Pleasanton, with his horses, would have been a spectator only; and Howard had lost so large a portion of the Eleventh Corps at Gettysburg, that he could scarcely have been relied upon to do effective work with his command. Such was the position of those who felt sanguinely inclined. Of the cons, were all of the fighting generals of the fighting corps save the First. This, then, was the feeling of these generals: All who would have had no responsibility or part, in all probability, hankered for a fight; those who would have had both part and responsibility, did not. The attack was not made.

At daylight on the morning of the 14th, strong reconnaissances from the Twelfth, Second and Fifth Corps were the means of discovering that between the enemy, except a thousand or fifteen hundred of his rear-guard, who fell into our hands, and the Army of the Potomac, rolled the rapid unbridged river. The rebel general Pettigrew was here killed. The enemy had constructed bridges, had crossed during all the preceding night, but so close were our cavalry and infantry upon him in the morning that the bridges were destroyed before his rear guard had all crossed.

Among the considerations influencing these generals against the propriety of attack at that time were probably the following: The army was wearied and worn down by four weeks of constant forced marching or battle, in the midst of heat, mud, and drenching showers, burdened with arms, accoutrements, blankets, sixty to a hundred cartridges, and five to eight days' rations. What such weariness means, few save soldiers know. Since the battle the army had been constantly diminished by sickness or prostration, and by more straggling than I ever saw before. Poor fellows! they could not help it. The men were near the point where further efficient physical exertion was quite impossible. Even the sound of the skirmishing, which was almost constant, and the excitement of impending battle, had no effect to arouse for an hour the exhibition of their wonted former vigor.

The enemy's loss in battle, it is true, had been far heavier than ours; but his army was less weary than ours, for in a given time since the first of the campaign it had marched far less, and with lighter loads. The rebels are accustomed to hunger and nakedness, customs to which our men do not take readily. And the enemy had straggled less, for the men were going away from battle, and towards home; and for them to straggle was to go into captivity, whose end they could not conjecture. The enemy were somewhere in position, in a ridgy, wooded country, abounding in strong defensive positions, his main bodies concealed, protected by rifle-pits and epaulements acting strictly on the defensive. His dispositions, his positions, even, with any considerable degree of accuracy, were unknown; nor could they be known, except by reconnaissances in such force, and carried to such extent, as would have constituted them attacks, liable to bring on at any moment a general engagement, and at places where we were least prepared, and least likely to be successful.

To have had a battle there, then, General Meade would have had to attack a cunning enemy in the dark, where surprises, undiscovered rifle-pits and batteries, and unseen bodies of men, might have met his forces at every point. With his not greatly superior numbers, under such circumstances, had General Meade attacked, would he have been victorious? The vote of those generals at the council shows their opinion. My own is, that he would have been repulsed with heavy loss, with little damage to the enemy. Such a result might have satisfied the bloody politicians better than the end of the campaign as it was; but I think the country did not need that sacrifice of the Army of the Potomac at that time,— that enough odor of sacrifice came up to its nostrils from the First Fredericksburg field to stop their snuffing for some time. I felt the probability of defeat strongly at the time, when we all supposed a conflict would certainly ensue; for always before a battle, at least it so appears to me, some dim presentiment of results, some unaccountable foreshadowing, pervades the army,—I never knew the result to prove it untrue,—which rests with the weight of conviction. Whether such shadows are cause, or consequence, I shall not pretend to determine; but when, as they often are, they are general, I think they should not be wholly disregarded by the commanders. I believe the Army of the Potomac is always willing, often eager, to fight the enemy, whenever, as it thinks, there is a fair chance for victory; that it always will fight, let come victory or defeat, whenever it is ordered so to do.

Of course, the army, both officers and men, had very great disappointment and very great sorrow that the rebel escaped,—so it was called,—across the river. The disappointment was genuine, at least to the extent that disappointment is like surprise; but the sorrow, to judge by looks, tones and actions, rather than by words, was not of that deep, sable character for which there is no balm. Would it be an imputation upon the courage or patriotism of this army if it was not rampant for fight at this particular time and under the existing circumstances? Had the enemy stayed upon the left bank of the Potomac twelve hours longer there would have been a great battle there near Williamsport, on the 14th of July. After such digression, if such it is, I return to Gettysburg.

As good generalship is claimed for General Meade in this battle, so was the conduct of his subordinate commanders good. I know and have heard of no bad conduct or blundering on the part of any officer, unless the unauthorized movement of General Sickles, on the 2d of July, may be so characterized. . . . The Eleventh Corps was outnumbered and outflanked on the first day, and when forced to fall back from their position, did not do it with the firmness and steadiness which might have been expected of veteran troops. With this exception, and some minor cases of very little consequence in the general result, our troops, whenever and wherever the enemy came, stood against them with storms of impassable fire. Such was the infantry, such the artillery. The cavalry did less, but it did all that was required.

The enemy, too, showed a determination and valor worthy of a better cause; their conduct in this battle even makes me proud of them as Americans. They would have been victorious over any but the best of soldiers. Lee and his generals presumed too much upon some past successes, and did not estimate how much they were due, on their part, to position, as at Fredericksburg, or on our part to bad generalship, as at the Second Bull Run and Chancellorsville.

The fight of the 1st of July we do not, of course, claim as a victory; but even that probably would have resulted differently had Reynolds not been struck. The success of the enemy in the battle ended with the 1st of July. The rebels were joyous and jubilant, —so said our men in their hands, and the citizens of Gettysburg,— at their achievements on that day. Fredericksburg and Chancellorsville were remembered by them. They saw victory already won, or only to be snatched from the "raw Pennsylvania Militia," as they thought they were when they saw them run; and already the spires of Baltimore and the dome of the national capitol were forecast upon their glad vision, only two or three days' march away through the beautiful valleys of Pennsylvania and "my" Maryland. Was there ever anything so fine before! How pleasant it would be to enjoy the poultry and the fruit, the meats, the cakes, the beds, the clothing, the whiskey, without price, in this rich land of the Yankee! It would indeed!

But on the 2d of July something of a change came over the spirit of their dreams. They were surprised at results, and talked less and thought more, as they prepared supper that night. After the fight of the 3d, they talked only of the means of their own safety from destruction. Pickett's splendid division had been almost annihilated, they said; and they talked not of how many were lost, but of who had escaped. They talked of those "Yanks" that had clubs on their flags and caps,—the trefoils of the Second Corps, that are like clubs in cards.

The battle of Gettysburg is distinguished in this war, not only as by far the greatest and severest conflict that has occurred, but for some other things that I may mention. The fight of the 2d of July, on the left, which was almost a separate and complete battle, is, so far as I know, alone in the following particulars: the numbers of men engaged at one time, and the enormous losses that occurred in killed and wounded, in the space of about two hours. If the truth could be obtained, it would probably show a much larger number of casualties in this, than my estimate in a former part of these sheets. Few battles of the war have had so many casualties altogether as those of the two hours on the 2d of July. The 3d of July is distinguished. Then occurred the "great cannonade,"—so we call it, and so it would be called in any war and in almost any battle. And besides this, the main operations that followed have few parallels in history, none in this war, of the magnitude and magnificence of the assault, single and simultaneous, the disparity of numbers engaged, and the brilliancy, completeness, and overwhelming character of the result in favor of the side numerically the weakest. I think I have not, in giving the results of this encounter, overestimated the number or the losses of the enemy. We learned on all hands, by prisoners, and by their newspapers, that over two divisions moved up to the assault,—Pickett's and Pettigrew's,—that this was the first engagement of Pickett's in the battle, and the first of Pettigrew's save a light participation on the 1st of July. The rebel divisions usually number nine or ten thousand, or did at that time, as we understood. Then I have seen something of troops, and think I can estimate the number somewhat. The number of rebels killed here I have estimated in this way: The second and third divisions of the Second Corps buried the rebel dead in their own front, and where they fought upon their own grounds. By count they buried over 1,800. I think no more than about 200 of these were killed on the 2d of July in front of the Second Division, and the rest must have fallen upon the 3d. My estimates that depend upon this contingency may be erroneous, but to no great extent. The rest of the particulars of this assault, our own losses and our captures, I know are approximately accurate. Yet the whole sounds like romance, a grand stage-piece of blood.

Of all the Corps d'Armée, for hard fighting, severe losses, and brilliant results, the palm should be, as by the army it is, awarded to the "Old Second." It did more fighting than any other corps, inflicted severer loss upon the enemy, in killed and wounded, and sustained a heavier like loss; and captured more flags than all the rest of the army, and almost as many prisoners as the rest of the army. The loss of the Second Corps in killed and wounded in this battle—there is no other test of hard fighting—was almost as great as that of all General Grant's forces, in the battles that preceded, and in the siege of Vicksburg. Three eighths of the whole corps were killed and wounded. Why does the Western Army suppose that the Army of the Potomac does not fight? Was ever a more absurd supposition? The Army of the Potomac is grand! Give it good leadership—let it alone—and it will not fail to accomplish all that reasonable men desire.

Of Gibbon's white trefoil division, if I am not cautious, I shall speak too enthusiastically. This division has been accustomed to distinguished leadership. Sumner, Sedgwick, and Howard, have honored, and been honored by, its command. It was repulsed under Sedgwick at Antietam, and under Howard at Fredericksburg; it was victorious under Gibbon at the Second Fredericksburg, and at Gettysburg. At Gettysburg its loss in killed and wounded was over 1,700, near one-half of all engaged; it captured seventeen battle-flags and 2,300 prisoners. Its bullets hailed on Pickett's division and killed or mortally wounded four rebel generals,—Barksdale on the 2d of July, with the three on the 3d, Armistead, Garnett, and Kemper. In losses, in killed and wounded, and in capture from the enemy of prisoners and flags, it stands pre-eminent among all the divisions at Gettysburg.

Under such generals as Hancock and Gibbon brilliant results may be expected. Will the country remember them? Attempts have been made to give the credit of saving the day at Gettysburg to this and that officer who participated in the battle, and even the President is believed to have been deceived by unfounded claims. But in the light of this truthful narrative can either the President or the country be insensible of the transcendent merit of General Meade and his brave subordinates?

About six o'clock on the afternoon of the 3d of July, my duties done upon the field, I quitted it to go to the general. My brave horse Dick—poor creature! his good conduct in the battle that afternoon had been complimented by a brigadier,—was a sight to see. He was literally covered with blood. Struck repeatedly, his right thigh had been ripped open in a ghastly manner by a piece of shell, and three bullets were lodged deep in his body; and from his wounds the blood oozed and ran down his sides and legs, and with the sweat formed a bloody foam. Dick's was no mean part in that battle. Good conduct in men under such circumstances as he was placed might result from a sense of duty; his was the result of his bravery. Most horses would have been unmanageable, with the flash and roar of arms about, and the shouting. Dick was utterly cool, and would have obeyed the rein had it been a straw. To Dick belongs the honor of first mounting that stormy crest before the enemy, not forty yards away, whose bullets smote him; and of being the only horse there during the heat of the battle. Even the enemy noticed Dick, and one of their reports of the battle mentions the "solitary horseman," who rallied our wavering line. He enabled me to do twelve times as much as I could have done on foot. It would not be dignified for an officer on foot to run; it is entirely so, mounted, to gallop. I do not approve of officers dismounting in battle, which is the time of all when they most need to be mounted, for thereby they have so much greater facilities for being everywhere present. Most officers, however, in close action, dismount. Dick deserves well of his country, and one day should have a horse monument. If there be an equine Elysium, I will send to Charon the brass coin, the fee for Dick's passage over, that on the other side of the Styx, in those shadowy clover fields, he may nibble the blossoms forever.

To find the general was no easy matter. I inquired for both Generals Hancock and Gibbon,—I knew well enough that they would be together,—and for the hospitals of the Second Corps. Oh, sorrowful was the sight to see so many wounded! The whole neighborhood in rear of the field became one vast hospital, of miles in extent. Some could walk to the hospitals; such as could not were taken upon stretchers, from the places where they fell, to selected points, and thence the ambulances bore them, a miserable load, to their destination. Many were brought to the buildings along the Taneytown road, and, too badly wounded to be carried further, died, and were buried there; Union and rebel soldiers together. At every house and barn and shed the wounded were; by many a cooling brook, on many a shady slope or grassy glade, the red flags beckoned them to their tented asylums; and there they gathered in numbers, a great army; a mutilated, bruised mass of humanity. Men with gray hair and furrowed cheeks, and soft-lipped, beardless boys, were there; for these bullets have made no distinction between age and youth. Every conceivable wound that iron and lead can made, blunt or sharp, bullet, ball and shell, piercing, bruising, tearing, was there; sometimes so light that a bandage and cold water would restore the soldier to the ranks again; sometimes so severe that the poor victim in his hopeless pain, remediless save by the only panacea for all mortal sufferings, invoked that.

The men are generally cheerful, and even those with frightful wounds often are talking with animated faces of nothing but the battle and the victory; but some were downcast, their faces distorted with pain. Some have undergone the surgeon's work; some, like men at a ticket office, awaiting patiently their turn, to have an arm or a leg cut off. Some walk about with an arm in a sling; some sit idly upon the ground; some at full length lie upon a little straw, or a blanket, with their brawny, now blood-stained, limbs bare, and you may see where the minie bullet has struck, or the shell has torn. From a small round hole upon many a manly breast the red blood trickles; but the pallid cheek, the hard-drawn breath and dim-closed eyes, tell how near the source of life it has gone. The surgeons with coats off and sleeves rolled up, and the hospital attendants with green bands upon their caps, are about their work; and their faces and clothes are spotted with blood; and though they look weary and tired, their work goes systematically and steadily on. How much and how long they have worked, the piles of legs, arms, feet, hands, fingers, about, partially tell. Near by appears a row of small fresh mounds placed side by side. They were not there day before yesterday; they will become more numerous every day.

Such things I saw as I rode along. At last I found the generals. General Gibbon was sitting in a chair that had been "borrowed" somewhere, with his wounded shoulder bare, and an attendant was bathing it with cold water. General Hancock was near by in an ambulance. They were at the tents of the Second Corps hospitals, which were on Rock Run. As I approached General Gibbon, when he saw me he began to "hurrah," and wave his right hand; he had heard the result. I said: "O General! long and well may you wave"; and he shook me warmly by the hand. General Gibbon was struck by a bullet in the left shoulder, which had passed from the front, through the flesh, and out behind, fracturing the shoulder blade, and inflicting a severe but not dangerous wound. He thinks he was the mark of a sharp shooter of the enemy, hid in the bushes near where he and I had sat so long during the cannonade; and he was wounded and taken off the field before the fire of the main lines of infantry had commenced; he being, at the time he was hit, near the left of his division. General Hancock was struck a little later, near the same part of the field, by a bullet piercing and almost going through his thigh, without touching the bone, however. His wound was severe, also. He was carried back out of range, but before he would be carried off the field he lay upon the ground in sight of the crest, where he could see something of the fight, until he knew what would be the result. And there, at General Gibbon's request, I had to tell him and a large voluntary crowd of the wounded who pressed around. I never had so enthusiastic an audience before. Cries of "good!" "glorious!" frequently interrupted me, and the storming of the wall was applauded by enthusiastic tears, and the waving of battered, bloody hands.

On the 6th of July, while my bullet bruise gained in the battle, was yet too inflamed and sensitive for me to be good for much in the way of duty,—the division was then halted for the day some four miles from the field on the Baltimore turnpike,—I could not repress the desire or omit the opportunity to see again where the battle had been. Never elsewhere upon any field have I seen such abundant evidences of a terrific fire of cannon and musketry as upon this. Along the enemy's position, where our shells and shot had struck during the cannonade of the Third, the trees had cast their trunks and branches as if they had been icicles shaken by a blast; and graves of the rebels' making, and dead horses, and scattered accoutrements, showed that other things besides trees had been struck by our projectiles. Along the slope of Culp's Hill, in front of the position of the Twelfth, and the First Division of the First Corps, the trees were almost literally peeled, from the ground up some fifteen or twenty feet, so thick upon them were the scars the bullets had made. Upon a single tree, in several instances not over a foot and a half in diameter, I actually counted as many as two hundred and fifty bullet marks. Such were the evidences of the storm under which Ewell's bold rebels assaulted our breastworks on the night of the 2d and the morning of the 3d of July. And those works looked formidable, zig-zagging along those rocky crests, even now, when not a musket was behind them. What madness on the part of the enemy to have attacked them!

All was bustle and noise in the little town of Gettysburg as I entered it on my tour of the field. From the afternoon of the 1st to the morning of the 4th of July, the enemy was in possession. Very many of the inhabitants had, upon the first approach of the enemy, or upon the retirement of our troops, fled their homes, and the town, not to return until after the battle. Now the town was a hospital, where gray and blue mingled in about equal proportions. The public buildings, the court house, the churches, and many private dwellings, were full of wounded. There had been in some of the streets a good deal of fighting; and shells had riddled the houses from side to side. And the rebels had done their work of pillage there, too. In spite of the smooth-sounding general order of the rebel commander, enjoining a sacred regard for private property,—the order was really good, and would sound marvelously well abroad, or in history,—all stores of drugs and medicine, of clothing, tinware, and all groceries, had been rifled and emptied, without pay or offer of recompense. Libraries, public and private, had been entered, and the books scattered about the yards, or destroyed. Great numbers of private dwellings had been entered and occupied without ceremony, and whatever was liked had been appropriated, or wantonly destroyed. Furniture had been smashed and beds ripped open, and apparently unlicensed pillage had reigned. But the people, the women and children that had fled, were returning, or had returned, to their homes,—such homes!—and mid the general havoc were restoring, as they could, order to the desecrated firesides. I heard of no more than one or two cases of personal injury received by any of the inhabitants. One woman was said to have been killed while at her washtub, sometime during the battle; but probably by a stray bullet, coming a very long distance, from our own men. For the next hundred years Gettysburg will be rich in legends and traditions of the battle. I rode through the cemetery on Cemetery Hill. How those quiet sleepers must have been astounded in their graves when the twenty-pound Parrott guns thundered over them, and the solitary shot crushed their grave-stones! I stood solitary upon the crest by "the trees," where less than three days ago I had stood before; but now how changed is all the eye beholds. Do these thick mounds cover the fiery hearts that in the battle rage swept the crest and stormed the wall? I read their names,—them, alas, I do not know,—but I see the regiments marked on their frail monuments,—"20th Mass. Vols.," "69 P.V.," "1st Minn. Vols.," and the rest,—they are all represented, and, as they fought, commingle here. So I am not alone,—these, my brethren of the fight are with me. Sleep, noble brave! The foe shall not desecrate your sleep. Yonder thick trenches will hold them. As long as patriotism is a virtue, and treason a crime, your deeds have made this crest, your resting place, hallowed ground.

11

FORREST'S PURSUIT AND CAPTURE
OF STREIGHT

By Robert Selph Henry

Nathan Bedford Forrest is perhaps most renowned for enunciating the tactical precept of "get there first with the most men." And he was personally a combat officer par excellence. Perhaps few general officers in all history have exerted so much personal leadership as he did.

Forrest was a man unaffected by odds, a man wholly dedicated to the simple tactical doctrine of "attack!" Nowhere is his personality better displayed or his leadership better exemplified than in the assignment given him to cut off the Federal raid under the command of Colonel Streight. In the gripping account that follows, Colonel Henry conveys all the desperate urgency and all the fierce energy of this intense cavalry leader.

The destruction of the Southern granaries and limited industrial facilities was always prominent in General Rosecran's thinking. It was regarded as crucial that Forrest, with his small force should thwart those efforts. Here, in extremely graphic style, is tactical crisis at its dramatic best.

In mid-April of 1863 the Union armies in the West began to use against the Confederates the pattern of long-distance cavalry raid developed by Forrest and Morgan, driving deep into enemy-held territory to strike at remote bases and lines of communication and supply.

Two such raids were launched simultaneously. One, that of Colonel B. H. Grierson of Illinois, from the vicinity of Memphis through the length of the state of Mississippi, was a distinct success in disturbing and disrupting Confederate communications at the critical time when Grant was transferring his army across the Mississippi and establishing himself in the rear of Vicksburg.

The other, that of Colonel Abel D. Streight of Indiana, starting from Nashville with intent to travel a circuit of nearly 1,000 miles by steamboat and muleback to get into north Georgia and there "cut the railroads which supply the rebel army by Chattanooga," ended in failure and captivity.

Streight had the longer and more difficult road to follow. He had, too, the problem of finding and fighting his way back—or rather, would have had, could he have reached his objective—while Grierson had only to keep going south to come out at Baton Rouge, Louisiana, already held by Union forces coming up the river from below. Grierson, moreover, had the good fortune to strike a virtual vacuum in the Confederate defenses, while Streight was to meet the fierce resistance of Forrest—an experience which was to be reserved for Grierson until the following year at Okolona and Brice's Cross Roads.

Streight's "Independent Provisional Brigade designed for special secret service" was made up of four regiments of infantry from Indiana, Ohio and Illinois, who were to be mounted, and two companies raised in north Alabama but designated as Middle Tennessee Cavalry (Union). On the afternoon of April tenth, as Van Dorn and Forrest were falling back from their fruitless demonstration against Franklin, Streight's command filed down to the steamboat landing at Nashville, loaded their stores, and drove aboard the 800 quartermaster mules on which a portion of the command hoped to ride diagonally across northern Alabama into Georgia. The balance of the command, it was planned, was to be mounted on horses and mules gathered up in the countryside through which they were to pass—one purpose of the expedition being, as was explained in a book published afterward by Colonel Streight, "to cripple the enemy" by "seizing the animals whose labor furnished subsistence for the rebel armies."

On the morning of the eleventh, Streight's flotilla of eight transports backed out from the landing at Nashville, turned in the stream and "sped irresistibly along," as one member of the expedition described the scene, "before the mighty force of the river's current and power of the steam engine," with the "spiral columns of white steam ascending from the exhaust pipes . . . forming behind us, over vale and hill, a milky track of the circuitous course of the Cumberland."

That evening the boats landed at a "heap of black and charred ruins" which "in the palmy days of peace" had been the village of Palmyra. There men and mules disembarked, while the steamers proceeded down the Cumberland to the Ohio, where they were to pick up forage and rations, and come up the Tennessee to Fort Henry, to which point the command was to march overland, gathering up horses and mules on the way.

At Palmyra the idyllic humors of the morning's start from Nashville first began to fade. It was discovered that the mules brought down on the boat were not so good as they should have been, many of them being wild and unbroken. It was found, also, that the infantrymen who were to ride them "were at first very easily dismounted, frequently in a most undignified and unceremonious manner." A day and a half were spent at Palmyra in this manner of equestrian exercise, while parties were out scouring the country for additional mounts.

At noon on the fifteenth, the day appointed to meet the boats, Streight arrived at Fort Henry, having picked up some 500 mounts as he marched across from Palmyra, and having lost through distemper and exhaustion about 100 of those with which he had left Nashville. At Fort Henry Streight met his first delay when the fleet failed to put in its appearance until the evening of the sixteenth. That night was spent in loading the 2,000 men and 1,200 animals aboard and, on the morning of April seventeenth—the same day on which Grierson left La Grange, near Memphis, on his raid into Mississippi—Streight's expedition started southward, up the Tennessee River to Eastport, Mississippi, head of navigation at the then stage of water.

At Eastport Streight was to meet an expedition under Brigadier General Grenville M. Dodge, sent out from Corinth to advance beyond the Muscle Shoals section of north Alabama as a screen and blind behind which he could disembark, complete his preparations and get started across the state of Alabama to his first objective at Rome, Georgia. The original plan called for the meeting on the sixteenth, but the delayed start and further delays to the fleet on account of low water prevented Streight from reaching the rendezvous until the afternoon of Sunday, April 19, late on his schedule by three full days.

Dodge, meanwhile, had moved out to Bear Creek, twelve miles above Eastport, with some 7,500 men. Thither Streight repaired on Sunday evening, leaving the unloading and coralling of his precious mules to subordinates. Returning to the bivouac at Eastport at midnight, he found that there had been a stampede among the mules, and that 400 had escaped. Two days were spent trying to round up the scattered mules, of which only about half were recovered—another two days lost on the schedule.

It was not until the morning of the twenty-second, therefore, that Streight moved up to the rear of Dodge's command, whose eastward advance up the Tennessee Valley was intended to cover Streight's movements until he was in position to cut loose on his independent dash for Georgia, to distract Confederate attention from that move and, if the move should be discovered, to keep the Confederates too busy to follow him.

During the nearly two weeks in which Streight was on the move from Nashville to Eastport, and getting started from there into Alabama, neither his movements nor those of Dodge were of concern to Forrest. A scout did report the passage of transports with troops up the Tennessee River on the seventeenth. Colonel P. D. Roddey, the Confederate commander at Tuscumbia, Alabama, engaged in stubborn resistance to the advance of Dodge in that direction, and relayed another scout's report that "transports were landing an army at Eastport" on the nineteenth. Both reports were duly passed on to General Joseph E. Johnston, supervising all Confederate Western operations, at his headquarters in Chattanooga.

Thus it happened that while Union forces from Mississippi and Tennessee, numbering nearly 10,000 altogether, were moving into northwestern Alabama against Roddey's 1,200 Confederate cavalry, Van Dorn and Forrest were left at Spring Hill, watching the Federal forces at Franklin. Relations between them, which had been growing more and more strained during the two months of their service together, came near to an open flare-up of personal encounter on the very last day on which they were to be together. That there was no such open break and the reasons why there was not reflect the good sense and patriotism of two high-strung, high-tempered soldiers of opposite and clashing temperaments.

Three accounts of this incident have come down, all from members of General Van Dorn's staff. From them it appears that Van Dorn reproached Forrest with having permitted some member of his staff to write articles for the Chattanooga *Rebel*, in which the honors at Thompson's Station were claimed for Forrest rather than Van Dorn, and with having improperly reported property captured at Brentwood which he now refused to turn over to the army authorities, as ordered. The story, as told by General Van Dorn to Captain H. F. Starke of his staff immediately after the incident, goes on:

". . . without mincing matters, I called his attention to the reports I had heard, and accused him of misrepresentation at headquarters. This he warmly denied and expressed his conviction of my too great willingness to listen to stories to his discredit. One thing led to another, until at length I threw off all restraint and directly expressing my belief in his treachery and falsehood, suggested that then and there was as good a time and place to settle our difficulties as any, and suiting the action to the word, I stepped to where my sword was hanging against the wall, snatched it down and turned to face him.

"Forrest (said Van Dorn with a smile) was really a sight to see. He had risen and advanced one step, his sword half drawn from its scabbard, and his face aflame with feeling. But even as I unsheathed my own sword and advanced to meet him, a wave of some kind seemed to pass over his countenance; he slowly returned his sword to its sheath, and steadily regarding me said, 'General Van Dorn, you know I'm not afraid of you—but I will not fight you—and leave you to reconcile with yourself the gross wrongs you have done me. It would never do for two officers of our rank to set such an example to the troops, and I remember, if you forget, what we both owe to the cause.'

" 'I never felt so ashamed of myself in my life,' General Van Dorn went on to say, 'and recalled by Forrest's manly attitude and words to our true position, I immediately replied that he was right, and apologized for having used such expressions to him. And so we parted to be somewhat better friends, I believe, than we have been before. Whatever else he may be, the man certainly is no coward.' "

While it may be doubted that General Van Dorn gave to the conversation quite the literary finish with which it was afterward reported by his staff officer to the Confederate Veterans' Association, there can be no doubt that from the incident Van Dorn gained, as he said, "a higher opinion of General Forrest than I have ever held before."

About eleven o'clock on the night of April twenty-third—the day, probably, of the near-clash between the Confederate commanders—orders from General Bragg reached Forrest at Spring Hill to take his Old Brigade southward to the Tennessee River, there to join Roddey and to take command of the combined forces opposing the threatening advance of Dodge's Union force. No one on the Confederate side, as yet, was concerned with what Streight was up to.

Before daylight of the twenty-fourth, the advance of the brigade was under way for the Tennessee River. Thirty-six hours later the brigade was ninety miles away, at Brown's Ferry, below Decatur, Alabama. There Dibrell's Eighth Tennessee, with a section of guns under John Morton, was detached to work down the north bank of the river to Florence, with orders to block any attempt on the part of Dodge to cross over or, if no such attempt developed, to make such a demonstration as might make Dodge apprehensive of a Confederate crossing to the south bank.

With the remainder of the brigade Forrest ferried the broad Tennessee on the twenty-sixth, and on the twenty-seventh marched westward through Courtland and on to the vicinity of Town Creek, between that point and Tuscumbia. There, on the twenty-eighth, Forrest joined Roddey in an all-day resistance to the crossing of that stream by Dodge's force.

That day's fighting at long range, in truth, was but part of the Union plan to give Streight a good start on his way to Georgia. The twenty-fifth and twenty-sixth he had passed at Tuscumbia, where the medical officers gave his command a thorough going-over, checking every man for physical fitness for the grind ahead. Through this winnowing his strength was reduced to 1,500 men, but they were picked men. At the same time he was furnished by Dodge with 200 more mules and six ammunition and ration wagons, according to Streight's account, or with 500 mules and twelve wagons, according to the account of Dodge. This left him still short mounts for 150 men.

At eleven o'clock on the night of Sunday the twenty-sixth, the day on which Forrest crossed the Tennessee River, Streight's column slipped out of Tuscumbia, heading south to Russellville, where it was to turn eastward to Moulton. The march was made in a hard rain and through mud and darkness which, Streight reported, made progress slow, especially as the pace of the mounted men was held down, both to permit the men on foot to keep up and to afford an opportunity for parties to scour the country along both sides of the line of march to bring in additional mounts.

All day of the twenty-seventh Streight's men plodded along through the hill country that lies to the south of the broad and level Tennessee Valley. That night, having made thirty-four miles from the starting point, the advance encamped at the village of Mount Hope in Lawrence County, where Streight received word from General Dodge that the Confederates had been driven off up the valley, and that he should push on. Not until ten o'clock in the morning of the twenty-eight, however, did all Streight's command come up to Mount Hope. More delay.

During that day James Moon, an intrepid scout of Roddey's headed northwest for the battle along Town Creek with the news that a column which he estimated at 2,000 had left Mount Hope that morning, marching toward Moulton, which would put them well into the rear of Forrest's left flank. The information reached Forrest at dusk, just about the time that Streight, by this time having all but fifty of his men mounted, was marching into Moulton.

At midnight of the twenty-eighth Streight marched away from Moulton, headed southeastward toward Blountsville by way of Day's Gap. During the same night Forrest's camp, a day's march north of Moulton, was a scene of most intense activity. From the fragmentary information which came in through scouts, and from his own observation of the course of the day's fighting along Town Creek, he had arrived at the sound conclusion that Dodge's force was but a blind, and that the real threat was from Streight. Still, with the limited knowledge which he had, it was not safe to hazard everything on such a conclusion. Roddey, therefore, was ordered to place his own command, plus Edmondson's Eleventh Tennessee and Julian's battalion, between Dodge and the assumed position of Streight's column, to prevent either from sending reinforcements to the other. Biffle's Eighth Tennessee and Starnes's Fourth Tennessee, temporarily under Major McLemore, with two of Morton's pieces and Ferrell's six-gun Georgia battery, which had been with Roddey, were told off for the pursuit of Streight. Orders were sent across the river to Dibrell to intensify his demonstration toward Dodge's rear, with the idea of causing him to retreat westward, while the remainder of the command was left in front of Dodge, to fight him if he came forward or to follow him if he fell back.

All night long these soldiers who for five days had marched and fought almost continuously worked to get ready for the test ahead. The portable forges of the farriers were fired up, and anvils rang as horses were shod. Ammunition was checked and inspected, the best animals were selected for the artillery and guns and caissons were double-teamed. Rations were cooked, two days' feed of shelled corn to be carried on the saddle was issued, supplies and gear of every sort were gone over, with Forrest himself planning, directing, overseeing the whole of the preparations. He did not know just who Streight was nor what he was up to but he did know that a formidable column was loose and headed into the South, where there were no Confederate forces, and that it had a long head start.

At dawn of the twenty-ninth Forrest marched for Moulton, some six hours after Streight had marched away from that little courthouse town of Lawrence County. Thirty-five miles Streight made that day, to rest in camp that night at the foot of Day's Gap, where the rough road climbed through a narrow and winding defile to the top of the plateau of Sand Mountain—the local name for the final southwestern extension of the great Appalachian chain.

"On the morning of April 30th, 1863," Colonel Streight's aide afterward wrote, the rains which had plagued their march were over and "the sun shone out bright and beautiful, as spring day's sun ever beamed; and from the smouldering camp fires of the previous night the mild blue smoke ascended in graceful curves, and mingled with the gray mist slumbering on the mountain tops above. The scene was well calculated to inspire and refresh the minds of our weary soldiers."

Colonel Streight, marching at the head of his column as it wound up the mountain, may well have felt some sense of elation, after all the vexatious delays of the three weeks since his men had marched aboard steamboats at Nashville. He had had good hunting the day before, with sufficient haul of horses and mules to mount his whole force at last, including the replacement of many of the failing and broken-down mules brought from Nashville. He was in a country of pronounced Union sympathies from which, indeed, most of the men of the two "Middle Tennessee" cavalry companies under Captain D. D. Smith had been recruited. "Many were the happy greetings between them and their friends and relations," he reported. He did not know that Dodge had begun his retirement to Corinth, Mississippi, the day before.

Ahead of Colonel Streight at sunrise on that last day of April 1863 the way seemed open to great results and much glory. Behind him, he thought, was the protection of Dodge's force to engage and hold off any possible Confederate pursuit—when, as he reached the top of the mountain two miles from his starting place, his ears were assailed by the boom of cannon.

Forrest, having marched a day and half the night to cover the fifty miles from the battle line along Town Creek, had bivouacked at midnight only four miles behind Streight, and at sunrise was driving in his rear.

The force immediately behind Streight was that which had been sent under Roddey to keep between him and Dodge, while the regiments of Biffle and Starnes were to climb the mountain by another gap to the northward and get upon Streight's flank or rear. Getting word of this movement, Streight put up a strong delaying fight with his rear guard at the head of the Gap, while the main column pushed ahead through a "country which was open, sand ridges, very thinly wooded, and afforded very fine defensive positions."

Selecting one such position, some three miles back from the brow of the mountain, Streight formed line of battle on a ridge, with his right resting on a precipitous ravine and his left on a marshy run. The mules and horses were sent to a place of safety in a ravine to the rear, skirmishers were sent out to front, flanks and rear, both to prevent surprise and "to prevent any straggling of either stray animals or cowardly men." The plan was for the rear guard, when everything was set, to retreat rapidly toward the center of the position, leading their pursuers into ambush.

The plan worked. As the Alabama Union cavalry fell back on the run, closely followed by Captain Bill Forrest's company of scouts, the Union lines rose from the underbrush where they lay and, with the addition of two 12-pounder mountain howitzers, poured into the charging Confederates a destructive fire. One of the wounded was Captain Forrest, who suffered a shattered thigh bone.

Reinforcements coming up, the Confederates advanced again, this time running the two guns of Morton's battery under Lieutenant Wills Gould to within 300 yards of the Union line. An effective countercharge by Streight's men drove the Confederates back in confusion, and ended in the capture of Gould's guns with their caissons—a fact which put Forrest in a towering, thunderous rage and which, indirectly, was nearly to cost him his life within the month.

As more and more Confederates came up after their terrific ride from the Tennessee River—barely 1,000 men had been in hand during the early stages of the battle at Day's Gap—Forrest formed a new line of battle for another charge to avenge the check his men had suffered and to recapture his guns. Raging up and down the line, he ordered the men to tie their horses to the saplings in the thin piny woods. No horseholders this time, he told them, and no use for horses if they did not bring back those guns.

At eleven o'clock in the morning, after a fight of some five hours, Streight decided that he had done enough fighting for the time and, fearing the approach of one of Forrest's flanking parties, skilfully withdrew from his position and "resumed the march," just in time to avoid Forrest's attack from the rear. The first blood and the first honors were Streight's, for, after all, his mission was not to fight barren battles on top of remote Sand Mountain but to make his way to Georgia and cut railroads.

Six miles beyond the battleground of the morning, with Forrest closing in on his rear again at Crooked Creek, Streight was compelled to lose time again by deploying in line of battle on a ridge called Hog Mountain, where, from about an hour before dark until about ten o'clock, Forrest attacked under a full moon, with the general order to his men to "shoot at everything blue and keep up the scare."

Forrest's force at Hog Mountain consisted of the Starnes and Biffle regiments, which had come up after their unsuccessful attempt to get in Streight's rear, the General's escort company, Captain Bill Forrest's scouts and the artillery. Edmondson's regiment had been sent away that afternoon to move parallel with Streight to the northward so as to head off any attempt to break back toward the Tennessee River in that direction, while Roddey and his men had been sent back to make sure that Dodge did not pounce upon Forrest's back as the latter had upon Streight's.

The Hog Mountain fight was one of bold and venturesome determination on both sides, carried on in the darkness by the light of the flashes of artillery and small arms. Forrest, leading in the very front of the fight, had horses shot under him three times. Finally, when a detachment of Biffle's regiment passed around Streight's flank and threatened his mule-holders, Streight once more "resumed the march," leaving behind the Confederate guns whose loss had so roused Forrest.

About midnight Streight set another ambush, leaving Lieutenant Colonel Gilbert Hathaway's Indiana regiment behind in a dense thicket alongside the road to check the pursuit by firing into it at short range. The ambush, Streight reported, caused "a complete stampede of the enemy," although Confederate accounts have it that the advanced point of the pursuing column sensed the ambush, which was located by scouts, and shelled out of the woods by two pieces of Ferrell's battery pushed forward by hand, without noise, along the road of soft sand shimmering in the moonlight.

Colonel Streight, as he explained, hoped that by "pushing ahead" he could get down from the top of Sand Mountain to a region where he "could feed before the enemy could come up with us, and, by holding him back where there was no feed, compel him to lay over at least a day to recuperate." Consequently, he marched on through the night. By two in the morning, however, Forrest was again crowding his rear to the point where it was necessary to halt, deploy and lay another ambush.

After another brisk affair in the moonlight Forrest halted until daylight to water and feed, and to give an opportunity for those with the weaker horses to close up. Meanwhile, Streight pushed on wearily to the village of Blountsville, forty-three miles from Day's Gap, where he arrived about ten in the morning of Friday, May first.

When Forrest's men took up the march again shortly after daylight of the same day, they had been on forced march or fighting ever since leaving Spring Hill a full week earlier. In the three days since they had arrived in front of Dodge at Town Creek, they had fought one day, worked one night, marched all the next day and night, and marched and fought still another day and most of the night.

The weariness with which men and horses picked up the march that morning can hardly be imagined. And yet pick it up they did, for Old Bedford led, and they picked it up with such spirit that well before noon, and before Streight's men finished feeding their animals in Blountsville, Forrest was driving in his rear pickets. The two commands went through the little village in a running fight and a whirl of dust. During his halt, Streight had sought to lighten his column by transferring ammunition from his wagons to pack mules and burning the wagons. So closely did Forrest press him, however, that the hungry Confederates managed to put out the fires before the store of provisions which the wagons had carried was entirely spoiled.

Beyond Blountsville, Streight took up the same tactics which he had developed the day before—marching ahead with his main body, setting ambushes with small parties of his rear guard and so forcing upon the pursuit a certain caution, at the same time continually scouring the country for mounts, both to supply himself and to insure that no fit animal should be left behind for the mounting of Forrest's men as their horses failed, using and then destroying bridges, obstructing the road. All these advantages of the pursued, Colonel Streight, an able man as well as brave, with a command of real soldiers, exploited with skill and persistence.

Beyond Blountsville the running fight went on all day until, late in the afternoon, Streight made another general stand to give the command a chance to get across the deep and difficult ford of the east branch of the Black Warrior River, under cover of the two howitzers emplaced upon the farther bank. From there he pushed wearily on toward Gadsden, plodding through the night "though the command was in no condition to do so," because of a report from scouts that another Confederate column was moving on a parallel road with evident intent to get ahead and cut him off. Forrest, on the other hand, sent no more than an advance guard forward to keep up the attack, while the main body was given three hours' rest at the crossing of the Warrior, refreshed somewhat by rations which Streight had lost when two of his pack mules drowned at the ford.

Marching again before midnight, Forrest was hard upon Streight's rear at the crossing of Big Will's Creek, in the valley below the southern point of Lookout Mountain. There Biffle's regiment, which had been in the advance, was allowed a short rest while the remainder of the command pushed on.

Four miles on in the direction of Gadsden, and about nine o'clock in the morning of May second—the ninth day of almost continuous fighting and marching for Forrest's men—Streight got across Black Creek on "a fine wooden bridge, which was afterwards burned by our rear guard. This, it was thought, would delay Forrest's forces long enough to enable us to reach Rome, Georgia, before he could again overtake us, as the stream was very deep and seemed to be unfordable."

While the bridge was yet burning, Forrest and his escort company, riding hell-for-leather at the head of the pursuing column, tore up to the stream, to be met with sharp fire from the opposite bank. It did look, for a moment, as if Forrest were balked. But only for a moment, for from a neighboring farmhouse, home of the Widow Sanson and her two daughters, came unexpected help.

"Can you tell me where I can get across that creek?" Forrest asked of Emma, sixteen-year-old daughter of the house.

Miss Emma knew, she said, of a trail about 200 yards above the bridge, and on the Sanson farm, where the cows sometimes crossed at low water, and offered to show it to the General if he would have a horse saddled for her.

"There is no time to saddle a horse; get up here behind me," he said, as he backed his mount up close to the bank on which she stood.

Over the momentary objection of her mother, who feared that "people would talk about" Emma if she went off with the soldiers, she swung up behind the General and guided him to the neighborhood of the lost ford, where, coming in sight of the Union sharpshooters, she suggested that they dismount to be less conspicuous. As they came close to the ford, creeping through the bushes, she happened to be in front. Forrest stepped ahead, saying, "I'm glad to have you for a pilot but I'm not going to make breastworks of you."

Amid a burst of fire—bullets passed through the billowing skirts of the young girl—she pointed out the marks and bearings of the ford. Returning to the house, Forrest ordered the widow and her daughters to seek safety from the Federal fire, while he went about the business of getting the command across the creek. When the Union forces marched on, fondly believing that they had placed an impassable stream between themselves and pursuit, the Sanson ladies returned to their house.

On the way they met Forrest, who told Emma that he had left a note for her in the house, asked for a lock of her hair, asked that they see that Robert Turner, a Confederate soldier killed in the skirmishing across the creek and "laid out" in their home, be buried in some near-by graveyard, got on his horse and with his men rode away in the implacable pursuit. "My sister and I sat up all night watching over the dead soldier who had lost his life fight-

ing for our rights," Emma Sanson wrote in the brave and simple
recital of her deed which she gave Doctor Wyeth thirty years afterward.

The note which Forrest left for her, written in a clear hand and
published in facsimile in Wyeth's *Forrest*, reads:

> "Hed Quaters in Sadle
> "May 2, 1863
> "My highest regardes to Miss Ema Sanson
> for hir gallant conduct while my posse was
> skirmishing with the Federals across Black
> Creek near Gadsden Alabama
> "N. B. Forrest
> "Brig. Genl   Comding N. Ala—"

Disappointed in their hope of some respite at Gadsden, east of
Black Creek, Streight's men seem to have believed that Forrest
was shown the ford by "a young man by the name of Sanson" who
had been "among a lot of prisoners captured by us in the morning
and paroled, who, as soon as set at liberty, made his way direct
to the pursuing force of General Forrest," in violation of his parole.
"From this incident," Streight's aide wrote, "the rebels manufactured the bit of romance" about Emma Sanson.

With Forrest at his heels Streight paused in Gadsden only long
enough to destroy army and commissary stores of the Confederacy
found there, and forced himself and his weary column on. "It
now became evident to me," Streight reported, "that our only hope
was in crossing the river at Rome and destroying the bridge, which
would delay Forrest a day or two and give us time to collect
horses and mules and allow the command a little time to sleep,
without which it was impossible to proceed."

From Turkeytown, eight miles east of Gadsden, therefore, he
dispatched "200 of the best mounted men selected from the whole
command," under Captain Milton Russell, to push ahead to Rome,
seize the bridge across the Oostanaula River there, and hold it until
the main command could come up.

Rome and rest looked a long way off but on Streight's men
plodded, in a continuous rear-guard skirmish all through the day
until four in the afternoon, by which time they had reached

Blount's plantation, twelve miles east of Gadsden. "Here I decided to halt," wrote Streight, "as it was impossible to continue the march through the night without feeding and resting." While details fed and watered the animals, the rest of the command formed line of battle on a ridge. After a skirmish in which Streight's second-in-command, Colonel Hathaway, was killed, Forrest drew back to a parallel ridge and began massing his men, Streight thought, for "a more determined attack."

The little battle at Blount's having revealed that much of the ammunition was worthless by reason of a wetting in fording some creek, and that much more was worthless because the paper cartridges had worn out and the powder had sifted away in the men's cartridge boxes or pockets, and darkness coming on, Streight decided to slip away "unobserved, if possible" and lay another ambush in a thicket half a mile to the rear.

The ambush failed when Forrest discovered it and started a flank movement around it. Streight and his men, many of them now without mounts and others with stock "jaded, tender-footed, and worn down," withdrew as silently as possible and started for another dreadful night of marching. After some delay for a skirmish at the village of Centre, they reached the ferry across the Chattooga River, a short distance above where it falls into the Coosa. Captain Russell had passed that way but had neglected to leave behind a guard for the means of crossing the considerable stream, and by the time the main body arrived citizens had spirited away the ferryboat.

The indomitable Streight turned wearily northward, with intent to cross on a bridge reported to be standing near Gaylesville, some seven or eight miles upstream. On the way it was necessary to cross extensive "coal choppings." Here the timber had been cut and burned for charcoal to supply the near-by Round Mountain Iron Furnace, where nearly 1,000 hands were engaged in making charcoal pig iron to be used by the foundry and machine shops at Rome in casting cannon and building engines for the Confederacy. One of Streight's scouting parties partially destroyed the furnace—the one tangible result achieved by the raiders—but the passage of the "choppings" that Saturday night was an ordeal which contributed to the disastrous end of the expedition as a whole.

The old choppings were a maze of wagon tracks running in all directions through the scrub second-growth timber. It was night, the guides were none too sure of their way at best, men and animals were staggering along, scattered, lost and wandering in a nightmare of utter confusion and weariness approaching exhaustion. Not until daylight did the command get across the Chattooga on Dyke's Bridge, which they burned, turned back southward toward the Rome road and pushed on beyond Cedar Bluff, with exhausted men and worn-out animals dropping by the wayside.

Toward nine o'clock on the morning of Sunday, May third, Streight decided that there was nothing for it but to halt for rest and feed, which he did at the plantation of Mrs. Lawrence in the Straightneck Precinct of Cherokee County, Alabama, and a little more than twenty miles short of his first objective at Rome, Georgia.

Through the Saturday night on which Streight's men toiled across the coal choppings, Forrest sent one squadron directly on their trail with orders to "devil them all night," while the remainder of the command took their rest.

While Forrest's men rested and Streight's toiled on, and Captain Russell's troop of 200 selected Federal soldiers pushed ahead to seize the bridges at Rome, messengers sent forward from Gadsden by Forrest were swinging well north of their line of march to reach Rome with warnings of their coming. Meanwhile, however, on the south side of the Coosa, a quick-witted volunteer was pushing forward on his own account to reach Rome first with the warning.

John H. Wisdom, forty-three-year-old rural mail carrier, returning from his rounds, drove up to the east bank of the Coosa River at 3:30 in the afternoon Saturday, to find the ferryboat (his own property, incidentally) sunk, and Gadsden, on the far side of the stream, in possession of Streight's raiders.

Hallooing across the river to a neighbor to tell his family that he was riding on to warn Rome of the approach of the Yankees, he turned his mail-driver's buggy and started on a ride of sixty-seven miles. Two hours later the approach of darkness found Wisdom and his rig twenty-two miles away at Gnatville. There the Widow Hanks undertook to care for his worn-out horse and to lend him a lame pony, the only mount she had, on condition that he ride it no farther than Goshen, five miles away, where he hoped to be able to get another horse.

At Goshen, twenty-seven miles from the start and forty miles from the finish, farmer Simpson Johnson let Wisdom have a horse for himself and sent his son along on another, to bring both back. Into the night Wisdom and young Johnson went at a swift gallop another eleven miles to the home of Preacher Joel Weems, at Spring Garden, where after some delay a new horse was had. Eleven miles farther the Weems horse carried Wisdom, on into Georgia, where, near Cave Spring, he left that horse with John Baker, from whom another was borrowed. Twelve miles the Baker horse made, when he too gave out, and, six miles from Rome, was replaced by another for the last lap. Just before midnight Wisdom galloped into Rome with his warning.

At the request of the local authorities he galloped through the streets to sound the alarm and waken the people. "Everybody jumped out of bed and the excitement was great," was the way Wisdom recalled the scene afterward. "A Citizen of Rome," writing in the Rome *Tribune* less than a week later, was stronger in his language. "Tremendous excitement, and be it said to the discredit of some, much liquor was wasted, doubtless to screw up their courage to the fighting point."

When the children heard "The Yankees are coming!" as one mother recalled the events of the night, they "jumped up and got under the bed. . . . There was one little girl who was terribly frightened. She had no idea whether the Yankees were men or horses, or what kind of animals they were. She just knew they were something dreadful."

"Bill Arp" (Major Charles H. Smith) in a nearly contemporary account of the Rome "battle" in the Atlanta *Southern Confederacy*, written in the style of dialect and unorthodox orthography so popular with humorists of the time, says that with the sounding of the alarm, "there were no panik, no skedadlin, no shakin of nees—but one universal determination to *do sumthin*. The burial squad organized fust and foremost and began to inter their money, and spoons and 4-pronged forks, and sich like about the premises."

Having buried valuables in one place, as one Roman lady re-
lated, "we would begin to imagine that because *we* knew where
these things were, the first Yankee that appeared would know too,
and often we would go and take them all up from there and dig
another hole and put them in that, so that our yards came to look
like graveyards."

Throughout the night and early morning hours, according to Bill
Arp's humorously exaggerated account, "reports were brought into
these Head Quarters, and all other quarters, to the effeck that 10,-
000 Yankees were kummin, and 5,000 and 2,000 and any other
number; that they were ten miles from town, and 6 miles, and 2
miles, and any other number of miles; that they were on the Alabama Road, and the Cave Spring Road, and the River road, and
any other road . . . that they had tuck the Steembote Laura
Moore, and Cherokee, and Alfaretta, and any other steembote;
that they had shot at a scout and hit him in the coat tail, or his
hosses tail, or any other tale. . . . In fak, a man could hear anything by gwine about, and more too."

But despite the intense excitement and real terror in the little city
which had never seen a Yankee soldier and, until Wisdom came
galloping in at midnight, had no idea there was one nearer than the
army lines 'way up in Tennessee, there did begin to emerge a state
of defense. There was no organized Home Guard in Rome, but
convalescent soldiers turned out from the military hospitals, and
citizens, including those from the neighboring country, were mustered with shotguns and squirrel rifles. The main dependence for
local defense, however, was upon cotton-bale barricades thrown
up across the bridges spanning the Etowah and Oostanaula Rivers,
which flow together at Rome to form the Coosa. Two ancient and
cranky cannon were resurrected and emplaced so as to sweep the
approaches to the bridges, it was hoped, while the roadway plank-
ing was covered with straw soaked in turpentine, to be fired if other
means of defense failed.

As the critical "Citizen of Rome" remarked, there was enough
preparation "to make a pretty formidable fight if they had been
under any sort of organization but the organization amounted to as
near none as possible." At that, while it would not have withstood
an attack pressed home by even a small body of troops, the show of

resistance resulting from Wisdom's warning did in fact play a considerable part in the final result of the Streight raid.

Shortly after sunrise on Sunday morning, May third, while Streight was still more than twenty miles to the westward, and just about the time Forrest's men were getting under way to close in for the kill, the advance party of the Union raiders, under Captain Russell, came over the crest of Shorter's Hill, within sight of Rome. Through their field glasses they saw the "fortifications" at the bridges and glimpsed the bustling activity in the town behind them. An old Negro woman, asked if there were any Confederate soldiers around, assured the invaders that the town was "full of sojers!" On the way Captain Russell had captured a garrulous mail carrier who, either believing or seeming to believe that the captain was a Confederate, had freely given him "much valuable information concerning the numbers and disposition of the troops and defenses of the city"—most of which were nonexistent. Captain Russell, therefore, "reconnoitered the defenses and military strength" of Rome, found them "indeed quite formidable," so reported by courier to his commander, and early on Sunday afternoon started back to join the main body.

Meanwhile, at sunrise of Sunday, Forrest and his men, now numbering fewer than 600 after their driving, punishing march all the way from Tennessee, rose from their rest, refreshed, and pushed on to Dykes Bridge. Finding the bridge burned, they forded the Chattooga, holding the ammunition high above their heads as they splashed across, and dragging the two guns of Ferrell's battery across on the bottom of the stream, with long ropes carried across to double teams on the far side—a method of crossing at which they had become adept in their pursuit of Streight across bridgeless streams.

By nine o'clock, but a short time after Streight had ended his all-night march with the halt at Mrs. Lawrence's, Forrest closed on his quarry. Even before Forrest struck, Streight had found it "almost impossible to keep the men awake long enough to feed." When his pickets were driven in, Streight abandoned breakfast for man and beast, and formed line of battle on a ridge a half-mile from the plantation house. "The command was immediately ordered into line," he reported, "and every effort made to rally the men for action, but nature was exhausted, and a large portion of my best troops actually went to sleep while lying in line of battle under a severe skirmish fire."

Sending McLemore to the right with the Fourth Tennessee, or what part of it had managed to stand the pace of the pursuit, and Biffle to the left with the Ninth Tennessee, Forrest and his escort, with a few troops besides, began a demonstration in the center against Streight's line.

His real reliance, though, was not on force with a two-to-one superiority of numbers against him, but on craft. Captain Henry Pointer of his staff was sent forward with a flag of truce to demand immediate surrender "to stop the further and useless effusion of blood."

"Most of my regimental commanders," Streight reported, "had already expressed the opinion that, unless we could reach Rome and cross the river before the enemy came up with us again, we should be compelled to surrender." A council of war was called to canvass the situation.

Streight knew that his men and mounts were "in a desperate condition," with not more than twenty of the animals drawn in Nashville still going, and the men "overcome with fatigue and loss of sleep." He believed, too, that he was "confronted by fully three times our number," a belief which Forrest was doing nothing to dispel. Sergeant William Haynes of the Fourth Tennessee, a young man of mien so solemn and inspiring of confidence that he was known by the nickname of "Parson," captured in the fighting of Saturday and closely questioned by Streight, had assured him that Forrest had with him his own brigade, Armstrong's, Roddey's and one or two other commands which Haynes could not recall. To add to all his other distress, word came to Streight that Captain Russell had been unable to take the bridge at Rome.

"Yielding to the unanimous voice of the regimental commanders," Streight asked for parley with Forrest, and they met in a patch of woods. Even then Streight refused Forrest's demand for surrender unless it could be demonstrated to him that he was indeed faced by a force superior to his own. At this juncture a section of Ferrell's battery, the only artillery Forrest had in reach, galloped up in full sight. When Streight protested against movement of troops nearer than a certain ridge while negotiations were going on under flag of truce, Forrest sent Captain Pointer to order the artillery back. The alert young captain, responding to a covert nod from his commander, enlarged upon the order to such an extent that the same two guns appeared, disappeared and reappeared at so many points as to seem almost a column of artillery.

As Forrest described the scene afterward, he was standing with his back to the guns, while Streight faced them. "I seen him all the time we was talking," Forrest is quoted as having said, "looking over my shoulder and counting the guns. Presently he said; 'Name of God! How many guns have you got? There's fifteen I've counted already!' Turning my head that way, I said, 'I reckon that's all that has kept up.' . . ."

As the conference continued, Forrest interspersed his talk with Streight with an occasional order to Captain Pointer for the disposition of some entirely imaginary command. Catching the spirit of the game, McLemore and Biffle, off the flanks, marched portions of their commands around and around the conical hills of that section until the weary and worried Streight, after returning for further consultation with his officers, finally came to the conclusion that the hills and hollows must be filled with armed Confederates.

Toward noon Streight yielded to the desire of his officers to give up the hopeless fight, and agreed to surrender upon condition that all his men be treated as prisoners of war, officers to retain side arms and personal baggage—terms which Forrest was perfectly willing to grant.

Forrest's men, indeed, were in but little better state than those whom Streight was so reluctantly surrendering. Streight's men were asleep in line of battle, it is true, but many of Forrest's were nodding as they stood with bridles in hand at the drooping heads of their horses. Forrest's men had come farther under forced draft, but they had been better handled, with the three opportunities for short rests which had been given them—and they were led by Forrest. But not until the arms were stacked, and Streight's officers and men were separated, with the Confederates interposed between them, could Forrest really breathe easy after his game of bluff.

The prisoners surrendered at Lawrence numbered 1,466. The

enlisted prisoners were put in charge of Biffle, whose regiment by that time was reduced to little more than 200 men, and were marched that afternoon to a bivouac halfway to Rome. With the officers in custody, Forrest pushed on to the town, on the way gathering in Captain Russell's force which he met as it marched back from its fruitless dash for the bridge. The addition of Russell's men brought the total bag of prisoners to nearly 1,700, or roughly three times the force Forrest had at hand.

Forrest, having sent couriers ahead to Rome with news of the surrender, reached there with the first batch of prisoners about six o'clock on Sunday evening, to be met with an exuberance of gratitude which insisted upon expressing itself, among other ways, in firing a salute from the guns which had been shotted and emplaced to rake the road from Alabama, along which Forrest himself was now coming—without remembering to remove the shot. Only bad aim prevented fatal results.

"I am told that when Forrest entered Rome with his prisoners," Kate Cumming wrote in her journal when she visited the hospitals there three months later, "he was met by the ladies and presented with a wreath of flowers, and the pathway of his gallant army was strewn with them."

"The excitement was worse than any camp meeting you ever saw," one Roman lady said of that evening. "Everybody was flying from one end of the town to the other. Suppers that were just ready to be cooked were never cooked or eaten; there was a general jollification. . . . Every lady insisted on going up and speaking to the General and shaking hands with him and his forces." Another account has it that several young women snipped off locks of his hair, and that had he yielded to the requests of all the ladies who asked for them, he would have been bald-headed.

When Mrs. George Ward went up to speak to the General, carrying her baby daughter, "he took her and kissed her. He told us that his prisoners were coming into town, and he wanted them to have rations. He said, also, that his own men had been riding hard . . . and he wanted something for them to eat at once."

Forrest was ever the quartermaster and commissary, and not even the exultance of conquest, the vast weariness of the flesh which must have been his on that evening, nor the adulation of the

ladies, diverted his mind from the business in hand. Officer prisoners he lodged in the county courthouse, enlisted men in bivouac
at the Choice House, site of the present-day principal hotel of the
city which, appropriately enough, bears the name "General Forrest."

Heeding Forrest's request for rations for his prisoners and his
own men, "everybody went home," Mrs. Ward continued, "and
there was just a regular wholesale cooking of hams and shoulders
and all sorts of provisions that we had, and everything was sent
down to the respective camps. We were quite willing to feed the
Yankees when they had no guns"—treatment which Colonel
Streight's aide thus acknowledged in his subsequent book: "We
remained in Rome until Tuesday morning, May 5, under orders
of General Forrest, who, to his credit be it said, furnished us with
sufficient rations for our subsistence, and also with comfortable
quarters."

Since Streight had cleaned the country of riding stock as he
came through, and Forrest had been unable to obtain remounts for
such of his animals as were broken down, he reached Rome with
fewer than 600 horses. Streight had three times as many horses as
Forrest at the time of the surrender. His animals, moreover, had
for the most part marched but one, two or three days, and had not
accomplished the whole exhausting march from Tennessee, as had
Forrest's. Using the best of the captured animals, therefore, to re-
mount those of his own men whose horses were done for, Forrest
sent the remainder direct to Chattanooga under escort, with the
request to General Bragg that they be returned to north Alabama
for distribution among the people from whom they had been taken
by the raiders.

Having turned over his prisoners to the troops sent up from
Atlanta by the provost marshal, and seen them started for prison on
the little Rome railroad on the morning of the fifth, Forrest and
his men turned to the business of rest and refitment, and to the
enjoyment of Roman hospitality.

A popular subscription to buy a fine horse to be given to the
General himself, the Rome newspapers announced, was oversub-
scribed in an hour or two, when it was found that A.M. Sloan, a
local citizen, had anticipated the popular movement by personally

presenting the General "his splendid saddle horse, for which he would not on any other account have taken the best negro fellow in the State." The money which had been raised was turned over to the General, therefore, for the benefit of the sick and wounded of the command.

Plans were announced, also, for a great picnic for "Gen. Forrest and His Brave Men," with appeals to all to come, bringing "sufficient supplies, ready cooked and prepared; bring for 20 men if you can, or for 10 men, or for 5, besides a sufficient supply for your own family which will attend."

But Forrest and his men were not to be there, for on the night of Tuesday, May fifth, only a little more than forty-eight hours after their arrival in Rome, word came that another raiding column had left Tuscumbia, headed toward Jasper and Elyton, site of the present Birmingham. In the early morning of the sixth, therefore, Forrest and his men were in the saddle again, backtracking through Gadsden to meet the new threat. The Romans were left to consume the bountiful basket dinners which had been provided, to observe an official day of thanksgiving and prayer for their deliverance, to start organizing a Home Guard company for future emergencies, and to tell over and over again the stirring story of the Sunday when Streight and his men came to Rome as prisoners, not as conquerors.

12

THE BATTLE OF SPOTTSYLVANIA COURT HOUSE

By Cyrus Townsend Brady

In 1864, the Northern Army had a new commanding general named Grant. He elected to establish his headquarters with the Army of the Potomac, though executive command of that army remained with General Meade. In the Spring another "On to Richmond" campaign was launched. The Federal forces crossed the Rapidan at fords above Chancellorsville and started through the Wilderness. This sub-marginal area contains a low grade of iron ore which had been smelted even in colonial times. To fire the furnaces the timber had been cut off and by 1864, as now, it was largely covered with scrub second growth which in many parts was virtually impenetrable; only occasionally is this mass of thickets broken by small clearings.

The Confederate forces lay west of the Federal line of advance. General Lee determined to attack while the Blue forces were canalized on the few poor roads running south and while the density of the growth prevented Grant from taking advantage of his vastly superior artillery. The Confederates struck the flank of the moving Blue column on the axis of two parallel roads crossing the Wilderness from west to east. There they achieved what, by previous standards, was a victory. According to the well-established pattern, the Yankees should withdraw across the river and a hiatus elapse before another engagement. But the incoming Northern command was new and sterner stuff. They did not with-

draw: they "sidled" to the left and moved on toward Richmond. Confederate cavalry discovered the direction of movement of the Federal wagon trains and Lee was able to predict, with great accuracy, the Union move. In a desperate race, Gray cavalry managed to beat the Blue advance to Spottsylvania Court House and throw a line of skirmishers across their front. The line held while arriving troops were frantically added to the colors on both sides. These troops dug in and a static situation was reached. Then the Federals, without artillery preparation, launched a surprise assault in great strength and penetrated the Confederate lines. Here was crisis indeed! If these lines were not restored the army would be destroyed, Richmond would be completely undefended and the Confederacy subdued. In this stirring scene was enacted, perhaps, the war's most dramatic single episode when General Lee attempted to lead the counter attack in person.

Cyrus Townsend Brady portrays those violent hours in graphic tenseness of crisis.

The Confederate lines at Spottsylvania Court House were traced in the shape of a great irregular crescent which ran roughly from west to east for half their length and then bent around to the south, the chord of the arc connecting the two ends of the circle being about four miles long. Nearly in the middle of the line, or at the northeast point of it, a tremendous salient half a mile wide at its base ran the same distance almost due north and south, culminating in a blunt obtuse angle. The existence of such a salient in such a line was a grave mistake. Its one advantage was that it was an excellent position for artillery.

The Confederate lines had been formed under fire, however, and in running them in the somewhat haphazard methods necessitated by the fact that they had to be placed during action, advantage had been taken of the topography of the land, which had been followed, as was usually the case, in disregard of strict engineering principles. Wherever the ground was found to be defensible the trained soldiers usually seized upon it and rapidly threw up temporary breastworks, which, when connected with other similar coigns of vantage, and strengthened, constituted the main line which the army must defend. Nor had there been in the two days of continuous battle much opportunity for rectifying the crooked, irregular lines. The tremendous assaults delivered by Grant and his overwhelming force could only be resisted by the most superhuman efforts on the part of the Confederates. They had no time for anything but fighting. To cling to the line they had made was a necessity. And it was commonly observed that when the men selected their own line they held it better than when it was traced by the engineers. They seemed to feel a certain affection as well as responsibility for it, and it was difficult or impossible to dislodge them from it.

Lee was as keenly alive as his officers to the vulnerability of the salient, and had given orders that a line of works should be built across its rear, so that in case of necessity it could be abandoned without impairing his main line of defence. Such few men as could be spared from the fighting line had been at work upon these new lines, but they were yet in a very incomplete state. Meanwhile the works in the salient had been strengthened by the men who held it until they were the most formidable in the whole line —which was proper, as the position naturally invited attack. The non-military reader will understand that once a line is effectively broken at any one spot the whole line becomes untenable, and the defending army must retreat under circumstances of terrible disadvantage, or be broken to pieces and annihilated where they are.

Grant, in the previous fighting, had tried both flanks of the line, and, finding them impregnable, had decided to concentrate a force and endeavour to break the line at the tempting salient. For this purpose he selected Hancock's corps. There was no finer corps in his army than the famous Second Corps commanded by Winfield Scott Hancock; indeed, there was no more splendid body of fighters in the Army of North Virginia itself than those Hancock had led in so many battles. By natural selection under fire he had assembled a body of soldiers who would go anywhere and do anything that a captain could ask of humanity. They may be fitly compared to Pickett's famous Virginia division. And it may be remembered that it was Hancock's men upon whom the assault at Gettysburg had fallen, and it was they who had repulsed the famous charge.

The heavy losses of the Federal troops were constantly made good by the arrival of fresh troops—when Lee lost a man his place could not be filled. Consequently Hancock was able to bring to the assault the full strength of his corps, numbering in all perhaps twenty thousand men. Early on the evening of the 11th of May he was ordered to withdraw from his position on the extreme right, pass around the rear of Warren's and Sedgwick's corps, who were to extend and occupy his abandoned lines, to the Brown Farm, a clearing about three-quarters of a mile due north of the apex of the Confederate salient. The open ground extended from Brown's Farmhouse to the face of the salient, the distance between the bordering groves of trees on either side being about four hundred yards.

The advance of Hancock's troops reached the Brown Farmhouse about midnight. The march had been made over a terrible road in a pouring rain. The weather conditions would have taken the mettle out of any but veteran and tried soldiery. The night was dark as pitch. Hancock spent the hours until four o'clock, the designated moment, in placing his men. When the time for the assault arrived it was still too dark to see, and he therefore waited until four thirty-five. Taking directions from a white farmhouse, the McCool house, seen dimly just within the Confederate lines, at that moment he ordered the advance.

With Barlow's division in two close lines of masses, Brooke's and Miles' brigades in front Brown's and Smyth's in the second line; with Birney's division in two double lines of battle on Barlow's right; with Mott's division in the rear of Birney, and Gibbon's division in reserve, the order was given to march forward. There were no obstacles in front of Barlow's division, his way being where the ground was open and clear. Birney's division had to wade through a morass and force its way through a rather open piece of woods. By hard marching they kept abreast of the troops in the open and all approached the salient together. As they converged upon it they naturally crowded together in masses of increasing density.

Certain threatening movements of Grant's left, made for the purpose, had caused Lee to believe that the next attack would fall on the right of his own line. He had therefore withdrawn most of the artillery from Ewell's troops, who held the salient. During the early part of the night General Edward Johnson, who commanded the division at the apex, had become convinced that his own front was menaced, and he had sent to Lee and asked for the return of the guns. Accordingly, orders had been sent to the artillery to be back at the salient at daybreak. The batteries were even then coming across the rough country at a gallop. The men in Johnson's division lay behind the breastworks ready for whatever might be demanded of them. The sentries were alert and watchful. Pickets were posted three or four hundred yards in front of the lines.

The works here had gradually been made very strong. The usual rough-and-ready fortifications made use of by either army as occasion demanded were merely shallow ditches with the earth piled up in front of them. Around the salient, however, the trees with which the country abounded had been cut down and banked with earth to a height of about four feet. Along the top of the embankment a headlog rose on stones, or wood blocks, so as to leave an open space of about three or four inches between it and the crown of the earthwork, as a sort of continuous loophole for firing through. In front of the work there was a rude abattis, or slashing, improvised from sharpened tree branches; not much of a protection, but still sufficient to annoy and perhaps check an assailing enemy when backed by such a fire as was certain to come from the veteran defenders.

The ground outside the lines sloped downward gently for about forty yards, and then it rose in still more gentle ascent all around the position. Within the salient the country was more open, although the farms and meadows were interspersed with clumps of trees. Outside the lines, save for two or three farms, the ground was marshy and heavily wooded. Little water courses, full from the heavy rains, ran here and there.

As became the commander of the most advanced and exposed section of the line, Johnson was awake early on the morning of the fatal 12th of May, and was engaged in an inspection of his men and lines before daybreak. Mounting the works, he stared northward through the grey, dull mist of the morning—the rain had stopped for the time being, but the mist was almost heavy enough to be

called a storm—toward the Union lines. As he did so his ear
caught the sound of distant cheering. It came to him dull and faint
in the heavy, sodden air. What could it mean? Why should men
be cheering there at that hour? There was no snapping of pieces
from his pickets—indeed the Union advance had been so rapid
through the dense fog that the men in the advance simply swal-
lowed up the guards in front of them before they had a chance
to fire—but Johnson was enough of a soldier to realize what that
cheering, which was drawing nearer, meant. The assault he had
anticipated was about to be delivered. Where were those missing
cannon? He threw one glance back into the salient; they had not
come. It was day, and they were not here. It was day and the
enemy was at hand. He would have given his life for the guns.
Well, he must do his best without them.

Instantly orders and shouts rang along the Confederate lines. The
men sleeping on their arms rose to their feet and made ready. For
a moment they stared into the impenetrable fog, while the cheering
came nearer and rose higher. An instant later and the grey cloud
was tinged with blue. An instant later and dark masses of men
shouldered their way through the mist, buffeting it aside as the
bows of a ship a wave, and fell like an avalanche on the Confederate lines.

Fortune had favoured them. They had reached so near the lines
before they were distinguished that although the breastworks
blazed with sudden fire on the instant and many fell, the momentum of the solid mass of twenty thousand men struck the line as a
great breaker crashes upon a shore. The first ranks of the assailants
were beaten into a human spray; men stumbled and fell in the
abattis, only to be trampled into human pulp by their oncrowding
comrades, as the wave of inundation swelled on, merciless, irresistible, overwhelming. The human torrent crushed through the abattis, surged over the breastworks and, bayonet in hand, fell upon
Johnson's men. The fighting was close and ghastly—with the bayonet mainly. The Confederates resisted desperately, but no line of
five thousand that were ever mustered could contend with four
times their number in mass, especially when without cannon. In a
short time those who were not killed or wounded were captured;
included in the latter category were Johnson and another Steuart,

the two general officers. There had been no surprise, simply a mighty, irresistible smash through a weak point brilliantly if unsuccessfully defended. The long lines of dead indicated the vigour and persistence of the defence. Their valour had been unavailing, however, for Hancock had at last broken the line!

Back of the second line of entrenchments that were being thrown across the base of the salient Lee had his headquarters. The sound of the battle in the early morning apprised him of what was happening. There was not a continuous roar of small arms punctured by artillery, but one long smashing volley, and then a strange sort of silence broken only by spattering shots, by yells and cheers that came to him faintly. He understood instantly. It could only mean that the Union troops were over the line and using the bayonet. There was no time or room for musket or gun fire. So swift and so sudden had been the terrible onslaught in the fog that but two or Johnson's remaining guns had been able to fire a shot before they were all captured.

It was evident to Lee that his line was broken. Just where and in what force the enemy were he could not yet decide. Some place on the salient, of course. A staff officer from the front galloped up and confirmed the news. In his excitement, with pardonable exaggeration, he declared that there must be forty thousand men already within the Confederate lines and that they had complete possession of the whole salient. Sending his staff officers in every direction to summon reinforcements, Lee galloped through numbers of flying stragglers, whom he attempted in vain to rally, toward the salient. Gordon's division had been previously ordered to reinforce Ewell's troops in the expectation of some such catastrophe as this, and Lee knew that they were stationed near the base of the salient. They were the troops which had been erecting the second line of defence. Followed by a single staff officer, Grafton, Lee on Traveller, his famous grey horse, rode at a tearing gallop for this splendid division.

And well he might ride fast and hard, for if the Federal troops had succeeded in seizing the salient, unless they could be driven out of it, or confined to the positions which they had now taken until the new line of breastworks at the rear of the salient had been so far completed that it could be held, the army of Northern Virginia was irretrievably ruined. If Grant could maintain his advantage and pour in his troops through that gap, by turning to the right or left, as the case might be, they could take the Confederate lines in reverse, and no troops on earth could resist them. The Army of Northern Virginia, the Confederacy, would end right then and there. Indeed it might be too late to save the army even by such prodigies of valour as he might expect from the men he had so often led to victory.

The cheers of the Federal troops grew louder as Lee raced toward the enclosure of the salient. They were evidently approaching the second position. The situation was even more disastrous than it had seemed at first. Far to the right and left of him the roar of guns told him that Grant was endeavouring by assault and cannonade to prevent the detachment of troops from those wings to reinforce the broken Confederate centre. If Grant could hold the Confederate troops on the right and left in their places in their entrenchments, his great preponderance of force would enable him to overwhelm the reserves that Lee was hastening to the danger point, the disaster would be converted into a rout, and then God save the Confederacy, for nothing could avail!

The situation was patent even to the private soldiers in the army, much more to the officers. Rhodes and Ramseur, of Early's corps to the right of the salient, had already got their troops in line, when a staff officer galloped up with Lee's commands. Best of them all, Gordon, a young man who had entered the war as the captain of an infantry company and now commanded a division, and who went out at Appomattox in the front of the last battle line in a position second only to that of Lee and Longstreet, was quick to see the necessity. Without orders he deployed his division in line of battle and was about to move forward when Lee galloped on the field. The face of the great captain was set and firm. There was no lack of composure in his bearing, but the light in his eye, the uplift in his face, signified a desperate determination, nay rather, a great resolve.

Taking off his hat, he rode his splendid grey horse to the head of the line, looked back at the men, and wheeled toward the Union lines. His purpose was patent to all. Realising the supreme effort required to save the day, he was about to lead those brave Georgians in person against the victorious enemy. It needed, in the general's mind, his personal presence to inspire this small division with ability to hurl back, or even hold in check, that enormous mass of men. It was the supreme moment of the war, and unless he could master it, he would go to a great death at the head of his men. He would win a victory or he would not survive a defeat.

Over to the right as he took this position he saw the missing cannon. The horses were on a dead run, the cannoneers were yelling like fiends. As they bounded over the uneven road the muddy cannon leaped, banged and smashed through the air as if they had been projectiles themselves. It was much lighter now, and although the mists were still heavy, the field of battle could be distinguished.

Some slight works in the rear of the McCool house held by one of Gordon's slender brigades had temporarily checked the enemy. In the excitement of the charge and the deadly hand-to-hand fight which had ensued before Steuart's line had been overwhelmed, the men of this division did not surrender until their arms had been literally torn from them and they had been borne down by sheer weight of numbers. It was hoped this delay would enable the artillery to get into action. They saw the guns whirl to the front in battery, but before they had a chance to fire the Union troops were upon them and the first detachment of artillery was captured in the twinkling of an eye.

All these movements, however, had taken time, and Hancock's corps had become badly disorganised in the advance and the fierce fighting, and had naturally got entirely out of control. They came surging through the salient enclosure more in the nature of a mob, or a series of mobs, by this time than anything else, expecting to take the broken line in reverse in the direction of the Court House and end things out of hand.

Lee turned to his men. At that juncture Gordon, who had been at the other end of his own line, galloped over to where Lee was restraining his impatient horse. With a reckless disregard of military etiquette he threw his own animal squarely across the face of Traveller. Reaching out his hand he caught the bridle of the general's horse and checked him. Lee flushed and started to speak, when Gordon, shouted out in a voice that could be heard half a mile away, and which was heard—as he designed it to be—by every man in his advance:

"General Lee, you shall not lead my command in a charge! No man shall do that."

He fairly hurled the words at his astonished commander, not giving him time to answer.

"The men behind you are Georgians, Virginians, North Carolinians," he cried, his voice rising tremendously as he spoke. "They have never failed you in any field. They won't fail you now. Will you, boys?"

The men didn't cheer then in answer to that question. They simply roared.

"No, no, no!" came from the line; "we'll not fail him!"

"General Lee," shouted Gordon imperiously, while yet the response echoed through the dull air of the morning, "you must go to the rear!"

He recognised the value of that life. Lee must be saved at all hazards, else whatever happened they were indeed lost. Under no circumstances was the great captain to be permitted to sacrifice himself like an ordinary soldier. Lee must go back!

Instantly the words were caught up by Gordon's men. They were greeted by the Rebel yell certainly, but this time it was not the incoherent, thrilling shriek so filled with menace which animated the men who voiced it, and gave pause to those who heard its terrifying cadences. It was this shout.

"General Lee to the rear! General Lee to the rear!" repeated again and again.

The men dashed forward and grasped the general's horse and strove, in spite of his involuntary effort to prevent them, to turn his face to the rear. Indeed they crowded around Traveller so closely that they actually started to turn him and then push the horse backward by main force. If necessary they would have taken horse and man and carried them both bodily to the rear. They were quite in the mood for such an achievement. It was such an evidence of affection and devotion as few captains had ever received on a battlefield.

Lee used to say whimsically that he never really discovered

where was the proper station of the general-in-chief in action, for wherever he went during the course of a battle some officer was sure to remonstrate with him, and the words that he heard most frequently when fighting was going on were these:

"General Lee, this is no place for you, sir; you ought not to be here!"

There was nothing left for Lee but compliance. He shook his head and slowly forced his way out of the ranks, taking position on a little hillock where the whole division could see him. He was as fearless, as reckless of death, as the commonest soldier, and they knew it. His hold on those men was irresistible. They could do anything now, and they would.

While the impression of the scene was still upon them, Gordon gave the word "Forward!" The division, enthused to the sublime, struck the disorganised and scattered troops of Hancock with tremendous force and drove them back, stubbornly contesting every foot of the way, the resistance growing stronger and stronger as the blue men were crowded together by the constricting walls of the angle. But Gordon was not to be denied. Slowly his men pressed on. The stress and strain were terrific. There was more hand-to-hand fighting over the ground that Edward Johnson had occupied that morning. Many a man, wounded and unable to get away, fell and was trampled to death by the press of feet.

As Lee had withdrawn from Gordon's front at the imperious behest of that gallant young commander, he had sent Grafton, who had witnessed the whole scene with a feeling almost of awe, posthaste to bring up some more artillery to take the place of the captured guns. After a few minutes' fighting, which Lee watched, with his heart in his mouth and a prayer on his lips, he saw with relief indescribable Cabell's artillery coming up on the run. They wheeled to the right, the officers saluting, waving their swords, shouting as they saw Lee on old Traveller, and dashed into action.

By this time Rhodes and Ramseur had also swung into the salient in a series of hurtling charges, and added their onslaught to the tremendous thrust of the Georgians under Gordon. By prodigious efforts they finally forced the Union troops out of the salient and over the works. But no further. To one side of that narrow line of earth and logs the maddened men in blue clung with the grip of an octopus. Upon it the frantic men in grey threw themselves with the demoniac energy of enraged tigers.

It was daylight now. All that long grey day, with the rain whirling down on them, the soldiers fought for that line. The Confederates had cleared the salient and regained all that they had lost except the extreme angles. They could not dislodge the Union troops from the outer face of that portion of the line, nor could the Federal soldiers in turn drive them from the inner face. With six feet of earth separating them they struggled through the long hours.

It was not a series of charges and countercharges, of successive advances and retreats, as was usually the course of engagements. It was not a battle in which the fortunes of war wavered from one side to the other, but it was a straight, continuous, steady, hand-to-hand fight of over twenty hours' duration, and of such a character as beggars description. Never before, never since, was there a battle like it.

Men stood behind the breastworks firing until they were shot down. Guns were run forward, by hand, after the horses had been killed, from either side, and fired until their very carriages were cut to pieces by musket fire. The sponges were dipped in blood which dropped from the iron muzzles as from a ravening animal's lips. Men drank the sickening compound in their consuming thirst in default of water. The slopes on either side were piled with men past action forever, to whom no one gave heed. The trenches were filled with dead, the ditches with blood. The horrible mud was mixed with trampled human lives. Wounded men fought with the ferocity of tigers or the courage of lions at bay, until they could fight no more.

Fresh troops were brought up constantly, although they were subjected to a fearful shattering fire from the guns, placed far enough back from the works on either side to shoot over friend and into the foe. Still that breastwork was lined with men who fought on with no note of time, knowing that the last hour would strike presently for them. Opposing colours were planted on it face to face and waved there until cloth and staffs were shot to pieces.

In the frenzy of their passion men would leap on the breastworks and fire down into the trenches on the other side. Sometimes their comrades would pass up gun after gun, which the heroes on the works would fire until they were shot down. Bayonets crossed, sabres were rammed through crevices and openings in the breastworks, and the men were as mad. The redoubt smoked like a volcano, writhed like a serpent, bled like a heart. And over all the rains fell and fell. In the whole history of warfare there never was such a prolonged, desperate battle period of fierce hand-to-hand fighting since the world began.

Neither side would give way. Officers and men fought side by side; organization was lost. It was not needed. Each man was soldier and captain at once; and the sole need was to fight, to fight with parched lips and sobbing breast, until merciful death stayed the hand.

The rifle and musketry fire was of such fierceness and intensity that the air was filled with sheets of lead and steel. A deep, continuous humming sound dominated the field—the song of the rifle bullet, the aeolian harp of death. A large tree back of the lines was cut down by musket fire and fell. Gun after gun was put out of action because everything wooden about it was destroyed by the small-arm bullets. The headlogs on the breastworks were shivered into paint brushes. The reeds and rushes and weeds and underbrush were cut down as cleanly as though they had been mowed.

The heroism on both sides was so great that the battle, in spite of its horrors, was an epic of magnificence. Every soldier on that dead line that lived from hour to hour because it was constantly remanned with fresh victims, was a hero or a demon. With faces ghastly white from fatigue, with mouths powder-blackened from biting cartridges, with bodies covered with mud from the gunstocks, until they could not tell blue from grey in the rain, the men fought on.

The Union troops were not withdrawn while there was a hope of driving the Confederates away, for if they were forced back from the lines again the Army of Northern Virginia would be lost. The Confederates would not be hurled from their position, for their salvation depended upon keeping the Union troops at bay until the lines in the rear could be completed. So the best troops of both armies were concentrated on either side of those lines in a struggle which needs the pen of Homer to describe it.

Meanwhile, far back of the salient, toiled frantically the wounded, the sick, the teamsters, the camp-followers, every one who could handle a spade, or an axe, or even shovel the earth with a tin cup. Lee's personal presence sometimes animated these humble toilers. He rode from place to place, from fighting line to working line, encouraging all, filling his men with unconquerable determination, with an ardour that nothing could quench and by which, as welcome night came on, the terrible wrestle ended in a victory for them.

The first success of the Federals had been nullified by the sacrifice of the Confederates. The battle gradually died away, leaving each army in possession of the face of the angle it had fought for. About three o'clock in the morning humanity could stand no more. There was silence on the field. What remained alive of the Confederate divisions that had held the line retreated from the Bloody Angle and occupied the new breastworks that had been built across the base of the salient, leaving to the Federals the now useless works. The battle was over, the Confederacy was saved—but at a terrible cost.

To complete this tale of the fighting in "Hell's Half-Acre," as the soldiers called it, the next morning the Union troops occupied the lines which had been so bitterly contested for. On both sides they found them piled with dead in the ditches to the height of four or five feet, a solid mass of bodies. Here and there convulsive movements, a muffled moan, indicated that there was some life in the horrible heaps.

The possession of the field and the honours of the conflict remained with the Federals, but they were barren honours, for behind the new earthworks lay the veterans of the South as grimly at bay as they had been before the great assault of Hancock.

13

THE BATTLE OF BRICE'S CROSS ROADS

By John A. Wyeth, M.D.

Nathan Bedford Forrest began the Civil War as a private soldier and ended it as a lieutenant general, the only participant who achieved this spread of rank. Without formal military education he possessed an innate tactical genius and a most combative personality. He very largely accomplished his own tactical dictum, of arriving at the right place first with the most men, by personal leadership and sheer strength of personality.

While the battle at Brice's cross roads may not be strategically among the most crucial moments of the Civil War, it does have a quality in hair-breadth escape from desperate crisis.

When Sherman was faced with practically everything the deep south could muster, the Federals, being superior in numbers, could form raiding columns to slice through the Gulf states. To oppose this the Confederates had only Forrest's cavalry as a counteragent. The achievement of that cavalry is at times incredible. Nowhere does the skill and force of Forrest's leadership show better than in the crisis when Federal General Sturgis with more than 3,000 cavalry and more than 4,000 infantrymen struck out to the southeast from Memphis to divert Forrest from Sherman's communications. The hard-riding gray troops intercepted him at an obscure cross road and won a most signal tactical victory.

The battle at Brice's cross roads, in Lee County, Mississippi, took place on the 10th of June, 1864. It has passed into history as one

281

of the most signal victories of the civil war, considering the forces engaged. On this field General Forrest displayed not only that bull-dog tenacity of purpose which characterized his aggressive method of warfare, but his remarkable ability as a strategist, and those original methods of fighting which then won success, and have since attracted the closest attention of students of military science.

The contending forces were, on the Union side, 3200 cavalry and 4500 infantry, with 22 pieces of artillery, commanded by General Samuel D. Sturgis; on the Confederate side, 4713 mounted troops, with 12 pieces of artillery, under General N. B. Forrest.

At Brice's the main highway leading from Memphis to Ripley, and on in a direction east of south to Fulton in Mississippi, inter-sects almost at a right angle another important road, leading from Corinth through Rienzi, Booneville, Baldwyn, and in a south-westerly direction to Pontotoc.

With the exception of two or three cleared patches of land, not exceeding six acres in extent, immediately around Brice's house, the country, which is only slightly undulating, for a mile in every direction was, at the time of the battle, not only heavily timbered, but there was an undergrowth of black-jack and scrub-oak so dense that in places the troops could with difficulty force their way through; and being then in full leaf, it was possible to approach within a few yards without being seen. About one mile northeast of Brice's the Corinth road, with a worm-fence on either hand for about a quarter of a mile, passed through a field, to the outskirts of which, on all sides, the dense undergrowth extended. This field was enclosed by a heavy rail fence, re-enforced on top with poles and brushwood. About the same distance on the highway leading from Brice's toward Ripley and Memphis the roadbed descended some twenty feet into the Tishomingo Creek bottom, along which stream there was a large cornfield, at that time in cultivation, and here this sluggish stream was spanned by a small wooden bridge.

At the urgent insistence of General Sherman the expedition under Sturgis had been sent into Mississippi. Its first object was to engage the attention of Forrest, and thus prevent any interfer-ence from the much-dreaded cavalryman with Sherman's com-munications in Tennessee. Sherman and Johnston, two great mas-ters in strategy, were playing a memorable game of war among the pine-clad hills of Georgia. Sherman, fiercely aggressive, with an army larger and better equipped, was slowly yet surely pushing Johnston back upon Atlanta. The latter, with matchless skill, was contesting every foot of ground, and inflicting heavy losses upon his antagonist; but, despite these losses, it was clear to the Union commander that he had this army of the Confederacy at his mercy if he could keep his troops well supplied from the North and West until the corn with which the Southern fields were teeming was sufficiently ripened to supply subsistence to his men and animals. The burden of his official despatches of that date was, keep "that devil Forrest" (as he termed him) "from my rear, and I will take care of Johnston in my front."

His anxiety from this source became at last so great that he went to the extreme of offering one of his brigadier generals a major general's commission if he would kill Forrest. "It must be done, if it costs ten thousand lives and breaks the Treasury." In case the wily fox could not be killed or crippled, he must be kept busy where he was.

Starting from Memphis on the 1st of June, with a train of 250 wagons and ambulances, General Sturgis, by slow marches over roads made difficult by frequent rains, had, at dark on the 9th of June, concentrated his entire command at Stubbs's farm, on the Ripley and Fulton highway, nine miles north of Brice's cross roads.

Forrest, surmising from the direction the Federal column had taken that its object would be the destruction of the Mobile and Ohio Railway from Corinth southward, had posted his troops in various detachments along this road from Rienzi to Baldwyn.

At 9 o'clock on this night he received information of Sturgis's encampment at Stubbs's place, and immediately ordered each detachment of his command to prepare three days' rations, to issue the full complement of ammunition, and to move at four o'clock in the morning, as rapidly as the condition of the roads would permit, in the direction of Brice's cross roads. It had rained almost daily for a week, and on the afternoon and night of the 9th it came down in torrents until after midnight, but at daybreak on the morning of the 10th of June the clouds had vanished, and when the sun came up it ushered in one of those hot, humid, and depressing days characteristic of this season of the year in this section of the South.

It will thus be seen that, in order to reach the battlefield, Bell's brigade, which formed one-half of Forrest's command, would have to march from Rienzi, twenty-five miles; Rucker's brigade, and Morton's and Rice's twelve pieces, eighteen miles, from Booneville; and the brigades of Johnson and Lyon, from Baldwyn, six miles to Brice's—while the army of Sturgis concentrated at Stubbs's was within nine miles of the cross roads.

By daylight the Confederates were in motion. Colonel E. W. Rucker narrates that General Forrest overtook him early in the morning, about seven o'clock, and rode by his side. He told Rucker that he intended to attack the Federals at Brice's. "I know they greatly outnumber the troops I have at hand, but the road along which they will march is narrow and muddy; they will make slow progress. The country is densely wooded, and the undergrowth so heavy that when we strike them they will not know how few men we have. Their cavalry will move out ahead of the infantry, and should reach the cross roads three hours in advance. We can whip their cavalry in that time. As soon as the fight opens they will send back to have the infantry hurried up. It is going to be as hot as hell, and coming on a run for five or six miles over such roads, their infantry will be so tired out we will ride right over them. I want everything to move up as fast as possible. I will go ahead with Lyon and the Escort and open the fight."

At 5.30 the Union cavalry under Grierson mounted their horses and moved out in the direction of Brice's. With fateful leisure the infantry cooked their breakfast, and did not march until seven o'clock. The advance-guard of Waring's brigade of Grierson's division encountered the Confederate outposts at the Tishomingo Creek bridge, drove these away, reached Brice's cross roads at 9.45, and pursued the flying Confederates, who, turning to the left at Brice's, ran in the direction of Baldwyn. Along this road Waring proceeded for a mile, until he came to the edge of the field through which it runs, and here he encountered the advance of Lyon's brigade, which, under Captain H. A. Tyler, had just arrived upon the opposite side of this clearing, about four hundred yards distant.

By 10 o'clock, when Lyon had thrown out his skirmishers, Forrest in person came up with his Escort, eighty-five strong, and with Gartrell's company of fifty men, and took command of Lyon's troops, which numbered 800 rifles.

Grierson, satisfied that the Confederates were in considerable strength, dismounted Waring's brigade, 1450 strong, which he posted behind the fence in the edge of the dense timber, about equally divided on the north and south side of the road along which Forrest was advancing. Two rifle guns and two howitzers attached to this brigade were thrown into position on a slight elevation just behind his line, and one hundred picked men armed with revolving-rifles were sent forward and concealed in the fence corners of the lane, about one hundred yards in advance.

To the right of Waring was dismounted Grierson's other brigade, under Winslow, numbering 1750, and the extreme right of this portion of the Union line was slightly "refused," or drawn back, in the direction of Brice's house. It will be seen that at this (for General Forrest) critical moment General Grierson had on the field 3200 cavalry, with four pieces of artillery in position and six others in reserve, confronted, four hundred yards away, by 800 mounted troops of Lyon's brigade, with 135 men on Escort duty, and with no Confederate artillery within eight miles.

Forrest was naturally an offensive fighter. He rarely stood to receive an attack. If his troops were mounted and the enemy moved first upon him, he always advanced to meet their charge. In a memorable interview with a Federal officer he said he would "give more for fifteen minutes of bulge on the enemy than for a week of tactics." He believed that one man in motion was worth two standing to receive an attack.

When he realized how strong the enemy in his immediate front were, his chief anxiety was that they might charge in force and run over his small command. Rucker was still some two miles in the rear, and Johnson was yet behind him. He immediately had Lyon's troops dismounted and thrown into line, and their position behind the fence strengthened by brush and logs. To prevent Grierson from attacking, it was important to make a show of force, and, with characteristic effrontery, having alternate panels of the worm-fence thrown down, he ordered Lyon to make a demonstration by advancing from the edge of the woods into the open field. Lyon threw out a double line of skirmishers, and marched boldly toward the enemy's position.

That Forrest's advance was "pure bluff" should have been clear to Grierson, for Lyon's right just reached the Baldwyn road, while his left extended only a little beyond the junction of Waring's and Winslow's brigades. He was thus widely overlapped on either flank.

Major E. Hunn Hanson, of Waring's brigade, says of this movement, "The Confederate line advancing was shorter than our own, its left ending in front of the left and centre of Winslow's brigade."

With artillery and small-arms the Union line opened upon the Confederates, who kept up their feigned attack for about half an hour, when they withdrew, without confusion, to the edge of the woods from which they had started, and there resumed their position behind the "lay-outs."

Major Hanson (above quoted) says, "The Confederates retired, with but little disorder, to the edge of the woods, and kept up a skirmish fire at long range for some time."

It was at this moment that Colonel E. W. Rucker, with his brigade of 700 mounted men, came on the scene. When within two miles of Lyon's position, hearing the cannonade, he put spurs to his horses and went rapidly forward with his hardy riders to the relief of his chieftain.

Forrest at once dismounted two of Rucker's regiments, the Seventh Tennessee and Chalmers's Eighteenth Mississippi Battalion, placing them in line to the left of Lyon's troops, opposing the centre of Winslow's brigade. The Eighth Mississippi, under Duff, was kept mounted, and thrown well over to the left toward the Guntown road to protect that flank of the Confederates from being turned. All told, the Confederates now had on the field 1635 men, with Grierson's division, 3200 strong, in line of battle, opposing them.

Forrest again ordered his lines forward, with the same purpose for which the original attack was made, and after some sharp firing, although not at close range, the Confederates again retired. Chalmers's battalion, mistaking the object of the movement, had advanced too far to the front, and received an enfilading fire from the right of Winslow's line, which threw it into confusion, but it rallied on the main Confederate line.

As the troops came back a second time, Colonel W. A. Johnson arrived with 500 Alabamians, being that portion of his brigade whose horses had not given out in the forced march they had just made from northern Alabama. Two days before the battle General Forrest had sent Colonel D. C. Kelley to meet this body of troops, with an urgent note to Johnson to push forward with his best mounted men and reach Baldwyn by the night of the 9th or the morning of the 10th, as he expected to fight Sturgis at Brice's cross roads at that time.

These troops Forrest directed to dismount, take position on Lyon's right, and move forward to engage the attention of that portion of the Union line. After some desultory firing, lasting not longer than five minutes, Johnson also retired.

Major Hanson says of this incident, "Later about 300 of the Confederates advanced against Waring's extreme left, but were easily repulsed."

It was now about 11 o'clock, and although Bell's brigade, which numbered more than the Confederate troops at the front, and the artillery under Morton were not within supporting distance, Forrest determined to close with Grierson in deadly earnest. He rode hurriedly along his entire line, with words of encouragement to his troops, telling them that he expected every man to move forward when the signal was given. It was not to be a feint, but desperate work and at close quarters. At the sound of the bugle the dismounted troopers sprang from the edge of the timber, leaped through the fence, and with a wild yell rushed into the open space toward the Union line. Such was their eagerness that the commands seemed to vie with each other as to which should first reach their antagonists. The men of Waring and Winslow seemed imbued with the same desperate purpose, for they stood their ground right manfully, their repeating rifles crackling away in a deafening roar, first at a distance, and then, as the lines came clashing together, into the very faces of the Confederates.

It fell to the gallant Rucker to make the first impression upon the Union position. At the head of the Seventh Tennessee and

Chalmers's battalion, he swept onward with such impetuosity that he carried his part of the line fully one hundred yards in advance of Lyon and Johnson.

Concentrating his fire in this part of the Southern line, Waring had hoped to check or break it here, and when under the fearful ordeal it wavered for a moment, he sprang forward with two of his regiments to drive it from the field. To make assurance sure, this vigilant officer brought up the 2d New Jersey and the 7th Indiana to fill the gap made by his counter-charge and to re-enforce his line. It was a brave and desperate venture, and worthy of the brave Waring. But Rucker's men were not to be denied. Stubborn of will, and apt pupil of his great commander, he had already won the confidence of his faithful soldiers. As the Union troops rushed forward, he shouted to his Southerners to draw their six-shooters and close with them hand to hand, and in one of the most fiercely contested short engagements of the war the Federals were finally forced to retire. The desperate character of this attack and the obstinate resistance with which it was met may be appreciated from an account by a participant, in J. P. Young's *History of the Seventh Tennessee Cavalry*: "The Federals occupied a wood on the far side of the field, behind a rail fence, greatly strengthened with logs and brush piled up against it. It was very hot and sultry when the command was given, and as we approached, the fence seemed ablaze with crackling breech-loaders. The fire was so terrific that the regiment staggered for a moment, and some of the men fell flat upon the earth for protection. They again pushed forward, reached the fence, and began to pull the brush away in order to close with the Federals. So close was this struggle that guns once fired were not reloaded, but used as clubs, and pistols were brought into play, while the two lines struggled with the ferocity of wild beasts. Never did men fight more gallantly for their position than did the determined men of the North for this black-jack thicket on that hot June day. Sergeant John D. Huhn, of Company B, being a few feet in advance, came face to face with a Federal, presented his gun, and ordered the Union soldier to throw his weapon down. Several Federal soldiers rushed to the rescue of their comrade. With clubbed guns they broke Sergeant Huhn's arm and struck him over the head until he fell senseless. Privates Lauderdale and Maclin of the Seventh Tennessee ran to his aid, shot two of his stout-hearted assailants, and drove the others away with clubbed guns."

Of these attacks Colonel George E. Waring, Jr., says: "They were exceedingly fierce. The first assault was repulsed. The second one, after a hand-to-hand fight, was successful, and forced back my right, although the whole 2d New Jersey and the 7th Indiana were brought into action. After falling back a short distance I succeeded in forming a second line, which was held until the infantry came up to relieve my command, the men being much fatigued and out of ammunition."

Of this incident Major E. Hunn Hanson, of the 4th Missouri (Waring's regiment), says: "The line of the enemy in view did not exceed 2500, and was somewhat shorter than our cavalry in position. They advanced, and were repulsed, and, with little disorder, fell back. Again marching upon the cavalry, when within fifty yards of Waring's line the centre of that command slowly gave way."

Forrest had only 2080 men on the field at that moment; and as every regiment but one was fighting dismounted, deducting the troops left with the horses, he had actually engaged in this fierce and successful attack not more than 1700 troops. Employing his usual tactics, he had strengthened his centre, and while the enemy's flanks were kept at bay, he had broken through the Union line at this point. Just as this was accomplished, Johnson and Lyon, with equal courage, had closed in with the left of the Federal forces, while Duff's Mississippi regiment, mounted, on the extreme Confederate left, was vigorously engaged in holding the attention of the extreme right of Grierson's line. As Waring's centre gave way, the gallant W. A. Johnson and his Alabamians advanced so rapidly and eagerly that he had gained a point fully half-way between his original position and the road leading from Ripley to Brice's, along which the infantry column coming to re-enforce Grierson was now advancing.

Still pushing onward, Rucker, leading this brilliant assault mounted, was too fair a target to escape. Several bullets passed through his clothing; his horse, five times wounded, fell at last from a mortal shot. His rider received a bullet in the abdomen, which, though exceedingly painful, was fortunately not a fatal wound; nor did he yield his position at the head of his troops until the field was won.

The Union cavalry was now beaten at all points of the line, and by twelve thirty Forrest had carried out the first part of his program, that he would have the Federal cavalry whipped by the time their infantry could get up.

At ten o'clock in the morning, when Forrest had come on the field, he despatched Major Charles W. Anderson, of his staff, toward Booneville with the order, "Tell Bell to move up fast and fetch all he's got," and for Morton to bring the artillery on at a gallop. Nor had he forgotten the famous movement upon the flank and rear of his opponent, which he always employed, and which in all probability was one of the chief factors in his wonderful success. He directed General A. Buford, his division commander, to take Colonel C. R. Barteau's 2d Tennessee Regiment of Bell's brigade, when it should have arrived within five miles of the battlefield, and to proceed across the country through the woods and byways until it struck the road over which Sturgis would pass from Stubbs's to the cross roads. Barteau says, "My instructions were to take my regiment, numbering then 250 men, across the country by out-of-the-way routes, to slip in upon the Federal flank and rear, and attack them in co-operation with Forrest's forces in front."

How well Barteau did his work, and what commotion he caused in the Union lines, will appear in the course of the narrative.

When the Confederates were first encountered General Grierson had sent a courier to Sturgis, who was then some six miles back, for re-enforcements, and this request was repeated with greater urgency when Rucker and Johnson came on the field and joined hands with Lyon in their desperate onslaught. It was, however, not until twelve o'clock that the Union commander in person came upon the scene, and more than an hour later when the head of the infantry column began to appear. These had been urged forward as fast as the condition of the road and the extreme heat would permit.

Colonel Hoge, who led the advance brigade of infantry, says: "It was impossible to keep up the rapid gait. I received a peremptory order to move forward rapidly, as the enemy was gaining ground, and the only thing that would save us was the infantry. Three-quarters of a mile from the field I received an order from Colonel McMillen in person to move forward at double-quick, which was done."

Coming upon the scene, Hoge's brigade—the 113th, 108th, 95th, and 81st Illinois Infantry, with Battery B of the 2d Illinois Artillery—were thrown into line, the battery being placed at Brice's house.

These re-enforcements had not all formed in line before the 1st Brigade, under Colonel A. Wilkin, also arrived. The 95th Ohio, 114th Illinois, 93d Indiana, and 72d Ohio Infantry were thrown into line at points most needed, while Mueller's section of the 6th Indiana battery, re-enforced by Chapman's full battery, were posted on an eminence in the rear of Brice's house. Battery E of the 1st Illinois Light Artillery and the 19th Minnesota Artillery were held in reserve at the cross-roads. Three thousand six hundred Union infantry, who as yet had not fired a shot, with three batteries of artillery additional, had come upon the scene, re-enforcing Grierson's division, which Forrest had already beaten, and this entire force was confronted by 2000 Confederates, which General Forrest had at hand. Behind this bulwark of infantry the Federal troopers, exhausted and beaten, took refuge, some quitting the field, as the records show, without orders.

Still back of these, and then in sight, was another infantry brigade, of colored troops, with artillery, under Colonel Bouton, held in reserve.

In crescentic line, and this in some portion of double formation, the Federal army now extended from well north of the Baldwyn road across to and some two hundred yards beyond or west of the road from Ripley to Guntown. At this propitious moment for the success of Forrest's battle, just as the Federal infantry were swinging into line, Morton came up with the artillery, and at his heels were General Buford and Tyree H. Bell, with the latter's full brigade of fresh troops, which, within the last six months, had been recruited within the Union lines in western Tennessee. The artillery consisted of Morton's and Rice's battery, which had traveled eighteen miles since daylight, over roads so muddy that for much of the distance it was with great difficulty the horses could drag the pieces along. For the last six miles it required the most vigorous urging with whip and spur to push them forward in a trot.

To the right of the road from Baldwyn, as Morton advanced in rear of Lyon's position, his batteries were brought into action and opened with telling effect. General Sturgis says of this particular period of the engagement: "Finding that our troops were being hard pressed, I ordered one section to open on the enemy's reserve. Their artillery soon replied, and with telling accuracy, every shell bursting over and in the immediate vicinity of our guns."

With fatal precision, scarcely excelled by the sharpshooter with his Whitworth globe-sighted rifle, Captain John W. Morton, the famous young artillerist, who had celebrated his twenty-first birthday on the bloody field of Chickamauga, with clear eye and steady heart was sending his shells with deadly purpose right to the spot.

Placing Buford in command of the right wing, where Johnson and Lyon were operating, Forrest, with Bell's troops, who had marched twenty-five miles since daylight to reach the battlefield, moved to the Confederate left and dismounted to the left of Rucker, extending his now strengthened line westward of the road leading from Brice's to Guntown.

Still further to the Confederate left, mounted, and guarding that wing, and ready to swoop around and upon the Union flank and rear, were two companies of Kentuckians, upon which, under their dashing leader, Captain H. A. Tyler, Forrest knew he could rely for most desperate work when the occasion offered. The other mounted companies, his famous Escort under Captain Jackson and Gartrell's Georgians, on headquarter duty with Forrest, were kept immediately with the general.

The two opposing armies now faced each other for the supreme effort. 7,700 Federal soldiers with 22 pieces of artillery confronted Forrest, who, with an audacity born of supreme confidence in his men as well as in himself, moved forward to attack them. As most of the Confederates fought dismounted, deducting those left with the horses in the rear, the Confederate commander could not have carried into action in this desperate encounter over 3500 troops, with 12 pieces of artillery—a proportion of less than one to two.

For some thirty minutes the sounds of war had ceased. A rifle here and there from some sharpshooter or venturesome skirmisher spoke out in vicious challenge, but the wild fusillade and the crackle and roar of hundreds and thousands of guns no longer swept to and fro along the double rainbow of men in deadly earnest for the undoing of each other. It was the calm before the storm; the ominous silence which precedes the cloudburst and the angry onslaught of the winds. The atmosphere was heavy with humidity, the day depressing and intensely hot. Not a cloud was in the sky to shield friend or foe from the burning rays of the sun. Nothing but the thick foliage intervened, and this was motionless, for not a breath of air was stirring. Forrest, in apt phraseology more forcible than elegant, had measured the heat when he said to Rucker that morning, in his forecast of the fight and of the day, "It is going to be as hot as hell." The troops, and animals as well, in both contending armies, had suffered extremely, and a goodly number had fallen from exhaustion and sunstroke.

On the Union side, Grierson's cavalry had been fighting steadily from ten to two, and fighting is terribly exhausting work. They had been roughly handled to boot, and had a right to be wearied and worried. On the Confederate side, Johnson's, Rucker's, and Lyon's men, who had knocked out Waring's and Winslow's brigades, were equally fatigued. Bell's famous brigade, which had just arrived, had traveled twenty-five miles to reach the battlefield, and for the last fourth of this journey its horses had been urged to the full limit of their endurance and speed. The Union infantry had also suffered much; in fact, more than any other troops upon the field. They had marched nine miles since seven o'clock, and under urgent appeals from Grierson and Sturgis three miles had been made at a trot, and the next and final mile at a double-quick.

Forrest was fully alive to the conditions which, in spite of his numerical weakness, favored him. He had no thought of giving his enemy an opportunity to "catch their wind." He had informed Buford that everything was ready on the left, and that he must push his end of the line (the right), and engage as much as possible the attention of the enemy in that direction. He added that they were massing in front of him, and that their left would not offer as much resistance as he and Bell would encounter. Johnson, on the extreme right of the Confederate line, was urged to crowd in as closely as possible on the road leading from Ripley to Brice's.

The two Federal brigades of infantry under Hoge and Wilkin had scarcely effected their alignment when over to their left the rifles of Johnson and Rucker told them the fight had reopened, and at this moment everything in the Confederate line of battle moved to the front. There was now no open country, except a few acres immediately about Brice's house. Through the thick and almost impenetrable undergrowth, just where Hoge had formed his sturdy Westerners in double array, both ranks lying prone upon the ground, for concealment as well as protection, there came, with guns trailing and bodies bent as close to the earth as possible, the rustling sound of a moving body of men among the foliage, as with difficulty they pushed their way forward. These were the Tennesseans, as stanch and brave a set of men as ever served in war, under Tyree H. Bell, the Blücher of this hard-fought field. When within only a few paces of the Federal line, which as yet they could not see, the rifles of Hoge's infantry burst forth, a withering flash and murderous roar, into the very faces of the Confederates. Under this fierce and sudden fire, which inflicted serious loss, a part of Bell's men gave way. Taking quick advantage of the momentary confusion he had caused, Hoge, with great gallantry, believing that the entire line of the enemy would yield if a general advance was made, ordered his whole force forward, directing his attack principally on the right of Bell and the left of Rucker's position.

Forrest, knowing the heavy fighting would be just at this point, had remained with the troops, and seeing the disaster which now threatened him, dismounted from his horse, called to his two Escort companies to dismount and hitch their horses to the bushes, and with these daring fighters gathered about him he rushed into the thickest of the fray, pistol in hand, to take his place in the front rank with his men. With equal dash and courage, Bell did the same; and with such examples, and under such leadership, the Tennesseans quickly rallied, and being re-enforced by Lieutenant Colonel D. M. Wisdom, who, with 250 men of Newsom's regiment, had been held in reserve behind this portion of the line, they checked the retreat and advanced again upon the enemy. Arrested in front of Bell, the Federal infantry pushed on in gallant style against the thinner line of Rucker; but this sturdy fighter had no notion of yielding the position he had won after such a fierce struggle. He knew from the way the rifles were crackling on his left that Forrest was hard at work there and was holding his own. As the Federal infantry came on with bayonets fixed, Rucker shouted, "Kneel on the ground, men, draw your six-shooters, and don't run." Against this plucky wall the onrushing Federals struck hard, but rebounded. They could not break through it, and in fierce and bloody hand-to-hand combat the bayonet was no match for the repeating-pistol, and the Union troops gave way as the whole Confederate line rushed forward with irresistible force.

As the centre of Hoge's line crumbled away in this terrific onslaught, Johnson, with Lyon's prompt aid, had pushed back the extreme left of McMillen's line, until it was now doubled back upon the Ripley road. At this important juncture Forrest received a message from the ever-watchful Buford which was invaluable to him. From the open position occupied by this officer on the extreme right he had observed a sudden movement of the Union cavalry from near Brice's house to the rear, and could now distinguish musketry off to his right, in the direction of Tishomingo Creek. Barteau was there with the Second Tennessee. He had arrived in the nick of time, and had struck the rear and flank of Sturgis's column. The brilliant strategy of Forrest was now to prove its value in deciding the fate of the Union army.

Of this moment Colonel Barteau says: "I succeeded in reaching the Federal rear just as the fighting seemed heaviest in front. I at once deployed my men in a long line, had my bugler ride up and down, sounding the charge at different points, and kept up as big a show as I could and a vigorous fire upon the Federals, until their complete rout was evident. I was in the flank and rear of their position when Waring's and Winslow's brigades came back."

This brilliant movement, executed with vigor and precision, had at this crisis of the battle not only thrown the reserve brigade of infantry and the train-guard into commotion, but had withdrawn from Forrest's immediate front practically all of Grierson's cavalry that could offer him effectual resistance.

Forrest's perception told him that the crisis of the day had come, and that now the battle must be lost or won. It was past four o'clock. How swift and unheeded is the flight of time when the storm of battle is raging! For more than two hours these desperate men of either army had been in murderous strife at close range, since Bell and Morton had arrived. With savage fierceness against heavy odds Forrest's men had fought, and it seemed that the extreme of endurance had been reached.

Riding along the rear of the line, encouraging his troops by telling them that the enemy were giving way, that their rear was attacked by Barteau, and that only one supreme effort was necessary to sweep them from the field, he hastened to the position of Morton with the artillery, upon whom at this moment he greatly depended. As he rode up to Morton, whose guns were then in action, the position being one at close range to the enemy and of great exposure, the artillerist ventured to say to his general that it was too dangerous a place for him, and suggested that he should go to the rear a short distance, where it was safer. He noticed that Forrest was much exhausted, and was surprised that he yielded to the advice of his subordinate. Riding back some thirty or forty yards, he called Morton to him as he laid himself upon the ground at the root of a big tree. Here he said to the artillerist that he believed he had the enemy beaten, and that while they were still holding on with considerable stubbornness near the cross roads, he felt convinced that one more vigorous charge along the whole line, in which the artillery should take an active part, would be successful. He said that he would order this charge within ten minutes, and directed him to take four guns, double-shotted with canister, and, as soon as the bugle sounded the charge, to hitch the horses to them, gallop forward as far as possible, and open upon them at close range. Forrest rode then further over to the right to give Buford his final instructions. General Buford said that when Forrest told him what part Morton was to play, he suggested that it would be dangerous to send the guns forward without any support; but Forrest replied, "Buford, all the Yankees in front of us cannot get to Morton's guns." After the battle and pursuit were over, two days later, when the artillerist was returning with his pets, Forrest rode up to him, laid his hand on his shoulder, and said, "Well, John, I think your guns won the battle for us." Flushing with pride at this great praise of the man he idolized, Morton said: "General, I am glad you think so much of our work, but you scared me pretty bad when you pushed me up so close to their infantry and left me without any protection. I was afraid they might take my guns." To this Forrest replied, as he rode away, "Well, artillery is made to be captured, and I wanted to see them take yours."

Hurrying back to Bell, he ordered Tyler with his two companies of Kentuckians, Captain Jackson of the Escort, and Captain Johnson with Gartrell's Georgians to charge around the Federal right flank when the firing became general along the line and to rush into their rear, and engage at pistol range any Federal troops between their right and the Tishomingo Creek bridge.

Forrest's famous tactics were now to be demonstrated, the fierce onslaught—from the front, with a charge upon both flanks and in the enemy's rear by a few well-chosen and desperate horsemen. As Gaus's bugle sounded the charge, Buford and Lyon and Johnson went forward with the right of the Confederate line, in face of the tremendous discharge of small-arms and artillery; and amid the wild yells of the successful Confederates the Federal line gave way, stubbornly for a little space, and then yielded in disorder. Morton, with his horses hitched to the guns, swept forward along the country road, so narrow that only four pieces could be employed, with such boldness that in all probability the Federal commander at this point felt he was heavily supported, and when within short range of the centre and right of the Union line he made his double-shotted guns tell on their ranks with frightful effect. Rucker's final charge on the center and Bell's quick rush to the left carried away the last vestige of organization on the part of the Federals, and their line was at last irreparably broken.

Colonel McMillen, commanding the infantry, says: "As the enemy on our right were being driven back by the 9th Minnesota and 93d Indiana, I directed Captain Fitch to put one section of his artillery into position on the Guntown road and sweep it with grape and canister. Soon after, the left and left center gave back in considerable confusion, the rebels, Johnson and Lyon, following them in force up to the road over which we had advanced, and from which they were kept by the 72d Ohio and Mueller's battery. I endeavored to rally the different regiments and get them to ad-

vance to their original position, but failed. I sent word to General
Sturgis I was hard pressed, and unless relieved I would be obliged
to abandon my position. I was informed that he had nothing to
send me. I therefore determined to retire and form another line a
short distance in the rear to keep the enemy from the cross roads
until the artillery could be moved."

As the Federals retired, Lieutenants Haller and Mayson, under
orders from Morton, pushed their guns still further by hand along
the narrow roadway to the front, firing as they advanced. Coinci-
dent with this, Buford, Lyon, and Rucker closed in from all directions upon the Union forces, now in confusion, crowding them to
the cross roads at Brice's house, where three pieces of artillery
were captured and turned upon the fleeing enemy.

General Sturgis, referring to this period of the engagement,
says: "I now endeavored to get hold of the colored brigade, which
formed the guard of the wagon train. While traversing the short
distance to where the head of that brigade should be found, the
main line began to give way at various points. Order soon gave
way to confusion, and confusion to panic. . . . The army drifted
toward the rear, and was beyond control. The road became
crowded and jammed with troops; wagons and artillery sank into
the deep mud and became inextricable. No power could check the
panic-stricken mass as it swept toward the rear."

About one-quarter of a mile north of the cross roads Colonel
McMillen endeavored to stem the current of disaster by throwing
the 55th Colored Infantry across the line of retreat. The 59th Colored Infantry and Lamberg's section of artillery were placed
somewhat in rear of them, and for the same purpose, but the on-
sweeping tide of the Confederates was running high, and could
not be withstood. The brave General Buford, with boldness and
ability, had pushed Johnson's Alabamians so far forward on the
extreme Confederate right that they struck the flank of Bouton's
Africans in the direction of Tishomingo Creek, and at the same
moment upon the extreme left of the Confederate line the troopers
of Forrest's Escort, under Jackson and Gartrell, with Tyler's two
Kentucky companies, mounted, with daredevil recklessness swept
around the right of the Federal line and rode squarely into the col-

ored infantry with their six-shooters, just as Johnson's troops came in range and opened upon them from the other side. To add to their discomfiture, Morton and Rice, pushing their guns by hand, were crowding along the main road from Brice's to the bridge, and now, within gunshot range, thundered away, with their guns double-shotted with canister.

Nothing could surpass the desperate earnestness of these heroic men who stood to their work throughout this hot and depressing day. Suffering intensely with thirst, they drank the blackened powder-stained water from the sponge-buckets, which was being used to cleanse and cool the guns, rather than send one needed man away. Even some of the wounded refused to go to the rear. James Moran, for instance, a mere lad, who was badly wounded, when told by Captain Morton to go to the hospital, replied: "Captain, I don't want to go. I can stand it until we run 'em away." McMillen's forlorn hope was demolished so quickly that he scarcely checked the onward rush of Forrest's men.

Rearward of this position, across the sluggish Tishomingo Creek, there was a narrow wooden bridge, which had become hopelessly blocked by the overturning of a wagon and the impaction behind this of several other vehicles.

On to this bridge, clambering over the wreckage of wagons and the fallen horses struggling to free themselves, mad with fright, the fugitives rushed pell-mell, the soldiers pushing each other off on either side into the stream in their wild efforts to escape. Others, seeing the hopelessness of attempting to cross the bridge, threw themselves into the water, and waded or swam across, while many were drowned, or shot as they were floundering in the water. The Union loss was fearful. Reaching the creek, the Confederates cleared the bridge by pushing the wagons and dead or wounded animals into the stream.

Meanwhile a detachment of Forrest's Escort, under Lieutenant George L. Cowan, had effected a crossing about a quarter of a mile below the bridge, and sweeping around upon the flank of the enemy, charged boldly in among the panic-stricken crowd of fugitives, and cut off and captured a large number of prisoners and some wagons. So far was Cowan within the Federal lines that he came in range of Morton's relentless guns, and it was only when the battle-flag of the Escort was waved that he was recognized, and the firing in that direction ceased.

The sun was now just above the western horizon, but Forrest had no idea of calling off the chase. The men who had been detailed as horse-holders, and were therefore comparatively fresh, were hurried to the front, and under the personal leadership of Forrest and Buford they went forward upon the heels of the beaten army. Two miles from the battlefield McMillen succeeded in rallying a portion of the first and second brigades, under the command of brave Colonel A. Wilkin, who, later on, fell on the bloody field of Harrisburg. This line, however, could not stand longer than to permit Bouton to pass through with his Africans, for Morton came upon the scene with two of his pieces, and after a single round the Federals vanished. From this point on resistance practically ceased.

Major E. H. Hanson, a Union officer who took part in this engagement, reports: "All through the night the beaten men kept on their way, reaching Ripley, twenty-two miles from the battlefield, on the morning of June 11. During the retreat the enemy captured fourteen pieces of artillery, our entire wagon train of 250 wagons, loaded with ammunition and ten days' rations. At Ripley an attempt was made to reorganize our troops into companies and regiments, but the enemy appeared on two sides before this could be accomplished, and we were only able to check them until the retreat could be resumed. It continued in this way to Collierville, Tennessee. The bitter humiliation of this disaster rankles after a quarter of a century. Our loss was 2240 men. The enemy may have numbered 3500 or 4000, but it must be reluctantly confessed that not more than this number is believed to have been in action. If there was during the war another engagement like this, it is unknown to the writer; and in its immediate results there was no success, among the many won by Forrest, comparable to that of Guntown."

Forrest's men who had done the fighting on foot were allowed to rest until 1 o'clock, while the horse-holders kept hammering away at the fleeing enemy, to give them no respite. At 3 A.M. Buford in force came upon their rear in the Hatchie bottoms, and here the balance of the wagon train and fourteen additional pieces of artillery fell into the hands of the gallant Kentuckian. Four miles from Ripley, Grierson had rallied a forlorn hope, but, with the Escort and the Seventh Tennessee alone, Forrest, leading the charge in person, attacked them, and after a feeble resistance scattered them "like chaff before the winds."

All through the day and until nightfall of the 11th the pursuit was continued, and only closed when, near Salem, in sight of the home of his youth, Forrest, completely exhausted, was seized with a fainting spell, fell from his horse, and remained unconscious for nearly an hour, to the great alarm of his devoted followers.

The battle at Brice's cross roads demonstrated the truth of the adage that "the battle is not to the strong." The Federals were not defeated for lack of courage, as the fighting qualities of these men, when properly handled, was in a succeeding engagement fully shown.

From ten until four, beneath the fierce heat of a Southern sun, the men of Alabama, Mississippi, Kentucky, and Tennessee had struggled in desperate and often hand-to-hand conflict with the sturdy soldiers of Indiana, Illinois, Minnesota, Iowa, and New Jersey; and while there can be no doubt that great credit was due to the splendid fighting qualities of the men under Forrest, and to his officers, as determined and courageous as himself, nothing on that day and against such odds could have saved his army from defeat and destruction but the marvelous genius of the "unlettered soldier."

He had fought on the field a body of veteran troops which doubly outnumbered him, and withal advantageously posted, as he had been the assailant from the beginning. To reach the battlefield the Federal troops had only nine miles to march; the greater portion of Forrest's command had marched twenty-five miles, and his artillery had made eighteen miles before they came into action. The vigorous and tireless pursuit was as wonderful as the victory on the field. It seems almost incredible that men could have endured what this little army of Forrest endured on those two days of June.

The artillery of Morton and Rice had started from Booneville at 5 A.M. on the 10th, had marched eighteen miles, and then for five hours had been engaged without intermission in this desperate conflict; had followed the enemy from the field until well into the night, and after seven hours of rest pushed onward, keeping up with and at times even in front of the advance-guard of Forrest's cavalry; had reached Salem on the night of the 11th, making sixty miles in thirty-eight hours, besides fighting for five hours of this time—a record possibly without a parallel in artillery fighting. So energetic had been Morton's pursuit that fifteen horses fell dead in harness from exhaustion.

Bell's brigade at 4 A.M. on the 10th had left Rienzi, marched twenty-five miles to the battlefield, fought from 2 until 5, pursued the enemy from the field, and at 8 P.M. on the night of the 11th camped at Davis's Mill, north of Salem, having made nearly eighty miles in forty hours.

No wonder the army of Sturgis had melted away in a wild stampede, until it was every one for himself. Few escaped, excepting those who had horses, or who cut them loose from the wagons and the artillery. The infantry suffered most heavily in killed and captured, while the colored troops, believing that no quarter would be shown them, scattered in all directions, taking to the woods and bottoms for safety.

In his enterprising book entitled *Whip and Spur,* the late Colonel George E. Waring, Jr., gives a vivid description of this flight of the Union army; and records an incident replete with humor. He says:

> The demoralizing roar of our own guns, and the howling over our heads of our own shells, together with the sharp rattle of musketry in our rear, hastened and saddened the ignominious flight of the head of our column. The ambulances with our groaning, wounded men came pouring into the village [Ripley], and, to our surprise, those women who had so recently given only evidence of a horrified hatred, pressed round to offer every aid that lay in their power, and to comfort our suffering men as only kind-hearted women can. We marched without rest,

and without sleep, and without food. The cavalrymen were mainly dismounted, and driving their tired jades before them.

During our last night's march, my brigade having the advance, and I being at its rear, Grierson ordered me to prevent the pushing ahead of the stragglers of the other brigades, who were to be recognized by their wearing hats (mine wore caps). Grierson's adjutant was at my side; we were all sleeping more or less of the time, but constantly some hatted straggler was detected pushing toward the front, and ordered back. Finally, close to my right, and pushing slowly to the front in a long-strided walk, came a gray horse with a hatted rider, an India-rubber poncho covering his uniform. I ordered him back; the adjutant, eager for enforcement of the order, remonstrated at the man's disobedience; I ordered again, but without result; the adjutant ejaculated, "Damn him, cut him down!" I drew my sabre, and laid its flat in one long stinging welt across that black poncho. "Who are you hitting?" Then we both remembered that Grierson too wore a hat; and I tender him here my public acknowledgment of a good-nature so great that an evening reunion in Memphis over a dozen of wine won his generous silence.

On the morning of the 11th at Ripley, General Sturgis writes, "Nothing was left but to keep in motion." On the 12th he was at Collierville, after a run of forty-eight hours, with scarcely a halt; and on the 13th, at 9 A.M., a fragment of his fleeing command was at White's Station. It had taken him nine days to march his command from this point to Brice's cross roads. The return trip was made in sixty-four hours.

General Washburn says: "The expedition left the railroad terminus on June 1st, and reached Brice's cross roads on June 10th. The force that escaped returned to this point in one day and two nights."

The Confederates lost heavily in killed and wounded. The report of the chief surgeon, Dr. J. B. Cowan, gives 493 killed and wounded. In Rucker's brigade the loss was 23 per cent., and in Lyon's command over 20 per cent. were killed or wounded.

General Sturgis in his official report, made on the 24th of June, gave his loss of killed, wounded, and missing as 2240. The detailed reports of his brigade and regimental commanders show his loss to have been 2612.

General Forrest captured 250 wagons and ambulances, 18 pieces of artillery, 5000 stands of small-arms, and 500,000 rounds of small-arm ammunition, and all the enemy's baggage and supplies.

14

SHERIDAN AT CEDAR CREEK

By C. W. Denison

The valley of the Shenandoah River, "The Valley" to Virginians, was the most important military corridor in the eastern theater of operations. As the Confederate armies moved up and down it (in both the Antietam and the Gettysburg invasions, it was the axis of advance) they could debouch from there through any of its many gaps to flank Federal forces in the Piedmont region. Jackson's campaign there had been conspicuously successful in compelling Union troops to defend Washington.

It is a rich land, producing much foodstuff for the hard-pressed Confederate commissariat.

In 1864, Early's Corps was sent there to emulate Jackson's activities of 1862 and to relieve the pressure on the Petersburg front. In part he was successful and a raid actually took him to within sight of Washington. By the autumn, Grant was sufficiently annoyed by all of this to resolve to finish with the Valley once and for all. He appointed an aggressive young cavalry general, Phil Sheridan to clean out the Valley and then close up his forces to reinforce the army before Petersburg. Sheridan mustered a splendid force and advanced slowly, but effectively. He is reported to have said that he would leave the Valley so that a crow flying over it would have to carry his rations on his back. Early, who was a fighter and a good tactician, had what, at least technically, was a corps in the Valley to oppose Sheridan's advance. At Cedar Creek he made his move. In a well-planned surprise attack, he fell on the Federal troops and initially achieved a complete success. The Federal forces were largely routed. Content with this initial success, his hungry troops began to plunder Federal wagons. Sheridan was in Winchester at the time and from there made his famous ride to the scene of the engagement where he rallied his forces and completely routed Early. The Valley was no longer Confederate.

Soon after midnight of Tuesday, August 18th, Early, having arranged his troops unperceived at Fisher's Hill, just beyond Strasburg, moved forward to the attack. The sharp rattle of musketry on the right, near the Middle road, before daylight, made the camp aware that our cavalry pickets were engaged with the enemy's skirmishers. But the firing died away, the movement in that quarter being in fact only a feint, and being regarded, also, as a demonstration like the previous one against Custer's pickets. The real attack was to fall upon our left. Kershaw's division was in Early's advance. Marching southeasterly from Strasburg a short distance along the Manassas gap railroad, Kershaw, with a selected column, then turned northerly again on the small road which crosses the North Fork by a ford about a mile to the east of the junction of Cedar creek with that river. Before dawn of Wednesday, the 19th, he was across the ford and marching past the left flank of Crook's corps, directly in the latter's rear, the whole maneuver being accomplished in the chilly and foggy morning without the knowledge of our army. Meanwhile, the rest of Early's command had marched straight down the turnpike from Strasburg to Cedar creek, with equal silence and celerity, and, like the flanking column, without alarming our pickets or officers of the day.

His positions being gained, close upon our picket line, the enemy, just before daybreak, rushed to the attack. So well protected was this flank with earthworks carrying artillery, that little fear had been entertained for it. But the enemy's noiseless advance and successful surprise counterbalanced the strength of the defences. Advancing in columns of regiments, he swept in upon Crook's picket line, and captured the greater part of it. Before the noise of the skirmishing had aroused the camp from its slumbers, the enemy's flanking column was fairly within the intrenchments of the eighth corps, and was capturing prisoners in large numbers, among his captures being the second battalion fifth New York heavy artillery, which was on the picket line. Once inside the camp, the enemy rushed to seize the batteries, and succeeded in cutting off and capturing many pieces of artillery, before the latter could exchange a shot. The left division of Crook's corps was now thoroughly broken up, and Kitching's provisional division of heavy New York artillery, which lay in Crook's rear, suffered a similar calamity. General Crook and Colonel Kitching endeavored to rally their commands; but the bewilderment of the troops in the unexpected attack, the large force of the enemy, and his success in turning our flank unperceived, showed that he could not be checked at this point.

Meanwhile, also, Early had emerged from behind the hills west of Cedar creek, where he lay concealed, and simultaneously with the attack in flank, rushed across the creek at the ford, and drove back Thorburn's division, which lay on the right of Crook's line, in front of the ford and against the turnpike. This combined movement sufficed to complete the disaster. The entire corps was routed, and the left flank of the army turned. Many of the regiments, however, were rallied, and the whole command falling back to the turnpike, was there got into line again as rapidly as possible, after the loss of many prisoners. But the enemy had now got all his artillery in position on the high ridges on the westerly bank of the creek, and, with accurate range, was pouring shot and shell in great profusion into both the eighth and nineteenth corps. On this side of the creek also, he continued his rapid advance, elated at his success, and delivered a constant and murderous musketry fire into our recoiling line as he advanced. He had soon gained and passed the turnpike, in his march along our line, and in heavy force, charged the batteries of the nineteenth corps. His impetuous attack was only too successful, and the left of the nineteenth corps also gave way, leaving a part of its artillery in his hands. Under this rapid musketry fire of the enemy in his vigorous advance, joined with his effective artillery from the opposite banks of the creek, and the fire from our own batteries which he had turned against us, our left and centre were thrown into confusion. Many prisoners were captured, and many casualties occurred in our ranks from his hot fire. All the trains were therefore started in haste along the turnpike to Winchester, and escaping capture, arrived there in safety.

It was now broad day, and it appeared that our disasters had only begun. For the enemy, having succeeded in rolling up the left of the line, and in severing Powell's cavalry division on the extreme left from the rest of the army, was now forcing back the entire centre, and occupying the intrenchments of the nineteenth corps as he had those of the eighth. He had captured a large part of our artillery also—eighteen pieces thus far—and not only deprived us of these means of checking his advance, but, to our double calamity, turned them on our columns, materially precipitating the retreat. Nearly all of his force was on this side of the creek, and a part of the flanking column, turning off from the pursuit of the eighteenth corps, found itself in the rear of Grover's second division of the nineteenth corps, which formed Emory's left, and held the right or northerly side of the turnpike. Hasty dispositions toward a change of front were made, so as to hold the pike, but they were of no avail. Emory was flanked, in his turn, and gave away to the rear. The sixth corps had been already ordered over from its position on the right, and quickly executed a change of front, which brought it at right angles to its former direction.

Steadily holding this new line, the corps was soon engaged in desperate conflict, and, by its gallantry, served to check the enemy's impetuous rush. But, after all, it only availed to cover the general retreat, which was now ordered. The enemy was creeping up along the pike, and already approached Middletown. Great efforts were made to get away the trains of the two left corps, and most of those of the nineteenth were saved. Most of the ambulance train of the eighth corps was captured during the first hour of the engagement. In the retreat, and in the effort to cover our trains, our troops suffered severely from the fire of the enemy, who pursued closely and with great vigor. The enemy now increased both his artillery and musketry fire to its utmost capacity, till the roar and carnage became terrific. He still pressed our left flank, as if determined to drive us away from the turnpike, that he might seize our trains, and insert himself between us and Winchester. His projects were aided somewhat by the necessity forced upon us to spend much time in maneuvering to reform the line, while he employed himself only in advancing and pouring in his destructive fire. As he pressed our left so much more hotly than the right, the cavalry divisions of Merritt and Custer, were sent across thither from the right, and now a severe contest took place near Middletown, in the thickly wooded and rough country in which our left had found itself.

It was now about nine o'clock, and our troops having got into line-of-battle again, were, for the first time, making desperate efforts to check the enemy. The eighth corps on the left, and the sixth in the centre, were receiving the brunt of the fierce onset. Merritt and Custer had also taken part in the thick of the battle. Both sides were using artillery as well as musketry, but the enemy brought to bear the greater weight of metal, having reinforced their own batteries with our captured pieces. As the enemy's troops closed in on our own, it was clear that the momentum he had acquired was swinging him again past our flank. The flanking column of the enemy pressed severely upon Thorburn's division and other parts of Crook's corps, and once more forced it back. The sixth corps held its ground well, but the whole line was giving away, and the enemy gained Middletown. He continued to press us back toward Stephensburg or Newtown, which lies next below Middletown, on the turnpike, and about five miles distant therefrom. His artillery was served with accuracy from the heights north of Middletown, which we had just vacated. Our principal aim henceforth was successfully to cover our trains and to draw away the army with as little loss as possible to Newtown, when another stand might be made, for General Wright had by no means despaired of the day.

At this time, about half-past ten o'clock, Sheridan rode upon the field from Winchester, where news of the battle had reached him. He had come in at great speed, being well assured by the sight that met him on the road that his presence was needed at the earliest moment. His arrival created great enthusiasm among both officers and men, to whom, in the general gloom, this was a ray of hope. He rode along the ranks, and was received everywhere with cheers. A temporary pause in the enemy's pursuit, and our own withdrawal from his fire, facilitated greatly the preparations to resist any further advance. These were promptly undertaken, just south of Newtown, between the latter point and Middletown. The line was left as Wright had formed it, except that one cavalry division, Custer's, was sent across to cover the right flank, where it was before the battle.

The lull in the fierce fighting which had commenced soon after our retreat to Newtown and Sheridan's opportune arrival, soon after noon came to an end. The enemy, having got his artillery up into range of our new position, now opened it with new vigor. About one o'clock, his troops were well in hand again, and once more came up on the charge. But this time he was doomed to disappointment. Our lines were ready and, after a long and desperate struggle, repulsed him handsomely, and even followed him back for a short distance. General Bidwell was killed and General Grover wounded, in this renewal of the heavy engagement. From two o'clock till three there was no advance of importance on either side. Incessant cannonading and the rattle of musketry filled up the hour; but all attempts of the enemy to force us back were fruitless.

About three o'clock, Sheridan determined to make a grand effort to throw the enemy out of Middletown, which, up to that time, he held, and once more to regain our camp at Cedar creek. The sixth corps was drawn up in the centre, along the pike, with Getty's second division in advance. The other divisions supported. The eighth corps was re-formed on the left of the sixth, and the nineteenth came up on its right, under cover of the woods. Merritt's first cavalry division was thrown out on the left flank, with Lowell's brigade in advance, and Deven following closely. Custer was on the right flank. Between three and four o'clock, Getty dashed forward on the charge, and the remainder of the line followed. A tremendous fire of artillery and musketry greeted our troops as they burst out of the woods. For a time it seemed impossible to withstand it. Our lines once surged back, broken, but were again re-formed, and, while such of our own batteries as remained, answered the enemy with vigor and effect, the gallant troops again pressed on. Despite determined and bloody resistance, they carried the town, and drove the discomfited enemy through it. This was the crisis of the day, and from that moment victory was ours. The enemy at once began his retreat, and it was only a question how far our men would have strength enough to pursue him, and what spoil he would leave in our hands. In this last charge fell the gallant Colonel Lowell, who had greatly distinguished himself during this Shenandoah campaign. His brigade also behaved very handsomely during the present battle.

The sixth and nineteenth corps and the cavalry now pressed the enemy from Middletown to Cedar creek. In his haste he threw away guns, haversacks, clothing, and other debris of a routed army. No time was given him to pause. The infantry were thrown rapidly into column for the pursuit, and the cavalry charged across the open fields. At Cedar creek the enemy attempted at last to hold us in check, and planted his batteries on the opposite banks, to hold the bridge and fords. But our forces pressed on, carried the fords and bridge, and drove him from the creek through Strasburg to Fisher's Hill. The cavalry distinguished itself in getting across the creek under fire. The briskness of the pursuit caused the enemy to abandon large quantities of cannon, caissons, and wagons, and threw his whole rear into confusion. In fact our troops had now a fair offset for their own defeat in the morning, and the enemy was put to flight in quite as much rapidity and disorganization as he had visited upon us at daybreak, and with much greater loss of material. The desperately resisted but successful charge at Middletown was, in fact, the turning point of the day. The enemy was put to flight, and all that was required was to pursue, and pick up prisoners and spoils. The hard fighting was over, and the loss which followed fell upon the enemy. The cavalry proved now of great assistance, and the enemy, in his haste to get away, abandoned all the cannon he had captured and much of his own. Our camp equipage fell into our hands again, and in fact, at each step the cavalry found cannon, caissons, small arms, or other material, and prisoners ready to be captured without a struggle.

From the arrival of Sheridan and the turn of the tide, we gained back nearly all that had been lost—except the prisoners and the small amount destroyed or carried off by the enemy—and captured still more than we had lost. The most accurate estimate gives our total captures and re-captures as follows:—twelve hundred men, sixty-four officers, forty-eight cannon, forty caissons, three battery wagons, three hundred and ninety-eight horses and mules, with harness, sixty-five ambulances, fifty wagons, fifteen thousand rounds of artillery ammunition, fifteen hundred and eighty small arms, many medical stores of the enemy, besides our own, ten battle flags, and some smaller captures of stores. One of the enemy's papers, admitting the defeat, says:

"All of the camp equipage captured on the creek in the morning was retaken by the enemy, and at Strasburg the captured artillery becoming, by the demoralization of the drivers, mixed up in the street with some ten or twelve pieces of our own, the whole of it was abandoned. The prisoners we had taken, the most useless and unacceptable of our captures, were alone left to us as trophies of the morning. By night our army was in New Market, worn with fatigue, and perplexed and mortified with the results of the day's operation, but growing cheerful by degrees, and sanguine of 'better luck the next time.' Our loss in men was not heavy. In this respect there is some consolation in knowing that the enemy suffered by far the heavier. In the morning's operations the slaughter of the enemy is represented as having been very great."

A part of our infantry reached Strasburg, but the main army bivouacked in the old camp along Cedar creek. The cavalry dashed through Strasburg to Fisher's Hill, and there stopped the victorious march. Wright having fallen, we pursued only three or four miles beyond the old camp ground.

It was on the decisive and glorious results of this hard-earned victory, that the following spirited poem was produced by Thomas Buchanan Read:

SHERIDAN'S RIDE.

BY THOMAS BUCHANAN READ.

Up from the South at break of day,
Bringing from Winchester fresh dismay,
The affrighted air with a shudder bore,

Like a herald in haste, to the chieftain's door,
The terrible grumble, and rumble, and roar,
Telling the battle was on once more,
And Sheridan twenty miles away.

And wider still those billows of war
Thundered along the horizon's bar;
And louder yet into Winchester rolled
The roar of that red sea uncontrolled,
Making the blood of the listener cold,
As he thought of the stake in that fiery fray,
And Sheridan twenty miles away.

But there is a road from Winchester town,
A good, broad highway leading down;
And there, through the flush of the morning light,
A steed, as black as the steeds of night
Was seen to pass, as with eagle flight,
As if he knew the terrible need;
He stretched away with his utmost speed;
Hills rose and fell, but his heart was gay,
With Sheridan fifteen miles away.

Still sprung from those swift hoofs, thundering South,
The dust, like the smoke from the cannon's mouth;
Or the trail of a comet, sweeping faster and faster,
Foreboding to traitors the doom of disaster.
The heart of the steed and the heart of the master
Were beating like prisoners assaulting their walls,
Impatient to be where the battlefield calls;
Every nerve of the charger was strained to full play,
With Sheridan only ten miles away.

Under his spurning feet, the road
Like an arrowy Alpine river flowed,
And the landscape sped away behind
Like an ocean flying before the wind;
And the steed, like a bark fed with furnace ire,
Swept on, with his wild eyes full of fire.
But lo! he is nearing his heart's desire;

He is snuffing the smoke of the roaring fray,
With Sheridan only five miles away.

The first that the General saw were the groups
Of stragglers, and then the retreating troops;—
What was done—what to do—a glance told him both;
Then striking his spurs, with a terrible oath,
He dashed down the line 'mid a storm of huzzas,
And the wave of retreat checked its course there, because
The sight of its master compelled it to pause.
With foam and with dust the black charger was gray;
By the flash of his eye, and his red nostril's play,
He seemed to the whole great army to say:
"I have brought you Sheridan all the way
From Winchester, down to save the day!"

Hurrah, hurrah for Sheridan!
Hurrah, hurrah for horse and man!
And when their statues are placed on high,
Under the dome of the Union sky,
The American Soldiers' Temple of Fame,
There with the glorious General's name,
Be it said, in letters both bold and bright,
    "Here is the steed that saved the day,
By carrying Sheridan into the fight,
    From Winchester—twenty miles away!"

15

THE FALL OF PETERSBURG

By James P. Matthews

After the desperate days and hours, when the battle of Spottsyl-
vania Court House was fought to a bloody draw, Grant con-
tinued his determined proposal to fight it out on that line even
though it would take more than the summer. Stubbornly he con-
tinued to move to his left. Desperately the Confederates continued
to get in front of him by a narrow margin. At last Grant de-
termined upon a really big envelopment. He literally stole a march
on Lee. In a most remarkable operation he moved to the south
of Richmond and after crossing the great water courses attacked
the forces at Petersburg. With this rail center in his hands, Grant
could invade Richmond from the south, a plan incidentally pro-
posed by General Scott early in the war. Under the most desperate
of circumstances the Confederates once more were barely able to
contain the attack. Petersburg became a siege when both sides
dug in. Sapping operations resulted in the crater but somehow the
gray lines held. Through the summer, fall and winter the siege went
on. The Federals consistently tried to overlap the Confederates'
south flank. This required the gray forces to stretch thinner and
thinner. Not only that but the constant attrition of battle casualties,
disease, discouragement and desertion steadily weakened the gray
forces. By the first of April, when the mud began to dry sufficiently
to permit efficient maneuver, those lines were stretched beyond
their tensile strength. A great Federal assault before dawn on
April 2 finally shattered them. While the account given here is

*concerned primarily with the death of one of the Confederate
Corps commanders it does imply vividly the dissolution of the
Army of North Virginia and also the requirements with which to
organize any military semblance to the final withdrawal, which
would terminate one week later at the village of Appomattox
Court House.*

It is seldom that all the details of a battlefield incident are so well
known as in the case of the shooting of General Hill. Of the four
men who accidentally met on the edge of a wooded swamp, skirt-
ing the Boydton plank road, on the morning of April 2, 1865, three
were still living at the time of the dedication of the Hill monument,
and two of them (one on each side), had written narratives of
the occurrence which fit together wonderfully well, although
neither of the writers was conscious of the other's existence. It is a
somewhat remarkable circumstance that the survivors were all citizens of Pennsylvania in 1892. The Southern soldier who lived to
tell the tragic story of the death of his chief and his own fortunate
escape, and the two Union soldiers, who refused to surrender to
him, would have been citizens of the same county, if boundary
lines had remained as they were at the beginning of the Revolutionary War.

To understand properly the circumstances that brought General Hill and Sergeant Tucker, his chief of couriers, into accidental
collision with two Pennsylvania soldiers, it will be necessary to
take a glance at the military situation as it existed on that eventful morning. The two armies, which had been fortifying against
each other for nearly ten months, and had fought a dozen terrific
battles for the possession of vantage points on the various parts of
the embattled line, had entered upon the final struggle. A portion
of General Lee's forces held the cordon of strong forts which had
been thrown around Petersburg, forming as it were a gigantic
horseshoe, with the corkers resting on the Appomattox River and
covering the roads to Richmond.

Grant's guns had been pounding away at the toe of the horseshoe for nine months, with no appreciable effect. The Southside

Railroad runs westward from Petersburg and connects with the Richmond and Danville Road at Burkville Junction. The possession of this road was as important to Lee as the direct road to Richmond, and to protect it a line of entrenchments and forts was extended for eight or ten miles to the south and west, which, up to April 1st, had availed to keep Grant away from his main line of communication and supply.

On April 1st, Sheridan, with a powerful cavalry force, passed around this line of works, and supported by the Second and Fifth corps, assaulted the extreme Southern projection of Lee's right wing at Five Forks. All the troops that could possibly be spared from defense of Petersburg were hurried out to this exposed position, where a great battle was fought, which ended disastrously to the Confederates. Johnson's and Pickett's divisions retreated to the westward, and never returned to Petersburg. A large section of Lee's right wing had been eliminated from the military problem, and for the purposes of offense and defense had ceased to exist.

The strong line of works, however, reaching from Petersburg beyond Hatcher's Run, and the impregnable horseshoe around the city covering the road to Richmond, still remained intact. Upon these works Grant opened a fierce cannonade, which was kept up until four o'clock on Sunday morning, when, upon a given signal, the Ninth corps, under General Parke, assaulted the works immediately in front of the city, while the Sixth corps moved upon the line of works running southward and westward to Hatcher's Run.

Outside of the main line of forts around the city was a trench bearded with Chevaux-de-frise. Logs were hewn square and bored on the four sides. Sharpened sticks were driven into these holes, so that each log represented a gigantic rake with four rows of teeth, one row always being ready to impale an advancing column, no matter on which side it might be turned. The logs were chained together at the ends, so that for miles there was a continuous line of these ugly obstructions.

When the order to charge was given, the pioneers went forward first, and with their axes broke the fastenings at the ends of the logs, and then lifted the free end around, thus making gaps through which the assaulting columns poured. The Ninth corps carried the outer line of works, but halted before the strong forts within, and taking shelter in the captured trenches, made no further progress during the day.

The Sixth corps assaulted simultaneously with the Ninth corps, and broke through the line of works two or three miles further out in the direction of Hatcher's Run. After the troops got inside and cleared the ground in front of them, they turned to the left, dislodged four brigades of Heth's division from their defences, and started most of Heth's division of Hill's corps in a rapid retreat in a northwesterly direction, their object being to reach Goode's bridge and cross over to the north side of the Appomattox.

The troops along that portion of the line which were assaulted by the Sixth corps were mainly of Wilcox's division and Heth's division of Hill's corps. Those stationed to the right of the breach retreated east and north to the inner line of strong forts around Petersburg. Those to the left of the breach went north and west in the direction of the Southside Railroad, as already stated, and later in the day were overtaken at Sutherland's Station, on the Southside Railroad, by Miles' division of the Second corps, and compelled to halt and fight a battle.

Lieutenant General A. P. Hill passed the night at his headquarters in the western suburbs of Petersburg, and was disturbed by the heavy firing on the Petersburg Lines in front of the city. He was exceedingly anxious to communicate with the commander in chief on the subject, and at daylight rode over to General Lee's quarters at the Turnbull House, on the Cox road. From there, accompanied only by two soldiers, Sergeant Tucker and Private Jenkins, he started to the right of his lines; his troops had been swept away from their line of defense, and there was not an armed Confederate soldier in the whole region between the breach in his lines and the Southside Railroad east of Hatcher's Run. On the west side the disorganized brigades of Heth's division were hurrying away in rapid retreat. If he had started an hour earlier and followed the same route, he would have ridden into Seymour's division of the Sixth corps. If he had started an hour later he would have struck the returning column, reinforced by two divisions of Ord's corps, which had crossed the works west of Hatcher's Run, and turning eastward, met the Sixth corps, which faced about and came back to the point where it had entered the Confederate lines.

When General Hill came to the lost ground in front of Wilcox's line it was not occupied, except by a few soldiers of Keifer's brigade, a portion of which had not turned westward with the main body after crossing the Confederate works, but had kept straight on in the direction of the Southside Railroad. When this detached fragment faced about and followed the remainder of the command, a few men dropped out and took possession of an old deserted camp that had been occupied by General Mahone's troops during the winter, and began to prepare a hasty breakfast. Corporal John W. Mauk and Private Daniel Wolford, of Company F, One Hundred and Thirty-eighth Pennsylvania Infantry, did not halt with the rest, but kept on in the direction of the Southside Railroad. These two men were coming back from their independent exploring expedition when General Hill and his sergeant of courier, George W. Tucker came up with them. Mr. Tucker, in the November (1883) number of the Southern Historical Papers, gave a very interesting, and no doubt, perfectly truthful, account of this meeting and its fatal result, in which he said:

"We went directly across the road into the opposite field, and riding due south a short distance, the General drew rein, and for a few moments used his field glass, which, in my still profound ignorance of what had happened, struck me as exceedingly queer. We then rode on in the same direction, down a declivity toward a small branch running eastward to Old Town creek, and a quarter of a mile from General Lee's. We had gone a little more than half this distance, when we suddenly came upon two of the enemy's armed infantrymen. Jenkins and myself, who up to this time rode immediately behind the General, were instantly upon them, when, at the command "surrender," they laid down their arms. Turning to the General, I asked what should be done with the prisoners. He said, "Jenkins, take them to General Lee." Jenkins started back with his men, and we rode on.

Though not invited, I was at the General's side, and my attention now having been aroused, and looking carefully ahead and around, I saw a lot of people in and about the old log-hut winter quarters of General Mahone's division, situated to the right of Whitworth house and on the top of the hill, beyond the branch we were approaching. Now, as I knew that those quarters had been vacant since about March 15th, by the transfer of Mahone to north of the Appomattox, and feeling that it was the enemy's troops in possession, with nothing looking like a Confederate anywhere, I remarked, pointing to the old camp, "General, what troops are those?" He quickly replied, "The enemy's." Proceeding still further, and General Hill making no further remark, I became so impressed with the great risk he was running that I made bold to say, "Please excuse me, General, but where are you going?" He answered, "Sergeant, I must go to the right as quickly as possible." Then pointing southwest, he said, "We will go up this side of the branch to the woods, which will cover us until reaching the field in rear of General Heth's quarters. I hope to find the road clear at General Heth's."

From that time on I kept slightly ahead of the general. I had kept a Colt's army pistol drawn since the affair of the Federal stragglers. We then made the branch, becoming obscured from the enemy, and crossing the Boydton plank road, soon made the woods, which were kept for about a mile, in which distance we did not see a single person, and emerged into the field opposite General Heth's at a point two miles due southwest from General Lee's headquarters, at the Turnbull House, and at right angles with the Boydton plank road, at the Harman House, which was distant half a mile. When going through the woods, the only words between General Hill and myself, except a few relating to the route, were by himself. He called my attention, and said, "Sergeant, should anything happen to me, you must go back to General Lee and report it."

We came into the field near its corner, at the foot of a small declivity, rising which I could plainly see that the wood was full of troops of some kind. The general, raising his field-glass, said, "They are there." I understood perfectly that he meant the enemy, and asked, "Which way, now, General?" He pointed to that side of the woods parallel to the Boydton plank road, about one hundred yards down the hill from where our horses stood, saying, "We must keep on to the right." I spurred ahead, and we had made two-thirds of the distance, and coming to a walk, looked intently into the woods, at the immediate edge of which were several large trees. I saw what appeared to be six or eight Federals, two of whom, being some distance in advance of the rest, who halted some forty or fifty yards from the field, ran quickly forward to the cover of one of the large trees, and, one above the other, on the same side, leveled their guns. I looked around to General Hill. He said, "We must take them," at the same time drawing, for the first time that day, his Colt's navy pistol. I said, "Stay there, I will take them." By this time we were within twenty yards of the two behind the tree, and getting closer every moment. I shouted, "If you fire, you will be swept to hell. Our men are here—surrender!" Then General Hill was at my side, calling, "Surrender." Now, within ten yards of the men covering us with their muskets—the upper one, the general; the lower one, myself; the lower soldier let the stock of his gun down from his shoulder, but recovered quickly as his comrade spoke to him (I only saw his lips move), and both fired. Throwing out my right hand toward the general, I caught the bridle of his horse, and, wheeling to the left, turned in the saddle and saw my general on the ground, with limbs extended, motionless.

Instantly retracing the ground leading his horse, which gave me no trouble, I entered the woods again where we had left them, and realizing the importance, and, of all things, most desirous of obeying the general's last order to report to General Lee, I changed to his horse, a very superior one and quite fresh, and letting mine free, kept on as fast as the nature of the ground would permit."

*   *   *   *   *   *   *   *   *   *

The Fifth Alabama Battalion, skirmishing, found the general's body, which was still slightly warm, with nothing about it disturbed. The Federal party were doubtless alarmed at what had been done, and must have instantly fled. The writer did not again see General Hill's body, which was brought to Venable's by a route still farther to our rear.   *   *   *   I learned that the ball struck the General's pistol hand, and then penetrated his body just over the heart. That cruel ball first cut off the thumb of General Hill's left (bridle) hand, leaving it hanging from the gauntlet.

The account which Corporal Mauk wrote out for Mr. Matthews confirms Tucker in all the main incidents of the tragedy.

16

LINCOLN IN THE CONFEDERATE CAPITAL

By Philip Van Doren Stern

For four tragic and sanguinary years, the Federal armies tried to take Richmond. When Petersburg fell, Richmond was no longer defensible. The Confederate civil government fled and the Blue forces moved in unopposed. The President of the United States personally went to see the city, for himself, a few days later. Surely climax had been reached when the President of the United States could walk the streets of Richmond. Here one of America's most distinguished contemporary historians describes that event in his own vivid prose.

Richmond lay before them now, magnificent in the grandeur of its destruction. The pillared Capitol, still intact, crowned the heights above the city, and the whole section along the nearest shore was just as it had been left by the fleeing Confederate Army. But the entire business area between the Capitol and the river was either in ruins or still aflame.

The barge headed toward Rocketts Landing. It got stuck on a rock, was pushed off, and then went on again. Confederate cannon and plundered supply wagons stood near the warehouses along the waterfront. Several dozen Negroes, who had been digging in a field, stopped work to watch the boat approach.

Some of the sailors jumped out to make the barge fast and help the President and Tad get ashore. The cutter was far behind; still farther down the river was Barnes with a few men in the gig from the Bat. They were rowing frantically upstream to try to overtake the Presidential party.

Twelve sailors, the President of the United States, his young son Tad, Rear Admiral David Dixon Porter, a Navy captain, an Army captain, a signal officer, and the President's bodyguard, William H. Crook, made up the party. The sailors were armed with carbines and bayonets, Crook had a Colt revolver, and the officers doubtless wore their side arms. But they still had no idea of what kind of reception to expect.

When the President stepped ashore, dressed in his long black coat and wearing his customary tall silk hat, some of the Negroes recognized him from pictures they had seen. There was a buzz of excited talk. Here, at last, was the man who had set them free; this was the long awaited Messiah whose coming had been foretold in many a secretly worded spiritual sung at nightfall on thousands of plantations throughout the South. Here, in person, was the Father Abraham of their hopes and dreams.

A white-haired old man rushed forward to throw himself at the feet of the President, mumbling incoherently as he tried to kiss his muddied boots. The others pushed forward, shouting. Their excitement was instantly communicated to scores and then to hundreds of Negroes who sprang up from nowhere to surround the President in a wildly exultant mob.

Lincoln was embarrassed; he urged the kneeling man to get up and spoke to the others, repeatedly having to raise his voice in order to be heard above the noise of the ever-growing crowd. Porter quietly told his men to fix bayonets and form a circle around the President. More and more Negroes kept swarming over the landing, laughing, shouting, and singing as they came. Porter said later that at one time they joined together to sing a hymn.

Nothing would satisfy them but to hear from the President himself that they were really free. They kept asking him again and again to tell them so. Finally he held up his hand for silence, and those who were near enough to see the gesture quieted down. He spoke briefly, assuring them that they were no longer slaves and that they must learn to act and live like free men. Everyone cheered; then, at a nod from Porter, the sailors opened a way through the crowd, and the President started to walk toward the center of the city. His admirers had no intention of being left behind. They followed, and, as they emerged from the waterfront district, more and more people joined them, white as well as black.

During the two-mile walk through the ravaged streets of the unpoliced city, the attitude toward the lightly guarded man who was making his way slowly up the hill was simply that of curiosity, even among the whites. Most of them were poor or middle-class people, for the aristocracy had fled or were staying behind shuttered windows.

Crook said of the crowd: "The only sign of welcome I saw . . . was from a young lady on a bridge that connected the Spotswood House with another hotel across the street. She had an American flag over her shoulders." But Porter claims that a man in shirtsleeves rushed up to greet the President with the words "Abraham Lincoln, God bless you! You are the poor man's friend!" Then he tried to seize Lincoln's hand, and Porter had to push him away. The admiral also said that a beautiful girl struggled through the crowd, "her clothes very much disarranged in making the journey," to hand the President a bouquet and a card inscribed: "From Eva to the Liberator of the slaves." Although Porter does not say so, she may have been of mulatto birth; it seems unlikely that any white woman then in Richmond would have dared to risk her future with such a gesture.

Crook does not mention these two incidents. In fact, the naturally suspicious bodyguard believed that he prevented an attempted assassination, for he said: "The blinds of a second-story window of a house on our left were partly opened, and a man dressed in gray pointed something that looked like a gun directly at the President. I dropped Tad's hand and stepped in front of Mr. Lincoln. I was sure he meant to shoot." But Crook admits that no one else was alarmed, including the President. And finally he says: "It is to the everlasting glory of the South that he was permitted to come and go in peace."

But the danger was still very real; in fact, it was increasing every minute, for the surprise of the unexpected landing was over. By this time, many people in Richmond knew that the Northern President was walking through the streets of their city with a very small guard, and it would have been easy for one or more of them to take over action. But no one did, and Abraham Lincoln was permitted to pass unharmed through the former citadel of the Confederacy.

The little group with its accompanying crowd pushed on up the hill. The day was hot, the air was thick with the acrid odor of smoke and burning wood, and the aging President had to stop several times to rest. At last they saw their first Federal soldier, a cavalryman, sitting idly on his horse, looking on with the same curiosity as the citizens. Porter sent him to General Weitzel for a cavalry escort, which soon arrived to clear the streets. For the first time, the President was adequately guarded in the newly captured city.

Barnes and his men soon caught up with Lincoln's party, and they all went on up Capitol Hill. George A. Bruce saw them when they passed the Governor's mansion:

"Between two and three o'clock in the afternoon . . . there arose from the street back of the house a great noise and tumult. . . . I walked through the garden to the wall which is about twenty feet above the street. . . . As I looked down, the first platoon of sailors, armed with muskets, was directly opposite to me. They were stretched out in open file and reached within a few feet of either sidewalk. In the center of the street . . . was Mr. Lincoln leading his little boy. . . . Farther down was the second file of sailors stretching across the street. Before, on either side, and behind were two or three hundred negroes, men, women and some children. . . . This was, I believe, the wildest spectacle ever seen, and a picture of Mr. Lincoln moving wearily up this steep hill in the center of it would be one of the most remarkable in history. . . . Hats were thrown in the air, clothing pulled off and abandoned, but the most peculiar feature was the sudden throwing of themselves flat upon the ground and remaining there for some seconds, which species of demonstration or worship must have seized upon a third of the whole crowd during the short time it was in my sight. I watched Mr. Lincoln as far as my eye could follow him, and I could not see that he either turned his face or eyes to either side. After the procession passed, the street was literally covered with abandoned hats and clothing."

The little group then walked on to the house Jefferson Davis had occupied as president of the Confederacy. A number of Union officers were there to greet Lincoln. He went inside to look around curiously at the interior of the house which Davis had quit less than forty-eight hours before. Then he entered Davis' tiny office, sat down tiredly at the Confederate president's desk, and asked for a drink of water.

For the first time since he had been elected, Abraham Lincoln could now feel that he was President of the whole United States.

As he sat there at the desk of the man who had been his counterpart and his enemy, Lincoln must have thought about the four years of war. From the first fiasco at Bull Run through all the disappointments of Shiloh, the Peninsular Campaign, Second Bull Run, Fredericksburg, the bungled chances to follow up victory after Antietam and Gettysburg, and the horrible slaughter that took place in battle after battle to the north of Richmond—when Burnside, Hooker, and even Grant were successively unable to beat down Lee's incredibly competent army—the war had been one long nightmare to a man whose letters and speeches show unusual sensitivity of mind. Now the terrible bloodshed was about to end.

After resting for a short while, the President asked Weitzel's aide whether Davis' housekeeper was still on the premises. When he heard that she was not there, he got to his feet and said with almost boyish anticipation: "Come on then, let's look at the house." They went through the rooms of the three-story mansion, which wartime hardship had reduced from former elegance to a state of shabby disrepair. One living tie to the Davis family remained. A little black-and-tan dog, which had belonged to their dead son Joseph, frolicked around the visitors as they explored the house.

As the President and his guides were descending the stairs, cavalry clattered up to the door, and General Weitzel entered, having hurried to the house as soon as he was told that the President was there. He introduced his staff officers, and the occasion was celebrated with a bottle of fine old whisky from Davis' well-furnished cellar. The President, as usual, did not drink.

Then a simple midafternoon luncheon was served, during which the state of affairs at the front was discussed. It was known that Lee was at Amelia Court House, hard pressed by his pursuers, and that his men were in desperate need of food.

Later, one of the Confederate peace commissioners, Judge John A. Campbell, who had been at the futile Hampton Roads conference in February, came to call on the President. Campbell had some ideas about reconvening the Virginia State Legislature. Lincoln was interested and made an appointment for him to call again the next morning, for he planned to stay in Richmond overnight.

George Bruce was among those asked to accompany the President on a tour of Richmond. According to him, one of the dark-colored, two-seated wagons used at corps and division headquarters was drawn up in front of the Davis house. Lincoln was seated in this with General Devens alongside him and with General Shepley, Admiral Porter, and Tad in the rear. Some twenty or thirty field and staff officers accompanied them on horseback. As they started toward the northern end of the city, General Weitzel and Crook rode close to the carriage, while the others followed in no formal order. They soon came to a private house where the funeral of a Confederate officer was being held. Bruce thought it was the ceremony for A. P. Hill, but although the Confederate general was being buried about this time, the actual interment was taking place on the other side of the James. Since the street was blocked, they drove on to Camp Lee and then went to Capitol Square, where they stopped in front of the Washington Monument. The equestrian statue of the first President faces west with the outstretched hand pointing in the general direction of Danville. Lincoln looked at the statue of his predecessor and then said without smiling: "Washington is looking at me and pointing at Jeff Davis."

At the Capitol, the Presidential party saw the upturned chairs and desks and scattered papers of the hastily departed Legislature. Negroes were bowling in the empty corridors, and vandals and souvenir hunters had already taken their toll of the furnishings. On the lawn, worthless thousand-dollar Confederate bonds were blowing across the grass. Huddled on the slopes below the building, refugees from the fire were still waiting with the few belongings they had saved.

They left Capitol Square and drove toward the river to show

the President the burned district. They had trouble getting through the fallen bricks and fragments of masonry which littered the streets. Then they went on toward the waterfront, stopping to look at Libby Prison and Castle Thunder, where Confederate prisoners of war were now being held.

Somewhere along the route the party heard a 35-gun salute coming from the river. The Malvern had succeeded in getting through the obstructions in the James and was anchoring off Rocketts for the night. The long, tiring, exciting day was ending. It was pleasant to reach the familiar ship and have dinner on board.

When Porter arrived on his flagship he noticed that the Commodore Perry, despite his orders, had come up the river and was anchored nearby. He was too busy to do anything about it until after dinner; then, before he could summon Captain Foster, that officer had himself rowed over to the Malvern in his ship's gig. As he stepped on board, the admiral's fleet captain whispered to him: "You'll get it, old fellow, for coming up here." But Foster seemed very cool and self-assured as he waited on deck.

He was ushered into the cabin where Admiral Porter, President Lincoln, and other high officers of the nation were seated at a round table. Foster saluted and then said, "Admiral, I have the honor to report the U. S. Steamer Commodore Perry at Richmond."

Porter glowered at him. "I thought I told you not to attempt to come up to Richmond, sir."

"I did not so understand you, sir. I understood you to say that when I backed off, I was not to attempt to come up the river."

"Well?" said Porter coldly.

"I did not back off. I came off bow first."

Lincoln suddenly burst out laughing. He got up and shook Foster's hand, saying, "Captain, I congratulate you on commanding the first Union ship to reach Richmond."

Porter was still angry yet there was nothing he could do but order the young captain to return to his ship. Although he threatened to review the case in the morning, before morning came he had conveniently—and sensibly—forgotten the whole matter.

Once he had the President safely on the Malvern, Porter realized how reckless he had been during the day in exposing him to very genuine danger. Guards were posted at the doors of his cabin, and Porter became increasingly apprehensive about his safety.

During the night several attempts were made to hail the Malvern from the shore, but when a boat was sent to answer the calls, no one was there. Since four men had deserted from the ship's third cutter that day, it may have been some of them trying to return to the ship. And their subsequent disappearance may have been the result of a sudden change of heart when they were faced with the prospect of the stiff punishment meted out by the Navy to wartime deserters. Porter interpreted the mysterious calls as threats of assassination. Thereafter, he later recalled, "every precaution was taken that no one should get on board the Malvern without full identification."

17

DEATH STRUGGLE AT SAILOR'S CREEK

By Walter Harrison

When the Confederate lines, before Petersburg, were stretched to their limit and overlapped by the Federals, General Lee, on April 2, 1865, gave the order to abandon them. The Gray fox broke loose and streaked westward. No doubt Lee hoped to be able to join up with other Southern forces. Grant and Meade gave the view-halloo and raced to head him off. At Sailor's (some spell it Saylor's) Creek, Blue forces caught up with Gray forces and a large portion of Lee's command was captured. The Army of Northern Virginia had only three days more to live after the disaster at Sailor's Creek.

After the defeat of Pickett's command at Five Forks, the enemy did not advance immediately upon the Ford road, which leads directly in rear of their position, crossing Hatcher's Run about three-quarters of a mile from Five Forks, and on to the South Side Railroad. Hunton's Brigade, which had been heavily engaged on the 31st, on the right of the main line, had been sent to Pickett's assistance, and arrived the evening of April 1st, just in rear of the battlefield, and held its position there undisturbed until the next morning. The morning of April 2d, General R. H. Anderson came up with several brigades of Bushrod Johnson's Division. I had collected about two hundred and fifty of the scattered remnant of

330

Pickett's command at the railroad crossing, and reported to General Anderson.

Nothing was then known of Pickett's fate; whether he or any of his command had escaped in the rout at Five Forks, except the few who were present.

Very soon, however, General Anderson received a dispatch from General Pickett, saying that he was at Exeter Mills, on the Appomattox River, with about eight hundred of his command, and would rejoin the army that day. We moved on then towards Amelia Court House, skirmishing continually with the enemy, who followed in our rear, and reached Deep Creek that night, where we were joined by General Pickett with the remnant of the division saved from Five Forks. With Hunton's Brigade, which numbered about 900, we had a division strength of 2200. This would make our division loss at Five Forks about 1600.

On the evening of the 3d, we received the disastrous intelligence of the evacuation of Richmond and its partial destruction by fire. It was impossible to keep this sad news from the men; and the despondence it created was at once manifest, so many of them had homes and families in that city, with all of the little remaining property they had in the world there, that they looked upon the loss of the Confederate capital as the last hope of success destroyed. And so it was truly. Nevertheless I dare to affirm here, that these devoted men still continued to press on in sullen determination, obeying the orders of their commanders, and following, if not blindly, yet resolutely, the will of their honored chieftain. I know it has been said that General Lee in his retreat to Appomattox Court House was deserted wholesale by his men, and more especially by the Virginia troops, who were nearer their homes, and consequently could reach them with little difficulty. But this is an unjust accusation, and comes chiefly from the mouths of non-combatants and recreant fellow citizens who had shirked all active duty during the war. I do not deny that there were many stragglers, and men who fell down by the wayside exhausted. These men were obliged to seek food and shelter wherever they could get it.

Having no supplies in the commissariat of the army, they wandered from the line of march in search of a piece of bread even, to satisfy the cravings of actual starvation. These applications, so generally made to the farmhouses throughout the country, created the impression that they were deserters. It may be true that the whole army was fast being demoralized, by hopeless struggling against an overwhelming enemy, by constant night and day marches, and by want of ordinary subsistence; but I do know the fact that, with reference to the remnant of my own division, we carried nearly as many men into the last fight at Sailor's Creek as we had left to us from Five Forks, and that those men behaved as well on that last battlefield as they had ever done in their first flush of glory, or under the better fortunes of an earlier day. The position of inspector-general on a battlefield enables him to judge, at least as well as any other officer, of the conduct of the troops engaged. At Sailor's Creek, the exigencies of the time required me to perform the duties of inspector, aide-de-camp, or whatever was asked of me by the general, who was very short of staff, and I declare here that I have never seen on a battlefield less straggling or disposition in the troops to fall back.

It was the decimated few of a noble command who hung on to the last; who went up to heaven, or fell into the hands of their victors, in a final blaze of glory.

I will not attempt to describe the sufferings of this march to Amelia Court House, and thence to Sailor's Creek; when for forty-eight hours the man or officer who had a handful of parched corn in his pocket was fortunate.

On the morning of the 6th, Sailor's Creek was reached, and a halt in line of battle was made for several hours. Sheridan, the inevitable, was in front of us with his thousands of cavalry, making his usual parade and demonstrations to delay us until his infantry friends could come up. Meanwhile we were pressing on our artillery and wagon-trains to get across the Appomattox River at Farmville. Mahone's Division was on our right, and Ewell's command on our left. Mahone received orders to move on but we had orders to stand still. Thus when Mahone did move there was a gap left in the line, increasing as he got further and further away. General Hunton, who was on the right of our division, notified General Pickett of this move, and General Pickett sent to General Anderson, asking permission to move on after Mahone. But General

Anderson had been directed to hold on in connection with Ewell's command. Thus we delayed; and while we were doing so, Huger's battalion of artillery, in attempting to cross the gap between us and Mahone, now more than a mile in advance, was attacked and bodily "gobbled up" by the enterprising Sheridan. General Pickett couldn't stand this sort of freebooting, so he pushed his division across Sailor's Creek, and let General Sheridan have the benefit of a charge of two of our brigades, followed speedily by the other two. This was rather more than the reiters wanted. It looked like another taste of Dinwiddie Court House. So they ran back again some half mile, leaving one or two of Huger's guns behind them. Colonel Frank Huger himself was carried off; but his adjutant, Grattan, saved himself (and a gun) on the back of one of the artillery horses. We formed line of battle across an open field, and held it for several hours against the repeated charges of Sheridan's dismounted cavalry. We were now in a completely isolated position, with both flanks open to the enemy, until Wise's Brigade came up on our left and covered that flank. About three o'clock the long-looked-for succor came to General Sheridan. Both cavalry and infantry began to work around to the right, and hem us completely in. The "toils were set," and the "stag of ten" was to die at bay. Finding that we could not move a peg on our line of march, General Anderson at last gave the order to Pickett to draw off his brigades to the rear and try to cut his way out in any manner he could. Wise's Brigade was deployed in rear of our line of battle to assist the movement. As soon as this was perceived by the enemy, a charge was made on every side, and the division, enveloped by overwhelming numbers, though still fighting to the last, was forced to yield. Many of the men broke their guns before submitting stubbornly to inevitable fate. Generals Corse and Hunton were taken prisoners with their brigades; Generals Stewart and Terry succeeded in getting off from the field. General Pickett, Surgeon M. M. Lewis, medical director of the division, who was with us all day upon the field, and myself would have been certainly captured but for a fortunate circumstance. A squadron or more of cavalry were riding directly down upon us, at about one hundred yards distance, when we succeeded in rallying a mere squad of men, who delivered a last volley in the faces of these horsemen, which checked them for a moment, and we escaped by the speed of our horses.

Thus ended the military career of Pickett's Division. But few escaped this last disaster at Sailor's Creek, and these broken down, nearly famished and mostly without arms. To follow them in their misfortunes, whether as prisoners of war, or to the surrender, at Appomattox Court House, of the few remaining to witness that last humiliation, would be useless.

Thousands have gone to their eternal home in imperishable glory. Others were spared to shed bitter tears over the loss of a sacred cause for which they had toiled, suffered privations, and poured out their blood, to return to the peaceful avocations of civilized life, after four years of excitement and strife. That they have become good citizens of a common country, who will doubt? Not the men who have met them in arms. The carping politician alone can distrust the brave soldier who has periled and lost all in defence of a cause he believes just.

To me, this simple narrative has been a labor of love, which I hope may prove acceptable to those to whom it is dedicated.

Associated with the division from its formation to its last day, I felt that this tribute was due, and that I might presume to undertake the offering of it.

Sensible as I am that the subject might have been far better presented in more able hands, I yet console myself in the belief that it has been, at least, plainly and fairly set out. Writing almost entirely from personal recollections, this little work may be open to many criticisms. In its confined scope it may have neglected to do justice to some especial merit; but I am conscious of endeavoring to avoid giving offence to any one, as also of endeavoring to avoid the too frequent use of the personal pronoun. I hope to have succeeded better in the former than in the latter. If not, a humble apology is all I can give for either offence.

18

SURRENDER AT APPOMATTOX COURT HOUSE

By General George A. Forsyth, U.S.A.

There is a grim finality about the word Appomattox. When the Gray remnants broke out of the Petersburg lines, they dodged westward trying to find breathing space, be re-supplied and possibly join with other Confederate forces still in the field. Grant had no intention of relaxing any of the pressure he had been applying so relentlessly for eleven months. With horse, foot and guns he not only applied pressure but sent forces streaking to intercept the Confederate line of retreat. At Sailor's Creek the already pathetically small Gray forces were almost halved. Struggling on to the west the few that were left found Union forces across their line of advance at Appomattox Court House and strong forces in their rear. It was the end of the line: valor and tactical skill could do no more. General Lee, under a flag of truce, was forced to see General Grant for terms of surrender, though he is reported to have said that he would rather die a thousand deaths. So in the humble parlor of the house of Wilmer McLean, who had moved from Manassas to avoid the disturbances of war, two great Americans sat down to arrange peace for the tortured nation. It was the war's most crucial moment, when the mud-splattered victor elected to display a great and far-reaching magnanimity.

When, on the night of the 8th of April, 1865, the cavalry corps of the Army of the Potomac reached the two or three little houses that made up the settlement at Appomattox Depot—the station on the South Side Railroad that connects Appomattox Court House with the traveling world—it must have been nearly or quite dark. At about nine o'clock or half past, while standing near the door of one of the houses, it occurred to me that it might be well to try to get a clearer idea of our immediate surroundings, as it was not impossible that we might have hot work here or near here before the next day fairly dawned upon us.

My "striker" had just left me, with instructions to have my horse fed, groomed, and saddled before daylight. As he turned to go he paused and put this question: "Do you think, Colonel, that we'll get General Lee's army to-morrow?"

"I don't know," was my reply; "but we will have some savage fighting if we don't."

As the sturdy young soldier said "Good-night, sir," and walked away, I knew that if the enlisted men of our army could forecast the coming of the end so plainly, there was little hope of the escape of the Army of Northern Virginia.

I walked up the road a short distance, and looked carefully about me to take my bearings. It was a mild spring night, with a cloudy sky, and the soft mellow smell of earthiness in the atmosphere that not infrequently portends rain. If rain came then it might retard the arrival of our infantry, which I knew General Sheridan was most anxious should reach us at the earliest possible moment. A short distance from where I stood was the encampment of our headquarters escort, with its orderlies, grooms, officers' servants, and horses. Just beyond it could be seen the dying camp fires of a cavalry regiment, lying close in to cavalry corps headquarters. This regiment was in charge of between six and eight hundred prisoners, who had fallen into our hands just at dark, as Generals Custer and Devens, at the head of their respective cavalry commands, had charged into the station and captured four railway trains of commissariat supplies, which had been sent here to await the arrival of the Confederate army, together with twenty-six pieces of artillery. For a few moments the artillery had greatly surprised and astonished us, for its presence was entirely unexpected, and as it suddenly opened on the charging columns of cavalry it looked for a short time as though we might have all unwittingly

fallen upon a division of infantry. However, it turned out otherwise. Our cavalry, after the first recoil, boldly charged in among
the batteries, and the gunners, being without adequate support,
sensibly surrendered.

The whole affair was for us a most gratifying termination of a
long day's ride, as it must have proved later on a bitter disappointment to the weary and hungry Confederates pressing forward from
Petersburg and Richmond in the vain hope of escape from the
Federal troops, who were straining every nerve to overtake them
and compel a surrender. Tonight the cavalry corps was in their
front and squarely across the road to Lynchburg, and it was reasonably certain, should our infantry get up in time on the morrow, that
the almost ceaseless marching and fighting of the last ten days were
to attain their legitimate result in the capitulation of General Lee's
army.

As I stood there in the dark thinking over the work of the twelve
preceding days, it was borne in upon me with startling emphasis
that tomorrow's sun would rise big with the fate of the Southern
Confederacy; and as I began to recall the occurrences that had
taken place since the 30th of March, I realized for the first time
what a splendid burst it had been for the cavalry corps. Its superb
fighting on the 30th and 31st of March at the battle of Dinwiddie
Court House, which had been the immediate precursor of the
great victory of the battle of Five Forks, won by it and the Fifth
Army Corps on the next day, had not only crushed the right of
the Confederate line and given us thousands of prisoners, but had
also turned the flank of the Army of Northern Virginia. This had
rendered its vast line of intrenchments utterly untenable, and by
compelling the retreat of the Confederate army from before its
capital, which it had defended so long and so successfully, had
forced the evacuation of Petersburg and Richmond. The cavalry
corps had then immediately taken up the pursuit.

The Confederate army, once out of its intrenchments and away
from its hoped-for junction with General Joe Johnston's forces,
and knowing that the Army of the Potomac and the Army of the
James were in full cry in pursuit of it, had time and again turned
and fought gallantly, desperately, even, against odds too great for
successful defence, and against troops better equipped, better fed,

and of equal gallantry in every respect, and what is more, against
men who knew that the capture of the Army of Northern Virginia
meant the close of the war, the end of the great rebellion, the
dawn of peace, and their return to their homes, their families, and
their firesides.

Scarcely had word reached us of the evacuation of Petersburg
and Richmond when, without a second glance at the map, General
Sheridan concluded that Danville, on the southern border of the
state, was General Lee's objective point, and determined at whatever cost, if within his power, that neither he nor his army should
reach it. Probably no man in either army was so well fitted by
nature and training to prevent this, if surpassing ability to handle
cavalry, an almost intuitive knowledge of topography; a physique
that was tireless, dogged tenacity, tremendous energy, and a courage that nothing could daunt, could bring about the desired result.
Quick to see and prompt to act, his decision as to the method to be
pursued by the cavalry corps was immediate and simple. It was to
pursue and attack the left flank of the retreating army at any possible point with the cavalry division that first reached it, and, if
possible, compel it to turn and defend its wagon trains and its artillery, then to send another division beyond, and attack the Confederate army again at any other assailable point, and to follow up
this method of attack until at some point the whole army would be
obliged to turn and deliver battle in the open field to its old opponent, the Army of the Potomac.

In vain had General Lee's worn and tired-out cavalry tried to
cover his line of retreat and protect his trains, for we were stronger
in numbers, far better mounted, and, with no reflection upon our
opponents, in a much better state of drill and discipline. Moreover,
we had the élan of victory and the hope of success, while each
succeeding hour they saw their numbers lessening and their hopes
fading. Gallant men they were, and, considering the circumstances,
bravely and well they fought; but victory for them, with their half-
starved men and worn-out horses, was no longer possible.

From the morning of the second of April, when General Merritt
with the first cavalry division caught up with the retreating enemy
on the Namozine road, near Scotts Corners, we had given them
little or no rest. At Greathouse Creek on the third, at Tabernacle

Church and Amelia Court House on the fourth, at Fames Cross Roads on the fifth, and when brought to bay at Sailor's Creek on the sixth of April, a portion of their army, under General Ewell, halted and gave battle to the cavalry corps and two divisions of the Sixth Army Corps. Despite their splendid and desperate fighting, nearly eight thousand of their men, with much of their artillery, were compelled to surrender. The cavalry had given them no rest whatever, and right on their heels came our infantry constantly attacking and assailing them whenever and wherever they could overtake them. Still they kept plodding wearily on, weak and hungry as they were, holding themselves well together, and turning and fighting bravely where and how they could, but with ever failing fortune and steadily diminishing numbers. Already many of us, besides General Grant, thought that it was asking too much of these gallant lads in gray to risk their lives longer in support of a confederacy that was tottering to its fall.

General Lee evidently thought otherwise. The next day, the seventh of April, after another fight with the cavalry, at Farmville, he abandoned the idea of reaching Danville, and swinging his retreating army north, from towards the Richmond, Prince Edward, and Danville pike, which had evidently been his objective point, he shaped his course for Lynchburg, Virginia, over the old Lynchburg and Richmond road. The keen perception of General Sheridan had been but a few hours at fault. Realizing that the Confederate general would probably send for supplies to meet his hungry army at some railway station on the road to Lynchburg, near his line of retreat, he at once decided that Appomattox Depot would be the place, and hurried off his scouts in that direction. The cavalry corps at once abandoned its series of flank attacks on General Lee's retreating army, and pushed out rapidly for that station on the South Side Railroad. Its march led over an old grass-grown dirt road by way of Buffalo River, which ran at times almost parallel with General Lee's retreating army, that was marching south, and for the same objective point, only about twelve or fifteen miles away. General Sheridan's opinion had proved correct, and there we were, the enemy's supplies in our hands, and the cavalry corps squarely across the path of the Confederate army on its way to Lynchburg.

Rapidly as I had thought over the campaign, it was later than I realized as I stepped into the little house near the depot at which General Sheridan had made his headquarters for the night. I found my chief stretched at full length on a bench before a bright open fire, wide awake, and evidently in deep thought. At that time he was thirty-three years of age, with a clean-cut face, high cheek-bones, fine black eyes, an aggressive chin, slightly aquiline nose, firmly set mouth, dark brown mustache, and close-cut black hair, short in stature—being about five feet two in height, very slight but wiry and muscular, with a tremendous breadth of shoulder and long powerful arms, long-bodied too, but with very short legs. He sat tall, though, so that when he was mounted he gave one the impression of being quite the average height.

Turning to the chief of staff, Colonel J. W. Forsyth, I said that if there was nothing for me to do I would turn in. He advised me to do so at once, and I accordingly sought my blankets, in the belief that the next day would be a memorable one, either in the way of a desperate engagement between the Confederate army and our cavalry corps (which was at this time, including the horse-artillery and General Mackenzie's cavalry of the Army of the James, about nine thousand strong), or possibly a general engagement between the two armies, in which case I thought there was no hope for the Confederates.

Just before daylight on the morning of the 9th of April I sat down to a cup of coffee, but had hardly begun to drink it when I heard the ominous sound of a scattering skirmish fire, apparently in the direction of Appomattox Court House. Hastily swallowing what remained of it, I reported to General Sheridan, who directed me to go to the front at once. Springing into the saddle, I galloped up the road, my heart being greatly lightened by a glimpse of two or three infantrymen standing near a camp fire close by the depot—convincing proof that our hoped-for reenforcements were within supporting distance.

It was barely daylight as I sped along, but before I reached the cavalry brigade of Colonel C. H. Smith that held the main road between Appomattox Court House and Lynchburg, a distance of about two miles northeast from Appomattox Depot, the enemy had advanced to the attack, and the battle had opened. When ordered into position late the preceding night, Colonel Smith had felt his way in the dark as closely as possible to Appomattox Court House, and at or near midnight had halted on a ridge, on which he had thrown up a breastwork of rails. This he occupied by dismounting his brigade, and also with a section of horse-artillery, at the same time protecting both his flanks by a small mounted force.

As the enemy advanced to the attack in the dim light of early dawn he could not see the led horses of our cavalry, which had been sent well to the rear, and was evidently at a loss to determine what was in his front. The result was that after the first attack he fell back to get his artillery in position, and to form a strong assaulting column against what must have seemed to him a line of infantry. This was most fortunate for us, for by the time he again advanced in full force, and compelled the dismounted cavalry to fall back slowly by weight of numbers, our infantry was hurrying forward from Appomattox Depot (which place it had reached at four o'clock in the morning), and we had gained many precious minutes. At this time most of our cavalry was fighting dismounted, stubbornly retiring. But the Confederates at last realized that there was nothing but a brigade of dismounted cavalry and a few batteries of horse-artillery in their immediate front, and pushed forward grimly and determinedly, driving the dismounted troopers slowly ahead of them.

I had gone to the left of the road, and was in a piece of woods with some of our cavalrymen (who by this time had been ordered to fall back to their horses and give place to our infantry, which was then coming up), when a couple of rounds of canister tore through the branches just over my head. Riding back to the edge of the woods in the direction from which the shot came, I found myself within long pistol range of a section of a battery of light artillery. It was in position near a country road that came out from another piece of woods about two hundred yards in its rear, and was pouring a rapid fire into the woods from which I had just emerged. As I sat on my horse quietly watching it from behind a rail fence, the lieutenant commanding the pieces saw me, and riding out for a hundred yards or more towards where I was, proceeded to cover me with his revolver. We fired together—a miss on both sides. The second shot was uncomfortably close, so far as

I was concerned, but as I took deliberate aim for the third shot I became aware that in some way his pistol was disabled; for using both hands and all his strength I saw that he could not cock it. I had him covered, and had he turned I think I should have fired. He did nothing of the sort. Apparently accepting his fate, he laid his revolver across the pommel of his saddle, fronted me quietly and coolly, and looked me steadily in the face. The whole thing had been something in the nature of a duel, and I felt that to fire under the circumstances savored too much of murder. Besides, I knew that at a word from him the guns would have been trained on me where I sat. He, too, seemed to appreciate the fact that it was an individual fight, and manfully and gallantly forbore to call for aid; so lowering and uncocking my pistol, I replaced it in my holster, shook my fist at him, which action he cordially reciprocated, and then turning way, I rode back into the woods.

Within two hundred yards I met one of our infantry brigades slowly advancing through the trees in line of battle. It was part of the Twenty-fourth Corps of the Army of the James, which had marched nearly all the previous night to come to our assistance, and these troops were, I think, the advance of the first division of that corps. I rode up to the commanding officer of these troops and told him where the battery, which was now doing considerable damage among his men, was located, and urged him to dash forward, have the fence thrown down, and charge the guns, which I was sure he could capture. This he refused to do without authority from division or corps headquarters, and while I was earnestly arguing the case, orders came for the line to halt, fall back a short distance, and lie down. I thought then, and do now, that the guns could have been captured with less loss than they finally inflicted on this brigade.

About this time the enemy's artillery ceased firing, and I again rode rapidly to the edge of the woods, just in time to see the guns limber up and retire down the wood road from which they had come. The lieutenant in command saw me and stopped. We simultaneously uncovered, waved our hats to each other, and bowed. I have always thought he was one of the bravest men I ever faced.

I rode back again, passing through our infantry line, intending to go to the left and find the cavalry, which I knew would be on the flank somewhere. Suddenly I became conscious that firing had ceased along the whole line.

I had not ridden more than a hundred yards when I heard some one calling my name. Turning I saw one of the headquarters aides, who came galloping up, stating that he had been hunting for me for the last fifteen minutes, and that General Sheridan wished me to report to him at once. I followed him rapidly to the right on the wood path in the direction from which he had come.

As soon as I could get abreast of him I asked if he knew what the General wanted me for.

Turning in his saddle, with his eyes fairly ablaze, he said, "Why, don't you know? A white flag."

All I could say was "Really?"

He answered by a nod; and then we leaned towards each other and shook hands; but nothing else was said.

A few moments more and we were out of the woods in the open fields. I saw the long line of battle of the Fifth Army Corps halted, the men standing at rest, the standards being held butt on earth, and the flags floating out languidly on the spring breeze. As we passed them I noticed that the officers had generally grouped themselves in front of the centre of their regiments, sword in hand, and were conversing in low tones. The men were leaning wearily on their rifles, in the position of parade rest. All were anxiously looking to the front, in the direction towards which the enemy's line had withdrawn, for the Confederates had fallen back into a little swale or valley beyond Appomattox Court House, and were not then visible from this part of our line.

Here and there over the field were small groups of medical officers and stretcher-bearers around a dead or wounded man, showing where the last fire of the skirmishers had taken effect; and as we passed along a portion of the front of the Fifth Corps, I think it was Chamberlin's brigade, we saw just in front of one of the New York regiments a group of sad-eyed officers gathered around the body of one of their number, a fine, stalwart-looking lieutenant, who they told us had been killed by the last shot from the Confederate artillery, just before the order was given to cease firing.

He was said to have been a fine officer and a good man, promoted from the ranks for bravery, and it seemed, under the circumstances, a particularly hard fate.

We soon came up to General Sheridan and his staff. They were dismounted, sitting on the grass by the side of a broad country road that led to the Court House. This was about one or two hundred yards distant, and, as we afterwards found, consisted of the courthouse, a small tavern, and eight or ten houses, all situated on this same road or street. Reporting my return, the General quietly acknowledged my salute with a pleasant nod, saying, in reply to my inquiry, that just then he had no immediate need of my services. I saluted, gave my horse to an orderly, and sat down on the grass with the rest of the staff. All nodded smilingly, one or two of my especial friends leaned over and shook hands with me, but not much was said, for we were a tired and thoughtful group.

Conversation was carried on in a low tone, and I was told of the blunder of one of the Confederate regiments in firing on the General and staff after the flag of truce had been accepted. I also heard that General Lee was then up at the little village awaiting the arrival of General Grant, to whom he had sent a note, through General Sheridan, requesting a meeting to arrange terms of surrender. Colonel Newhall, of our headquarters staff, had been despatched in search of General Grant, and might be expected up at almost any moment.

It was, perhaps, something more than an hour and a half later, to the best of my recollection, that General Grant, accompanied by Colonel Newhall, and followed by his staff, came rapidly riding up to where we were standing by the side of the road for we had all risen at his approach. When within a few yards of us he drew rein, and halted in front of General Sheridan, acknowledged our salute, and then, leaning slightly forward in his saddle, said, in his usual quiet tone, "Good-morning, Sheridan; how are you?"

"First-rate, thank you, General," was the reply. "How are you?"

General Grant nodded in return, and said, "Is General Lee up there?" indicating the Court House by a glance.

"Yes," was the response, "he's there." And then followed something about the Confederate army, but I did not clearly catch the import of the sentence.

"Very well, then," said General Grant. "Let's go up."

General Sheridan, together with a few selected officers of his staff, mounted, and joined General Grant and staff. Together they rode to Mr. McLean's house, a plain two-story brick residence in the village, to which General Lee had already repaired, and where he was known to be awaiting General Grant's arrival. Dismounting at the gate, the whole party crossed the yard, and the senior officers present went up on to the porch which protected the front of the house. It extended nearly across the entire house and was railed in, except where five or six steps led up the centre opposite the front door, which was flanked by two small wooden benches, placed close against the house on either side of the entrance. The door opened into a hall that ran the entire length of the house, and on either side of it was a single room with a window in each end of it, and two doors, one at the front and one at the rear of each of the rooms, opening on the hall. The room to the left, as you entered, was the parlor, and it was in this room that General Lee was awaiting General Grant's arrival.

As General Grant stepped on to the porch he was met by Colonel Babcock of his staff, who had in the morning been sent forward with a message to General Lee. He had found him resting at the side of the road, and had accompanied him to McLean's house.

General Grant went into the house, accompanied by General Rawlins, his chief of staff; General Seth Williams, his adjutant general; General Rufus Ingalls, his quartermaster general; and his two aides, General Horace Porter and Lieutenant Colonel Babcock. After a little time General Sheridan; General M. R. Morgan, General Grant's chief commissary; Lieutenant Colonel Ely Parker, his military secretary; Lieutenant Colonel T. S. Bowers, one of his assistant adjutants general; and Captains Robert T. Lincoln and Adam Badeau, aides-de-camp, went into the house at General Grant's express invitation, sent out, I believe, through Colonel Babcock, who came to the hall door for the purpose, and they were, I was afterwards told, formally presented to General Lee. After the lapse of a few more moments quite a number of these officers, including General Sheridan, came out into the hall and on to the porch, leaving General Grant and General Lee, Generals

Rawlins, Ingalls, Seth Williams, and Porter, and Lieutenant Colonels Babcock, Ely Parker, and Bowers, together with Colonel Marshall, of General Lee's staff, in the room, while the terms of the surrender were finally agreed upon and formally signed. These were the only officers, therefore, who were actually present at the official surrender of the Army of Northern Virginia.

After quite a length of time, Colonel Babcock came to the door again, opened it, and glanced out. As he did so he placed his forage cap on one finger, twirled it around, and nodded to us all, as much as to say, "It's all settled," and said something in a low tone to General Sheridan. Then they, accompanied by General E. O. C. Ord, the commanding general of the Army of the James, who had just ridden up to the house, entered the house together, the hall door being partly closed again after them, leaving quite a number of us staff officers upon the porch.

While the conference between Generals Grant and Lee was still in progress, Generals Merritt and Custer, of the Cavalry Corps, and several of the infantry generals, together with the rest of General Sheridan's staff officers, came into the yard, and some of them came up on the porch. Colonel Babcock came out once more, and General Merritt went back to the room with him at his request; but most, if not all, of the infantry generals left us and went back to their respective commands while the conference was still in progress and before it ended.

Just to the right of the house, as we faced it on entering, stood a soldierly looking orderly in a tattered gray uniform, holding three horses—one a fairly well bred looking gray in good heart, though thin in flesh, which, from the accoutrements, I concluded belonged to General Lee; the others, a thoroughbred bay and a fairly good brown, were undoubtedly those of the staff officer who had accompanied General Lee, and of the orderly himself. He was evidently a sensible soldier too, for as he held the bridles he was baiting his animals on the young grass, and they ate as though they needed all they had a chance to pick up.

I cannot say exactly how long the conference between Generals Grant and Lee lasted, but after quite a while, certainly more than two hours, I became aware from the movement of chairs within that it was about to break up. I had been sitting on the top step of the porch writing in my field notebook, but I closed it at once, and stepping back on the porch leaned against the railing nearly opposite and to the left of the door, and expectantly waited. As I did so the inner door slowly opened and General Lee stood before me. As he paused for a few seconds, framed in by the doorway, ere he slowly and deliberately stepped out upon the porch, I took my first and last look at the great Confederate chieftain. This is what I saw: A finely formed man apparently about sixty years of age, well above the average height, with a clear ruddy complexion —just then suffused by a deep crimson flush, that rising from his neck overspread his face and even slightly tinged his broad fore-head, which, bronzed where it had been exposed to the weather, was clear and beautifully white where it had been shielded by his hat—deep brown eyes, a firm but well-shaped Roman nose, abun-dant gray hair, silky and fine in texture, with a full gray beard and mustache, neatly trimmed and not overlong, but which never-theless almost completely concealed his mouth. A splendid uniform of Confederate-gray cloth, that had evidently seen but little serv-ice, which was closely buttoned about him, and fitted him to per-fection. An exquisitely mounted sword, attached to a gold-em-broidered Russian-leather belt, trailed loosely on the floor at his side, and in his right hand he carried a broad-brimmed soft gray felt hat, encircled by a golden cord, while in his left he held a pair of buckskin gauntlets. Booted and spurred, still vigorous and erect, he stood bareheaded looking out of the open doorway, sad-faced and weary; a soldier and a gentleman, bearing himself in defeat with an all-unconscious dignity that sat well upon him.

The moment the open door revealed the presence of the Con-federate commander, each officer present sprang to his feet, and as General Lee stepped out on to the porch, every hand was raised in military salute. Placing his hat on his head, he mechanically but courteously returned it, and slowly crossed the porch to the head of the steps leading down to the yard, meanwhile keeping his eyes intently fixed in the direction of the little valley over beyond the Court House, in which his army lay. Here he paused, and slowly drew on his gauntlets, smiting his gloved hands into each other several times after doing so, evidently utterly oblivious of his sur-roundings. Then, apparently recalling his thoughts, he glanced deliberately right and left, and not seeing his horse, he called in a hoarse half-choked voice: "Orderly! Orderly!"

"Here, General, here," was the quick response. The alert young soldier was holding the General's horse near the side of the house. He had taken out the bit, slipped the bridle over the horse's neck, and the wiry gray was eagerly grazing on the fresh young grass about him.

Descending the steps the General passed to the left of the house, and stood in front of his horse's head while he was being bridled. As the orderly was buckling the throatlatch, the General reached up and drew the forelock out from under the brow band, parted and smoothed it, and then gently patted the gray charger's forehead in an absent-minded way, as one who loves horses, but whose thoughts are far away, might all unwittingly do. Then, as the orderly stepped aside, he caught up the bridle reins in his left hand, and seizing the pommel of the saddle with the same hand, he caught up the slack of the reins in his right hand, and placing it on the cantle he put his foot in the stirrup, and swung himself slowly and wearily, but nevertheless firmly, into the saddle (the old dragoon mount), letting his right hand rest for an instant or two on the pommel as he settled into his seat, and as he did so there broke unguardedly from his lips a long, low, deep sigh, almost a groan in its intensity, while the flush on his neck and face seemed, if possible, to take on a still deeper hue.

Shortly after General Lee passed down the steps he was followed by an erect, slightly built, soldierly looking officer in a neat but somewhat worn gray uniform, a man with an anxious and thoughtful face, wearing spectacles, who glanced neither to the right nor left, keeping his eyes straight before him. Notwithstanding this I doubt if he missed anything within the range of his vision. This officer, I was afterwards told, was Colonel Marshall, one of the Confederate adjutants general, the member of General Lee's staff whom he had selected to accompany him.

As soon as the Colonel had mounted, General Lee drew up his reins, and, with the Colonel riding on his left, and followed by the orderly, moved at a slow walk across the yard towards the gate.

Just as they started, General Grant came out of the house,

crossed the porch, and passed down the steps into the yard. At this time he was nearly forty-two years of age, of middle height, not over-weighted with flesh, but nevertheless, stockily and sturdily built, light complexion, mild, gray-blue eyes, finely formed Grecian nose, an iron-willed mouth, brown hair, full brown beard with a tendency toward red rather than black, and in his manner and all his movements there was a strength of purpose, a personal poise, and a cool, quiet air of dignity, decision, and soldierly confidence that were very good to see. On this occasion he wore a plain blue army blouse with shoulder straps set with three silver stars equidistant, designating his rank as Lieutenant General commanding the armies of the United States; it was unbuttoned, showing a blue military vest, over which and under his blouse was buckled a belt, but he was without a sword. His trousers were dark blue and tucked into top boots, which were without spurs, but heavily splashed with mud, for once he knew that General Lee was waiting for him at Appomattox Court House, he had ridden rapidly across country, over road and field and through woods, to meet him. He wore a peculiar stiff-brimmed, sugar-loaf crowned, campaign hat of black felt, and his uniform was partly covered by a light-weight, dark blue, waterproof, semi-military overcoat, with a full cape, unbuttoned and thrown back, showing the front of his uniform, for while the day had developed into warm, bright, and beautifully sunny weather, the early morning had been damp, slightly foggy, and presaged rain.

As he reached the foot of the steps and started across the yard to the fence, where, inside the gate, the orderlies were holding his horse and those of several of his staff officers, General Lee, on his way to the gate, rode across his path. Stopping suddenly, General Grant looked up, and both generals simultaneously raised their hands in military salute. After General Lee had passed, General Grant crossed the yard and sprang lightly and quickly into his saddle. He was riding his splendid bay horse Cincinnati, and it would have been difficult to find a firmer seat, a lighter hand, or better rider in either army.

As he was about to go out of the gate he halted, turned his horse, and rode at a walk towards the porch of the house, where, among others, stood General Sheridan and myself. Stopping in front of the General, he said, "Sheridan, where will you make your head-quarters to-night?"

"Here, or near here; right here in this yard, probably," was the reply.

"Very well, then; I'll know where to find you in case I wish to communicate. Good-day."

"Good-day, General," was the response, and with a military salute General Grant turned and rode away.

As he rode forward and halted at the porch to make this inquiry I had my wished-for opportunity, but my eyes sought his face in vain for any indication of what was passing in his mind. Whatever may have been there, as Colonel Newhall has well written, "not a muscle of his face told tales on his thoughts"; and if he felt any elation, neither his voice, features, nor his eyes betrayed it. Once out of the gate, General Grant, followed by his staff, turned to the left and moved off at a rapid trot.

General Lee continued on his way towards his army at a walk, to be received by his devoted troops with cheers and tears, and to sit down and pen a farewell order, that, to this day, no old soldier of the Army of Northern Virginia can read without moistening eyes and swelling throat.

General Grant, on his way to his field headquarters on this eventful Sunday evening, dismounted, sat quietly down by the roadside, and wrote a short and simple despatch, which a galloping aide bore full-speed to the nearest telegraph station, that on its reception in the nation's capital was flashed over the wires to every hamlet in the country, causing every steeple in the North to rock to its foundation, and sent one tall, gaunt, sad-eyed, weary-hearted man in Washington to his knees, thanking God that he had lived to see the beginning of the end, and that he had at last been vouch-safed the assurance that he had led his people aright.

INDEX

Names and places are shown as given in the text as taken from the original publications of a century ago by contemporary reporters and writers. Differences of spelling occur even within the same report. Changes of rank were frequent so that a man listed as a general is also listed in his lower ranks. The indexers have maintained as far as possible a true guide to this anthology and the publishers offer this explanation in extenuation of irregularities.